Blood & Iron

WONDERFUL PONTOON BRIDGE CONSTRUCTION

The engineers of the French Army have achieved wonderful per-
fection in the construction of pontoon bridges. This picture shows a
completed bridge being towed into position on a river in France.

Blood & Iron

A War Correspondent's Impression of the First Months of the Great War on the Western Front to the Second Battle of Ypres

Wilson McNair

LEONAUR

Blood & Iron
A War Correspondent's Impression of the First Months of the Great War on the
Western Front to the Second Battle of Ypres
by Wilson McNair

First published under the title
Blood & Iron

Leonaur is an imprint
of Oakpast Ltd

ISBN: 978-1-78282-479-4 (hardcover)
ISBN: 978-1-78282-480-0 (softcover)

http://www.leonaur.com

Publisher's Notes

The views expressed in this book are not necessarily
those of the publisher.

Contents

To
My Father
I Dedicate this Book

Preface

To know the truth concerning any great event it is necessary to know the atmosphere in which it took place. Divorced from its native air it is changed out of recognition and becomes a dead fact as compared with a living reality.

The war is too near as yet for treatment from the strictly historical point of view; but already we are in process of forgetting the feelings which we experienced during those early days of war, when the world was still "new to the game." These feelings are of vital importance, and will remain so. It is certainly true, for example, that a record of the emotions awakened by the great days of the Marne and Aisne is essential to a true conception of these days and to a proper understanding of their significance.

One of the chief objects of this volume is, therefore, the realisation of some of these emotions as the author himself experienced them, and as they were experienced by his friends. He has drawn very freely upon his friends' experiences, because one man, after all, sees only an infinitesimal part of this "game of war." To these friends, acknowledged and unacknowledged, he offers his thanks.

London, January, 1916

CHAPTER 1

A Night of Heroes

The scene is a *café* in the Boulevard Waterloo in Brussels and the hour is midnight, the midnight between August 5th and 6th, 1914. The *café* is full of men and women: men of the suburbs in morning dress, with round, heavy faces, and men of the shaggy bearded type that denotes the Fleming, men in uniforms, the dark blue of the infantry and the green of the cavalry. The women are for the most part of the less reputable order, but they are more soberly dressed than we might have expected—with a few exceptions—and they do not seem to care so much tonight what impression they make upon the cavaliers who accompany them.

They are excited, those women, with the feverish, nervous excitement which belongs to stress of emotion. They laugh nervously, and their laughter has a strange, unnatural ring in it. They have lost their coquettishness, most of them, and so you are able to see their drabness beneath their guise of opulence. They are become for the hour human and real, and the transformation is not without its pathos.

The men and the women are talking volubly, gesticulating with their hands in the manner peculiar to the Latin races. Some of the men are drawing little maps upon the white marble tops of the tables, and the women are bending over them to follow the demonstration; the maps show, all of them, one point marked "L" with a ring of tiny circles surrounding it, and a long line, bent like a half moon, approaching towards it. If you listen you will hear the explanation of it all in the rough accents of the north. "That is Liège, that point marked with the capital 'L.' And this ring of circles is the ring of the forts—the forts which Leman is holding now, at this moment, against the War Machine of the *Kaiser*. The half-moon is the German army."

"But," says a woman's voice, "why do the Germans not pass between the forts?"

"The infantry is entrenched there: and the guns of the forts command the ground."

This last remark is overheard by a man in uniform sitting near, and he approaches to join in the discussion. He is a Belgian officer, and today it is well to belong to that company—today for the first time for a whole century. His light grey eyes, which recall the eyes of the slow, sure men of the Norfolk and Suffolk coasts, are alight with a pride that is quite new and strangely inspiring.

He strikes an attitude—it is only boyish and charming, and has no "swagger" in it—and launches forth upon the great story which Liège has sent to Brussels this very afternoon, and which Brussels, with trembling joy, has sent out to the ends of the world for a testimony to her honour.

At another table an old man in the uniform of the Civil Guard is discussing the policy of the Government with deep earnestness. But his face is full of joy as he speaks. "The Government did their duty," he says, "and Liège has proved it. The German bubble"—that is the word he uses again and again—"has burst. The War Machine moves so smoothly that a single grain of grit in the wheels works disaster." He brings his fist down upon the table then with a bang which causes many heads to be turned in his direction. He raises his glass and drinks. It is damnation to the Germans which he is toasting. He has already drunk a good deal and his mind is not so clear as might be; but his hatred burns with a good, steady flame. After a few moments he rises to his feet and begins to speak in a loud, slightly thick voice. Cheers greet his words; he is encouraged, he speaks louder, he shouts, and still the cheers approve him. Suddenly he sits down again as if a little surprised at his enthusiasm, and another man thrusts himself upon public attention.

The heat in the place is suffocating, and the smell of beer and spirits and food—the curious penetrating smell of ham—cause a feeling of revulsion. The room is ablaze with light, and the roof is full of tobacco smoke which hangs like a pall over the company. Men and women come and go—the same kind of men and the same types of women. The talk continues in an unceasing flood, the same talk of victory and violence. Women clench their little hands and utter words of hate in jubilant voices; they are more patriotic than the men, these women of doubtful reputation, and much more bloodthirsty. Sometimes they seem like wolves in their bitter fury. But at other moments they are a sorrowful spectacle because one does not expect honest emotion of any of them. And they are in deadly earnest tonight.

Suddenly a diversion occurs; a motorcar has stopped at the door and a young officer, muddied from head to foot, has entered the *café*. It is whispered, guessed, believed in a breath that he is from the front. He is surrounded in a moment and a hundred questions are put to him. He cannot answer all of them manifestly, and so he smiles, the slow smile of his race which has always something of the sorrowful in its gaiety.—"From the front, yes, from Liège. . . . No, Liège still holds and the slaughter goes on merrily enough. . . . The stacks of German dead mount up . . . so. . . . (He raised his hand in a quick gesture full of complacency.) The guns are not yet satisfied, and the banquet is not yet over. . . ."

He fights his way through the crowd towards the back of the room where are some empty tables. He is still greatly good-natured but tired evidently. The crowd surges behind him still asking him questions. He seats himself with legs extended; the glint of his spurs, where the mud has spared them, is like a beacon to the women. They surround him; some of the bolder throw their arms round his neck and one of them kisses him to his confusion. A woman's voice is heard singing the first lines of the Brabançonne, and instantly the whole company begins to sing. The young knight joins himself in what is of the nature of an ac-colade. Then people from the street crowd in to find out what is the matter, and the door becomes blocked with a mass of people which extends right out into the roadway as though some monster were spewing out human beings from its extended jaws. All are singing and waving hats and handkerchiefs, and half of them do not know why they are doing it.

Out in the street a great moon is riding high above the towers of Brussels—the towers which rose up to meet the moons of years as full of storm and danger as this one—the towers which rang out, a hun-dred years ago, the wonderful message of Waterloo. The great boul-evard is nearly empty, and the smell of the tarred road is heavy on this sultry August night. Outside the *cafés* there are little knots of people who stand talking to one another as if reluctant to end their conversa-tion; a woman passes on the arm of a soldier, a painted woman with red lips and expressionless eyes. But she also is talking about the war tonight. Down the great sweep of the roadway a motor-car with its exhaust-pipe open rushes as though the fate of the nation hung upon its mere speed. It is full of officers in gold-slashed uniforms, old men with swords held between their knees. A *gendarme* moves slowly along the pavement exchanging greetings with the passers-by.

There is an ale shop over the way near the Royal palace. The ale shop is full of soldiers who have been brought to the great square in front of the Hôtel Flandre. Their rifles, with bayonets fixed, are stacked in little groups of three in the square. The men are going up to the front, they say, in the morning. They are big fellows, some bearded, some clean-shaven. The bearded men have a stern appearance which is belied by their kind expressions; the boys are of the English type, fair-haired and open-faced. Most of them speak Flemish, but there are a few Walloons in the regiment. They too talk incessantly of the news from Liège—of the forts and the slaughter of the massed Germans on the glacis, and of Leman and the king who told his people that Caesar said the Belgians were the bravest race in Gaul. It is a bare and dirty little room with sawdust on the floor and cigar-reek in the atmosphere. There are wooden benches for the customers with wooden tables in front of them, stained by many a catastrophe. The ale is from Munich, dark and good, but tonight it is called Belgian beer with a wink at the potman and a broad smile into the pewter tankard that holds it.

Listen to the talk of those men and you will gather a little of what this day has meant to the nation that yesterday was called scornfully an "arrangement." They are telling one another that Belgium has been born again or rather born anew. They confess to the first stirrings of nationality; they speak no longer of their differences, but of their union. Some of them at least, for many are too tired to speak, and others of the peasant class have little knowledge of the meaning of events. They are a very curious people, very childlike and simple. They hold the simplest ideas. Germany on this night is beaten and the end of the war is in sight. Belgium has vanquished Germany.

It is in vain that the little Frenchman who has found himself in the company expostulates, declaring that the German blow has not yet fallen and that the future is dark as night. They smile with vast incredulity, or they are indifferent. They have the peasant sense of man against man, and some of them know the German and despise him. The Flanders peasant is a big man and a simple man, and his ideas are simple. Being better men than the Germans, it is natural that they should defeat the Germans. They will go on defeating them.

There is a long road leading out through the suburbs of the city towards the east. The moon looking down upon this road discovers the march of armed men and touches a thousand bayonets with her

14

silver. Men, and still more men, white-faced and stern in the dim light, move with the swift hours towards the place where death has put in his scythe for the great reaping, drawn by some strange chemotaxis, as it seems. The windows of the suburban houses gleam out garishly against the moon. In the houses are well-dressed men and women who have sat up late to watch the road and to rejoice over the news. They are less gay than the throng in the *cafés*, those people, and less simple than the soldiers in the tavern, but their joy and their pride are not less. The first news from Liège has caught them also as it caught the world like an inspiration. They cannot rest in this hour of their country's glory.

So windows are thrown open even in the darkness and flowers that have no colour and no perfume under the moon are cast out upon the marching men. You may hear now and again the far strains of the Brabançonne, and sometimes the chant rises very near to you and is taken up from open windows by hidden figures that have gazed out during hours upon the road. The soldiers come and go no man knows whence or whither. Along the railway lines strange lights may be seen moving and great trains roll continually eastward. The troops which a day or two ago held the frontiers—the French frontier and the frontier of the sea, as well as that between Belgium and Germany—are being pressed into a single army; an army of barely two hundred thousand men, to face the greatest army which ever moved across the face of the world.

It is a night of heroes this—perhaps the most wonderful night in history. Around you men are hurrying to the scenes of death, hurrying in trains and in motorcars, afoot and on horseback. All the engines of man's making have been pressed into the service of destruction; they pant and storm towards their goal, shrilling through the quiet woods as though death were a carnival, not an hour of which might be lost.

In the trains are men who have never known war and have not yet learned to fear it. Home-loving men whose military duties have consisted in guarding a palace or a Senate house, and who have not so much as dreamed that this day awaited them. Very young men for the most part, but a few of them the husbands of wives and the fathers of children. They do not wish this thing; their hearts are sick with loathing of it.

The trains rumble away; at last the *cafés* are closed and the streets emptied. The empty streets resound to your footfalls, and you can hear the dull flapping of the flags overhead which do honour to the glory of Liège. Before you is the vast bulk of the Palace of Justice, and stretching away below the ancient city with its exquisite town hall and its splendid *place*. Scarcely a sound disturbs the peace of the scene. Brussels has grown tired even in her triumph; tomorrow will be the greatest day in all her years, and she must prepare herself against it and against the terror which will follow when the embers of victory are cold.

CHAPTER 2

The Birth of a Nation

Because the Germans failed to bring up their heavy guns to the first assault against Liège, the forts held out and the town was not taken. When the big guns came the error was rectified. But the error remained nevertheless like a millstone around the German neck. It cost time and it cost reputation. Out of the German error came a new Belgium united and determined, flushed with confidence and confirmed in courage and determination.

The new Belgium was born in a night—August 5th-6th. In the morning Brussels had become another kind of city from the Brussels of the history books and the Brussels of the tourist. The change was not, perhaps, immediately apparent, but it was real. If you have seen a boy addressed for the first time as a man you have seen the kind of change I mean; the exact change is perhaps paralleled when a weaker man defeats a stronger through sheer force of desperation.

I stood that morning in the great square by the Hôtel de Ville and watched the scene for a long time. A strange scene it was in this peaceful city. In front of the Hôtel de Ville with its marvellous gold tracery, paced on sentry duty a member of the civil guard who had been a business man in London a week ago—a chubby-faced boy with a merry smile and charming manners. But he was a man now, a Belgian. In the great courtyard a cavalry regiment was awaiting orders. The horses stood in groups on the side of the yard, their beautiful coats gleaming in the sunlight. People stopped and pressed into the archway to look at them and to talk to the soldiers who lounged about smoking cigarettes. Market women had their barrows in the square—barrows laden with vegetables from the rich country around Alost and Ghent, with great masses of blossom, red and white roses and carnations that perfumed the atmosphere. Business was brisk on this gay morning and the buyers plentiful. In the course of their buying they would often look up where the flag of Belgium floated lazily on its flagstaff above the hall. They smiled when they looked up. The newsboys ran amongst them selling the morning papers; the long-drawn shouting of the names of the papers mingled pleasantly with the clamour of the mart. Men bought edition after edition and read the news with eager, strained faces. They passed the papers on to their friends when their own anxiety had been satisfied.

The game of war was a merry game when one was winning it. The war machine looked less dreadful on that morning than ever before or since. All the people, the boy on guard who had been a clerk in London town, the soldiers who smoked the cigarettes while their horses fretted, the market women with their bare arms and ugly sunburnt faces, the men who loitered to read the latest news, all of them were becoming a part of the organisation which is called warfare; already the moods and emotions of yesterday were dead things. A vast complexity of emotions,—the noble emotions of patriotism and love of home, of self-sacrifice and honour, and the baser feelings of hatred and anger,—assailed them. Fear too and pride vied with one another for the mastery of their spirits. At one moment they laughed like boys at a game; at the next their faces were overcast with a great shadow of doubt and foreboding. Sometimes they seemed to struggle for breath as the future presented itself in all its horror: again a brighter view suggested a more cheerful mood.

Watch the face of this people in its hour of crisis and you will gain the knowledge that it is in fact a strong and united people with the soul of a nation. The impression will come to you slowly, but it will abide. You will think as you look that a word spoken might have saved all the anxiety which is already so manifest. If the Germans had been given leave to march through Belgium there would have been no anxiety, no terror, no death; prosperity would have walked with the marching armies, and even afterwards the reckoning would not have been over-burdensome. A word spoken might have spared all this blood and agony at Liège and the longer agony of mothers and wives waiting as Belgian women never waited before in living memory for news of their men folk. You will think too that there was a strong Germanic strain in this people and that therefore capitulation was made easier than it could have been in any other land.

Why was the word which might have won these advantages left unspoken then? Why was it that upon Monday morning before the sun was up over the city the Government of Belgium had decided to defy the bully whose threats they had heard for the first time at sunset on Sunday? Why did the people accept the sentence of *"honour or death"* so gladly in street and *café*—the people who knew all the power of Germany and all the terror of her arms? If you ask the grave-faced *burghers* who pass in and out of the Town Hall on this morning of mornings they will tell you.

They will point to the men and women in the Square and bid you note the type—the type which in the dim past disputed this land with Caesar; which bled and died for it at one time or another against the Spaniard, the Austrian and the Frenchman. They will say:

> Belgium has always been conquered but never beaten; the spirit of the nation survives a thousand tyrannies. In everything we are divided save in one thing—our love of liberty. Yesterday we were Catholics and Socialists, Walloons and Flemings. Today we are Belgians.

I thought as I wandered through the streets and watched the thousandfold activities of the city that this stand of Belgium against the German was one of the great miracles of history. It was a stand like that of Horatius at the Bridge over the Tiber, like that of the stripling David against the giant of Gath. Infinitely sorrowful these happy streets were, for who that knew the strength of the foe could doubt the issue? One seemed to see the days of blood and ruin that lay ahead like a thunder-cloud upon the horizon. I remembered another day, years before, when I stood on the quayside at Kiel and watched the German Fleet steaming into the harbour, the long grey ships looking like a menace even in those remote hours—and yet another day in Hamburg when I sat in a *café* on the Alster and listened to the pure doctrine of Pan-Germanism from the lips of a colonel of infantry. Brussels lay like a sheep on the butcher's trestle; the knife that was sharpened for her slaughter had been made ready these many years.

Yet the glory and triumph lost nothing of their splendour because they were set against a background of gloom. Those who have seen a bullfight in one of the great Spanish rings, Madrid or Seville, know that the only great moment of the spectacle is provided when the doors of the arena are opened and the little Andalusian bull trots slowly out to his death-fight. At that moment he stands as the type of a good warrior, and the strength and vigour of him are pleasant to see; at that moment he is a noble thing with, as it seems, a noble purpose in life. Later, as he reels bleeding from the horrible work of butchery which is forced upon him, the beauty and the strength are destroyed. Anger and hate have stepped naked from their cloak of romance and the business is revealed in all its sickening cruelty and disgust.

So it was, I think, with Belgium. On that Thursday morning you saw a people stripped for battle, for the battle of life against death, freedom against tutelage. Already the first blows had been struck, and because the conflict was still an equal one the honours remained with the little nation. But the hours of disaster approached hot-foot, the hours when this people must wither beneath iron heels and bleed to death at the hands of merciless conquerors.

There is a by-street running between the old town in the hollow and the new Brussels on the hill, a mean street with a car line laid along its upper length and the houses of poor artisans facing one another farther down. At the end of the street is a shop where are sold little religious trinkets ("*Bondieullerie*" as they are called prettily) and religious books. I was looking in at the window of the shop at a great white crucifix in ivory which filled the whole frontage when I heard for the first time the voice of war in all its realism and bitterness. It was the shrill scream of a woman I heard, and the sound rings yet in my memory as something strange and horrible, more strange and more horrible because of its association with the white figure upon the great white cross.

People in the street began to run as soon as the shriek was heard; as men and women will always run when a human drama of real human interest is afoot: I followed them; a crowd was gathered close at hand round a couple of men who seemed to be engaged in the work of dragging some heavy body along the pavement. The men were policemen, and between them they held a woman by the arms. The woman had thrown herself back and was therefore in a reclining posture with her legs stuck out in front of her on the pavement. Her face was as pale as ashes, and her eyes seemed to be starting from her head. At intervals she uttered the piercing shriek which I had heard a moment before.

She was a fat woman with fair hair and ear-rings. Her ear-rings were jewelled and they sparkled pleasantly in the sunlight. Her nose was broad, and being almost bloodless, had a waxy look like the nose of a dead person. There was a little blood on her lips because she had cut one of them in her struggle with the police. Her clothing was torn too and a white round shoulder was exposed through one of the rents.

20

She was fashionably dressed, too fashionably, and the powder which had recently covered her face was smeared over a black necktie she wore.

The policemen were big men; they did not relish this new work which had been forced upon them. Their faces wore strange, puzzled expressions. It was brutal work even though the woman was a spy, and they were, clearly, ashamed of it. But the work had to be done—in the name of war. The crowd felt at first just as the policemen did. There were young men in the crowd and also old men who might be grand-fathers; there were women and young children. The crowd hesitated a moment because its instincts were against the rules of war and the work which war exacts of those who wage it.

And then a shrill voice shrieked out the words *"espionne allemande"* and followed them with a bitter imprecation. In a minute the attitude of crowd and policemen changed.

Faces already soft with pity grew flint hard. Out of the shame they felt, men became more brutal. An angry growl, like the growl of a wild beast that is hungry, escaped their lips; the little fists of women, fists adorned with rings and bangles, were thrust into the face of this other woman and terrible threats rang in her ears.

"Kill her, shoot her, tear her to pieces," shrieked these women who, but yesterday, would have ministered to her had she fainted in the same place. "Away with her," said the men. "She's not fit to live."

A taxicab was called; screaming and kicking the woman was hoist-ed up and deposited inside of it. I heard her screams as the cab drove away: as the cab drove away a young girl with a pretty face shook her fist at it; you could see the light of hatred shining in her eyes. She turned aside and her eyes fell upon the face of Christ hanging in His agony upon the cross. She paused a moment. She crossed herself; she shuddered.

Do not blame these honest Belgian people because it is of war that we tell. Of war which is the negation of kindness and the sepulchre of pity. Rather pass into the church so near at hand and listen to the murmur of women's prayers for men, which is the other side of this terrible kaleidoscope of noble and base, strong and weak, sweet and bitter. The women are kneeling in a little circle before an image of the Virgin which looks down at them coldly from its white pedestal; there are little tapers in a great brazen candelabra on the right side of the statue, a little taper for a life and may Our Good Lady have mercy! An old man places the tapers on the candelabra, he moves with palsied steps, but deliberately because he has had much practice in this work. The women in the intervals of their devotion follow him with their eyes. Some of the women are crying, crying softly as children cry; these are the young wives perhaps; the older women are often dry-eyed because they have seen life already and have come to know it. And life and war have many points of similarity.

A priest passes very softly along the stone flags like a familiar spirit.

You can see the light burning in front of the altar; and the figure of Christ hanging upon His Cross, this time a cross of pure gold, gleams under the light. There are women who bow to this Presence also and cross themselves devoutly; women who murmur their thanks for victory and their prayer for salvation in the same breath.

Are these the women of the street in front of the little *Bondieullerie*, the women who cursed that other woman and ravened for her blood? It is possible, who knows? Your heart quails and your eyes are dim as you harbour this thought; the face of war is inscrutable truly as the face of death.

This was the beginning: there was a whole world of sorrow to come after. Swiftly it came. That night I saw a mother arrested in the Rue Royale and heard the screaming of her child, a little girl in a white dress with a doll clutched in her arms. The screaming of a child goes with a man through many days. The woman was a spy; they took her away. I saw a manhunt, too, along the housetops, and the crowd clamouring in the street below for his blood. I saw the face of the man, a big German face accustomed to smiles; it was flabby and dreadful looking in its terror. If you have seen the butchering of a pig you will realise what I mean. Another man pursued by a crowd, his clothes torn from his back, his body kicked and bruised, furnished yet another recollection; and the baying of the crowd recalled exactly the "music "of hounds on a hot scent. They were running the Germans to earth in Brussels as they were running Englishmen and Frenchmen and Russians to earth in Berlin; there was spy-hunting afoot in all the cities of Europe, the hunting of women and of men who fled before their devourers in white terror and found no eye to pity and no arm to save.

The thing had its grim humours, however, if you cared to forget the imminent horror of it. When the war began the Belgian Boy Scouts had been mobilised, and they swarmed now everywhere throughout the city. If you called on a minister at his *bureau* a boy scout conducted you to his presence; if you went to a passport office again a boy scout scrutinised and dealt with you. They were in the *cafés* and in the streets, at the hospitals and the railway stations, upon the tramway cars and around all the public buildings.

They were universally popular, perhaps because they are a British institution. All British institutions are popular in Belgium. The people petted them and talked about them and smiled on them, and the newspaper men wrote articles in which their patriotism and their quick-wittedness were belauded to the skies. One newspaper, I think *Le Soir*, had an article telling how a boy scout tracked a German spy and caught him while in the act of setting up a wireless installation on a housetop. From that hour every boy scout in Brussels became a spy-hunter; spy-hunting appealed to the scout instinct, and there was the chance of honourable mention if one were successful.

The thing became a plague within twenty-four hours, for boys are terrible when their native instincts are enlisted and sanctioned in a war against the larger social laws. These boys had no pity and no humour; what boys in such circumstances would have? They followed the most innocent people and spread terror wherever they went. I saw an old gentleman of obviously innocent character being tracked along the main street of the town by a stealthy boy who conducted the operation in Red Indian style, dodging from shop door to shop door. His victim soon discovered the plight he was in and then his efforts to escape became ludicrous. He was too fat to hurry and so he tried the expedient of buying things he did not want in all manner of shops. He bought tobacco at least twice within the space of ten minutes. At last the boy ran out of his hiding-place and confronted the man, demanding to see his papers.

In an instant a crowd collected. The unfortunate man had no papers. You heard the angry growl of the crowd rising in a crescendo above the expostulations of the victim and the shrill talk of the boy. The crowd began to jostle, to threaten, to abuse. The boy lost his head and shrieked the fatal word "spy." A scuffle began which but for the arrival of a couple of *gendarmes* would have gone badly for the victim. The *gendarmes* knew the fat gentleman and released him.

On another occasion a couple of telegraph mechanics who had gone on to a roof to mend a wire had a nasty experience which I witnessed from the street. A boy scout managed to reach the roof of the building they were working on and when the crowd in the street saw him and guessed his intentions they began to shout directions to him.

The two men lost their heads and very nearly their lives also, because they tried to escape from the boy and the crowd across the roofs.

Finally the boys wrought their own undoing. They stopped in a single afternoon a member of one of the Ministry Staffs and, it is said, M. Max, the *burgomaster*. Next day M. Max put an abrupt end to the reign of terror.

The anger of the people was rising. But yesterday they were the pleasantest, the most easy-going of all the peoples of Europe. Belgium was the home of liberty, and a man did and went as he willed. But the poison of war was working subtly. Brussels, the home of international spying, became a prey to the spy terror which is the most demoralising of all base emotions. Spies were everywhere, and every man began to feel himself unsafe. Every man began to be suspicious, and suspicion made kind men hard and weak men brutal. It rode upon men's backs in the street like a curse, and it spoiled even the taste of victory and heroism in men's mouths.

You could feel the poison at work; you could even see the change which it wrought upon the people and upon the face of the city. The joy of the early days was turned to a bitterness that was brother to fear. Safety seemed to have vanished even from the open streets. Everywhere were watching eyes and listening ears, doubting minds. If you lingered by a shop door the passers-by viewed you with quick suspicion; if you lingered long they gathered about you. In a moment you might be the centre of one of those furious crowds which have neither reason nor pity.

The poison corrupted wherever it spread as fear and hatred corrupt. Like an evil presence war spread her black wings over this city. At night you might see fierce mobs destroying the shops of the enemy or chasing suspects through the street; men but yesterday turned soldier, paced the streets and demanded proof of identity at the bayonet point.

This transformation is one of the most hideous of the features of war. It is like the process of a soul's damnation made universal to all souls and quickened within the space of a few days. Damnation comes too by force; there is no escape from it. As you look upon their faces men are debased, brutalised—out of the very nobility of their spirits, out of their heroism and out of their self-sacrifice is wrought the abomination.

How else can be explained the days of terror which supervened throughout all Europe upon the first clash of arms? Here are mothers weeping and praying for their sons, there are women tearing the clothing from women's backs and scarring them with their nails; here are men facing the most stupendous odds for the sake of honour and liberty, and there are men hunting fellowmen through mean streets as a dog hunts rats.

Here you may listen to the loftiest and noblest sentiments which the lips of man can give expression to; there are blood-calls and the shoutings of the mob frantic with hatred. It is woe surely to the minds which planned this corruption of espionage and this drama of oppression; those who pray and those who shout, what responsibility have they and what real share in this orgy?

But the orgy continues, sometimes fiercely as when the law is given by casual crowds, sometimes sternly and coldly as when authority steps in to take control. You read of the arrest of spies disguised as priests, as nuns, as red-cross nurses, there is always the laconic comment.

"La fusillade les attend."

And these are men and women!

Yet there is another side to the story. Here is a young Belgian officer whose name is known throughout the whole country, a member of the lesser nobility, an athlete of wide reputation. His wife and his child are in the town of Liège now, while the guns are booming and the Germans at the gates. A young wife—he will show you a miniature he carries upon a chain round his neck,—a girl with the sweet face of a child. Will she escape from the hell that is brewing? He has exhausted frantic efforts to find her and she is not to be found. Has she escaped already? Great shells have fallen into the town, and what of the child in that terror? His face is drawn with agony. It is more than can be borne. The Germans! He clenches his fists, the blood seems to rush even to his eyes. "My God, it is to the death this business. Their spies are everywhere, but please Heaven we shall hunt the rats out before the world is a week older."

The moon is still in the heavens; but it is a waning moon. The streets of the city are empty except around the doors of the *cafés*. Again I am walking these empty streets wondering at all the changes I have witnessed in so short a space of time, at one moment thrilled by the splendid heroism of this people which has come so quickly to nation's manhood, at another pitiful for all the sorrow that is come upon it, again filled with rage at the betrayals and treachery of the enemy who is not only without but also within the gates, this enemy with his thousand ears and eyes secreted all over the city and the land, this enemy whose strength is duplicity and whose right hand is cunning. Like the others, I have begun to lose something in this maelstrom of feelings; I am not pitiful towards spies, men and women, as I was a few days ago. I do not care so long as they are cornered and caught. Let them shriek; it is better so than that the innocent who have not schemed nor plotted should be laid upon the rack. In this war sentiments can have but a small place, sentimentality no place at all.

It is astonishing indeed what a man can bear to look upon unmoved. The other evening, I scarcely remember how long ago, the German inhabitants of Brussels were rounded up, and marched to a circus to spend the night before being entrained and sent back to their own country. What a motley throng that was, old and young, rich and poor, fat and lean. Gross-bodied merchants with pale, flabby faces, greatly careful of their skins in this terrific hour and no less disturbed concerning the possessions that have been, perforce, relinquished after long years of toil and labour, you could almost see the fat hands clutching at this vanished wealth; you could see the tears that coursed down their heavy faces.

The women were a grievous spectacle, especially those who had children hanging about their skirts; yet there were young girls who contrived to be coquettish even in this hour and to cast languorous glances at the Belgian soldiers who shepherded them. Some of the men and women were very old and some of them were ill and had to be carried on hastily improvised stretchers. Many of the children were mere babes carried tenderly in their mother's arms. They spent the night in a circus under strict guard; and during the night in the circus an old woman died and a child was born into the world.

CHAPTER 3

The Coming of the Terror

The noise of the city, if you shut your eyes, is no whit altered; you cannot detect war in these cheerful sounds, the clanging of a tramcar bell, the hoot of motorcars; the rolling of wheels, the tinkle of the bells under the necks of the horses, the hum of the *cafés*, the sound of many feet upon dry pavements. But open your eyes on this tenth day of war and you will see that the subtle process of fear and doubt has begun to leave its indelible marks upon Brussels. The news is no longer good news as it was a week ago. You hear no more concerning the heroic forts of Liège nor of the thousands of German dead that lie on the slope of the forts, before the town. Liège has fallen and every man is aware of it.

The Belgian Army is falling back across the green canal by Diest towards Tirlemont and Louvain; little by little the screen of defence is being withdrawn from Brussels. It is in vain that the newspapers assure their readers that the situation remains good in every particular; that the French are on the frontier and the English upon the sea. Men shake their heads and a great weight of foreboding settles down gloomily upon their spirits.

There are evil rumours, too, running about the streets of the city; rumours that make strong men faint of heart. They tell of villages burned and men and women put to the sword. Of women turned to the base uses of a brutal soldiery, and children whose tormented bodies have furnished in their undoing a laugh for the devils, their tormentors. It is horrible, this whispered terror, which no locked door can exclude and no discipline of mind discount. There is no longer any safety or any security in the world; and the familiar places are become terrifying. The instinct to flee away from sight and sound of the approaching doom has begun to drive men as sheep are driven.

27

In street and market and *café* you may see the same anxiety manifesting itself, the anxiety of men for their womenfolk, gnawing at the vitals, of women for their children, of the rich for their possessions, of the poor for their homes. All these are in deadly danger; the hands of the spoiler seem already to be thrust out towards them. The pavements are as crowded as ever, but the people have lost their customary restfulness; they hurry, looking furtively about them; uneasiness is expressed in every action; a discerning eye will not fail to observe that preparations for flight have already begun in the city and in many of the shops.

The heart of Belgium quails; but the heart of Belgium is not afraid nor turned from its allegiance. "The English will come," they say in the streets; "we shall have another Waterloo upon the old fields of victory. The terrible fleet of England will keep our coasts inviolate."

In the streets it is always of England they talk, with what faith, what wistfulness! A hundred times a day you are asked the same questions: "When do they come, the Highlanders?"

"Have you seen them? It is said that they passed through in the night and have gone up to the front."

"Today or tomorrow they will come and save us, is it not so?"

What to reply to these questions? You do not know. In your face it is written that you do not know. The Belgian will presently smile his slow, patient smile and shrug his shoulders—"*Tout est caché.*" He must accept the inevitable.

But the hours of waiting are slow hours and the enemy is approaching. On one day you may see the little princes walking in the *boulevards* with their tutor and hear the cheers that follow them; on the next, it is said that the queen has taken her family away with her from the doomed city. There are rumours that the government is about to leave for Antwerp and a long line of motorcars moves out through the long twilight upon the Antwerp road. It is in vain that the newspapers deny the rumours and repeat their happy assurances; the evidence is against them.

But at night in the *cafés* it is still possible to be merry over one's dinner. There are still beautiful women in the *cafés* and well-dressed men. And there are soldiers to discuss the news with, when there is anything in the news that is worth discussing. Here, for example, in the great *café* of the Palace Hôtel, beloved by English tourists, is a young flying officer. Baron ———, who is perhaps the first man to have witnessed a battle from an aeroplane in Europe. He is of the type that

Englishmen love, calm and steady, a trifle cynical, without the least self-consciousness. This very day he has flown over the woods and valleys around Diest and been a witness of a struggle there being waged. He laughs a little when you ask him to tell you his impressions.

"But that is the misfortune," he says in excellent English, "there is so little impression. You can see men—like ants. It is all silence too, because the noise of your engine drowns every other sound. You say to yourself, 'If this is war, it is a poor show; a struggle of the insects among the grass.'"

A little later he returns to that metaphor which, it is evident, has pleased him: "A struggle of insects among the grass," he says, "that exactly is war as you see it from an aeroplane."

The first wounded came to Brussels in the cool of a splendid August day. It seemed as if the sky was spread for their coming—all gold and crimson and saffron, like a banner of war spread upon the dim fields of night. The people knew of their coming and awaited it in the great square in front of the Nord Station which in peace times is the traveller's first vision of Brussels. The people had come to offer its tragic welcome to its soldiers.

For long hours the crowd waited, scarcely seeming to move. The train was late upon its journey, but the Belgian people have a deep fount of patience. The crowd consisted of the ordinary Bruxellois, though the number of women present was greatly in excess of the number of men. Some of the women were very poor and many of them were mothers leading children by the hand. The children regarded the matter from the point of view of children, that is, they thought that they were being taken to see a show of some kind and they clamoured to be lifted up so as to be able to view the proceedings over the heads of the crowd.

I do not think that I have ever experienced a crowd so quiet. The silence in the square was oppressive, like the silence you sometimes encounter in hospital wards at night when it is known that a death has taken place, or like the silence which attends the act of burial in a country churchyard. It was almost a presence this silence; a gathering of the spirits of men and women into some great indeterminate shape which brooded over their mere bodies possessing and compelling them. The chimes of a church clock which told the quarters sweetly near at hand had a strange significance and struck sharply upon the mind, as the tinkle of the Mass bell strikes at the great moment of sacrifice; and the sound of the traffic in the near streets which came faintly over this muted place only deepened the stillness and the tension.

There was a tongue given to this silence, however, when a long line of motor ambulances and motorcars, which had been hastily converted to serve the purpose of ambulances, crept down the hill from the Hôpital St. Jean and passed through the rows of the crowd into the station. This was the first sight which many of these people had been afforded of the actual form of war; like a statue unveiled the form stood forth from its coverings of language and romance, stark and terrible. The red crosses upon the cars, which deliberate hands had painted in anticipation of coming slaughter, seemed to be painted now in blood. The people reeled at the sight, ordinary, mundane as it now seems to all of us—for in those days the people were not inured to the spilling of blood and the wrecking of bodies; the eyes of the men grew cold and stern, and the women's eyes were full of tears and their faces soft with pity. You heard a murmur that was an expression at once of regret and grief and fear, a strange murmur recalling the uneasy sighing of the sea before a gale.

After that a long time passed, or it seemed that a long time passed, before the ambulances reappeared upon the great square. When the first car moved slowly out of the station and it was seen that it was in fact loaded with wounded men a groan, like the groan of a man under the knife, broke from the crowd. It was a terrible cry to hear, because you knew, as you listened to it, that it came from lips that were set against emotional expression. It was like the stab of a sharp knife, quick and deep; the stronghold of self-restraint had been assailed and taken as it were at a single blow.

The cars crept back silently through the crowd and the crowd shrank from them and then pressed forward again, divided betwixt fear and curiosity. There were faces at the windows of some of the cars, queer, vacant faces, with closed eyes or eyes that looked but did not see. There were faces so pale that you wondered whether death had not already finished his work. If you were near enough you heard terrible sounds coming from the inside of the open ambulances. And all around you you heard now the crying of women and the shriller crying of children, who cried because they were frightened and because their mothers cried. The ambulances moved up the hill in the golden dusk that enveloped them like a haze; the people melted away; spirits of desolation passed like a chill wind through the streets of the city.

The Hôpital St. Jean is built around a central quadrangle where are old trees and lawns and flowerbeds. They brought the ambulances here and unloaded them in an atmosphere sweet with the perfume of roses. Quiet orderlies who had been drilled for the work removed the stretchers from the waggons and cars, and carried them slowly to the wards. It was now that you saw the first horror of war and knew the first sickening sense of its presence.

There were boys on those stretchers who had come straight from the carnage of Liège, boys with yellow hair and blue eyes like English boys, and faces that were as pink and white as the faces of girls. One of them had a shattered arm that lay by his side limp and pitiful; a great bandage, hastily applied, covered half the face of another; by his pallor and the curious twitchings of his face you could guess that this man was grievously wounded about the body, his eyes were very wistful when they looked at you as though he told you that he was young as yet and did not wish to die. But his lips were firm and proud. Another lay in what seemed to be a deep coma flaccid and inert, the reservoirs of his strength exhausted.

In the wards nurses made ready for the work they had waited for during a whole week. Sweet white beds were spread to receive the poor bodies, and there were little trays of instruments set out and barrows loaded with dressings and bandages; the operating theatres were likewise prepared against their grim work.

One by one they brought the stretchers to the beds.

Night fell and the lamps in the wards were lighted; the yellow light fell graciously on the white beds and on the white faces of the men in the beds. So many faces and so different—the bearded men of Flanders and the heavy clean-shaven men of the Eastern provinces. Nurses in their white uniforms that suggested a religious order moved from bed to bed under the lamplight. How softly and serenely they moved and how deftly they performed their work! A surgeon with his assistant came into the ward; they were dressed in long white operating aprons. Methodically and noiselessly the toll of suffering was reckoned. As they passed from man to man the assistant wrote the diagnosis of his chief upon the case-boards which hung above each patient. When they reached the man who had gazed so wistfully in the quadrangle the surgeon shook his head.

Afterwards a barrow painted all white and with little rubber-tyred wheels was rolled into the ward and the man with the wistful eyes was taken away to the operating room.

It is so quiet in this ward and so homelike that you cannot believe that all the terror and agony which rage without do not belong to some nightmare. This ward, like every hospital ward, surely it stands as the expression of man's love for man; and the doctors and nurses are the ministers of a compassionate sentiment which has overflowed from the heart of humanity. War is far away now, here in this clearing-house of war. War, the shameful thing, is put away because the shame of it has been discovered and its mockery and tinsel are appraised at their worth.

There is a German in the ward, in the far bed on the right-hand side next the door. They have put him in the same ward with their own people for this night at any rate, though tomorrow they will remove him to a ward by himself. He is a tall fellow and fills all his bed, and he has a round face and a big jaw and hair like a brush, stiff and hard. His leg is broken and the Belgian surgeon has taken infinite pains to set it so that the German may have a good leg again as soon as possible. The Belgian surgeon was very tender in the handling of that leg; as tender as when he handled the legs and arms of his friends in the other beds. And the German thanked him when it was all over and the leg was bound in its splints.

Had they too, the surgeon and his patient, forgotten the fact of war in this quiet hour under the lamps when men suffer and die and grieve for one another that suffering and death are mingled in every man's cup? Yesterday at Liège it was different. The German was mad then; he told me in his broken French that he was quite mad, and I am not disposed to doubt his sincerity. He said he had one wish only—to kill. He lies very quietly now watching everything out of his little, restless eyes, which have a trace of uneasiness in their hurried glance. Perhaps these other men may experience the killing instinct just as he experienced it? But no, it will not come to a man in this place at any rate. So he goes to sleep and to dream, when his pain will let him; and then his face is quite simple and boyish as it may have looked when he slept at night in his father's house on the other side of the Rhine before they did this thing which has made all the world foul and hideous.

When you leave the hospital the streets seem grotesque to you, because the streets and all the people in them are given over to this business of war, the end of which for a man himself you have seen. But you are not proof against the delirium that runs in the streets and bends every spirit to its influence. The hope and the fear that are abroad grip you as they are gripping everyone round about you, and once more, like a piece of flotsam that has been cast ashore, you are sucked back into the whirlpool of hate and despair.

Brussels is shedding her delusions now with every hour that she measures of her freedom. The end is within her sight. She is dull and merry by turns, as they say the condemned are, who await execution of sentence. She is dull stoically, without scandal, and she is merry in a curious, aloof way that tells the secret of Belgium's history—that this people has learned the uses of war not by hearsay but from its blood. This people, after all, has a hereditary disposition towards exile. And despair has come to it often in the years that are past. Despair comes now upon the heels of triumph before even the glow of victory is cold.

Yesterday there were German prisoners marching in the streets of Brussels, dull, dirty men with muddied uniforms and bare-headed, because their helmets had been taken as souvenirs. They marched stolidly, not looking to right or left, because the shame of their position weighed on them. The people of Brussels looked at them from the footways, but did not demonstrate against them: the people of Brussels could read the truth now through the rosiest of the rosy pictures. . . It was a strange spectacle that column of marching, muddy prisoners and those quiet people on the footways watching it.

There is a *café* in the city that was once a guardroom of Alva's soldiers. A cellar it is, which you approach down a short flight of steps from the street; and the street is one of the lesser streets of the town. The place is full of memories of other days, and even today you may meet all manner of interesting men and women here—men and women who move behind the set scenes—men and women who understand, who know. The *café* has one of the best cooks in Europe—or had, because I have no knowledge concerning his fate since the occupation began. His soups were things to talk about, and his chocolate *soufflé* was a work of art as the term is understood in the narrowest circles. He was a good fellow, and he loved you if you showed a discriminating interest in his creations. He would not spare himself in that case to make you happy.

I dined in the old cellar on many occasions: the last occasion was Thursday night, a week before the end of things as they measure time now in what is left of Belgium. We had the *soufflé* that night by special request, and I fancy it was the last occasion on which the *soufflé* was made, at least with a good conscience. It came to us in a great earthenware pot; light as thistledown it was and exquisite as old sherry. We had the cook up afterwards and made speeches to him as he stood beaming and bowing in the gloomy middle distance of his vault.

I recall the incident because that night I met a very strange man indeed in the cellar *café* and had a long conversation with him. A being quick and nervous in his speech, a trifle furtive, amazingly well informed. He may have been a Frenchman or he may have been an Italian—or even a Turk. He had a rare assortment of passports in his wallet—passports for half the countries in Europe that an ordinary man has never as much as set his eyes upon. He knew Brussels as few of her citizens did, and his fund of news was remarkable.

But what held my interest was his exposition of the situation as he had come to know it. He spoke of the situation as grave beyond any powers of exaggeration. The Germans, he said, were going into Belgium in numbers that were almost innumerable; the Belgian Army was reeling back in front of them, fighting, it is true, like heroes, but hopelessly outnumbered and outgunned. The Belgian Army would not attempt to cover the city; it would wheel back to the northward and save itself behind the fortifications of Antwerp. Brussels was already a *ville ouverte* and the barricades which they had begun to erect in the suburban roads were so much wasted effort. They would not be used.

There was little hope of defeating the march upon Brussels because the Allies were not ready. The French might get as far as the frontier—with luck. The British perhaps would join forces with them in that region. But the German avalanche would be difficult to stop—it was doubtful whether it could be stopped. The future of Europe was, indeed, in terrible jeopardy; all things were possible, and most of the things that were probable were of evil omen.

There was no doubt that this was the truth: they knew it in the Government offices and at the Ministries; they knew it in the great business offices and were already making their preparations; they were beginning to know it more and more, certainly in the streets. The abounding life of the city still pulsed and throbbed, but the chill of death was near and it was coming nearer. It was spreading from the Eastwards where already the enemy was master of important towns and flourishing villages, from which he had driven forth the inhabitants as cattle are driven forth. It had spread all over this land even to the frontiers of the sea at Zeebrugge and Ostend.

Ostend was no longer the Ostend of summer memory. The crowds were still there in their summer clothes, and there were still little chil-

dren to paddle in the sea and build sand castles and fly their gaily col-
oured kites. There were still women ready to prove that all things may
be bought for gold, but a gloom that made all this pleasure-market
hideous in its emptiness had settled over the face of the town. On
Sunday, August 16th, when I walked for an hour in the evening along
the famous *digue*, I saw already the coming of the terror that was soon
to change these gay shores into a place of death and agony. Here, even
more than in Brussels, the people feared. Long years expended in the
piling up of profit had made them greedy of their possessions and very
careful in the disposing of them. Some of them were already in process
of flight to England; and others were nearly ready to flee; in the minds
of all anxiety was working bitterly, and upon the face of all was written the terror that rankled in their breasts.

The *digue* is empty for it is night: a soft wind blows in from the sea
across the long yellow sands. The town sleeps uneasily under a cloud-
less sky that is full of stars—this frivolous pleasure-town where all
Europe was wont to come merry-making. You see the long spires of
the churches piercing the blue night, and you hear the tinkle of soft-
tongued bells calling the hours. Out seaward there are strange lights
that flash a message indecipherable and mysterious, and far away you
hear the booming of a ship's siren. It is the end for Ostend also as it
is the end for all this pleasant land: the long, long years of peace are
rolled away like a concluded scroll: the days of sorrow and danger, of
shame and bitterness and death are at hand. You think as your footfalls
ring emptily upon the pavement in front of the famous Casino of the
lines of *Verhaeren*:

> It is the flabby, fulsome butcher's stall of luxury
> Times out of mind erected on the frontiers
> Of the city and the sea.

Will the fire that is already leaping to consume the old world, its
pleasures and its lusts, give in its place a new world fairer and nobler
made?

And now there are but three days left to Brussels in which she may
call her spirit her own. Monday (today) and Tuesday and Wednesday are all that are left to her. She has fought and prayed and hoped,
and the sound of her bitterness has been echoed through the whole
world—but there is no salvation and no help for her in the whole
world.

How changed the city is? If you speak to your fellow-diners in the *cafés* now they will no longer tell you of the great deeds that warm their hearts to hear and to recount. They will tell you instead stories of barbarism and horror that are coming to the city every hour from the country that has been invaded. The name of the Uhlans will be continually on their lips, and you will gather that these horsemen have become an obsession as terrible and as terrifying as in the days of 1870 when the French peasantry of Champagne fled before them. You will hear how the Uhlans carried pillage and rape into Tongres, Herve, Micheroux, Soumayne; how they fired the little villages that line the highway between Liège and the city, how they drove their long lances through the bodies of fleeing men and women, and how the women were caught and torn from their men and made the partners of most hideous carousal.

In Soumayne they shot men and women in batches without reason or object. They shot a little girl here with the men in the corner of a field near her home; but it may be that her fate was better than that of her sisters who were not shot. For in the night it was the habit of the Uhlans to visit private houses, the doors of which were ordered to be kept open all night. When they started forth upon these visits the soldiers were, more often than not, drunk.

At Herve they burnt houses, and lest the women and children should try to escape there were men posted with rifles to shoot into the doorways and windows.

On tables in the public square of Liège fifteen women were raped in daylight, and their agony made sport for the brutes who stood about to witness it.

A story was told me of the murder of a child, a little boy with fair hair. They drove a fixed bayonet through this boy and then the owner of the bayonet shouldered his rifle and the child, which still lived and moved, was carried aloft until it died.

As you listen to these stories, the truth of which is beyond dispute, you grow sick at heart. But there is worse to come, so that afterwards you will scarcely be able to remember what you have heard. There is the burning and sacking of Louvain to come, and the awful massacre of Dinant, and the scourge of Semspt and Rotselaer and Wespelaer and Tamines. The *café* lights grow dim and the garish decorations seem to mock you through the cloud of tobacco smoke which rises up around them. These white tables with their gleaming silver and their flowers and their costly food—the things which civilisation has evolved and sanctioned—of what meaning are they? Twenty miles away from this place civilisation is dead in a welter of the blood of children; human wolves blood-glutted, but still bloodthirsty, are ravening for more women and more children.

In the great square by the station, which faces the hotel I am staying at, the refugees from the eastern towns and villages are being gathered as they come to the city. They come by trains, by horse vehicles, on foot. The trains are crowded with them, fifteen and twenty people in a compartment huddled together like sparrows in the presence of a hawk. They throng the verandahs at the ends of the third-class carriages, holding on to the railings; they are even upon the roofs of the carriages. These are the fortunate ones who have managed to gain a place in the train and so to escape. They did not win that place, at least in many cases, without a fight, and there were grim scenes at some of the stations where the trains came from when it was seen that the accommodation was not sufficient for all who wished to travel. Some of the trains were the last trains out, and when the train left you behind, you and your children, you had to walk through a country in which armies were already moving, an army falling back and an army pressing forward. You had also to take the chance of meeting the dreadful horsemen with their death's-head helmets whose mercy is as the mercy of tigers.

So you fought for room in the train at least for your old folk and your children, and you left the poor baggage which you had brought with you on the platform of the station. When the train moved away from the station you shut your eyes and thanked God swiftly and silently for the deliverance accorded to you, though you had lost everything you possessed in the world in utter ruin.

The roads to the city were full of the fleeing peasants, of the old who toiled along bitterly and of the children who cried because they were hungry and there was nothing to eat, and they were not allowed to sit down and rest.

They came to the great square, most of them, about evening, when the lights of the city were being lit and the *cafés* were receiving their usual crowd of diners. They came to the square as to a haven of rest and safety. Here, surely, in the capital they would find a secure retreat. They brought their luggage, those of them who had luggage, and piled it up to await the moment at which the journey must be resumed in the morning. The luggage consisted of all manner of things, useful and useless. Of household goods tied up in blankets and shawls, of pots and pans strung together, of pieces of furniture brought upon hand-barrows, of treasures valued through many years which it had seemed impossible to leave behind to destruction. The barrows in Shoreditch of a Saturday night do not contain so motley a collection of odds and ends as did the great square in Brussels on that autumn evening. And the people themselves were stranger than their possessions.

You have to go to poets like Verhaeren for a description of these Belgian peasants herded in this city area with their dumb, hopeless eyes full of fear as the eyes of an animal when it approaches the shambles. They are peasants, tillers of the soil, ignorant and stupid; they have never before journeyed from their homes; their homes are their world, and this night it is not only exile which faces them but something nearly akin to death—a change terrible in itself and full of unknown terrors for the morrow.

Verhaeren has said of them that they are a greedy people.

Keen on the slightest gain; and mean
Since they cannot enrich themselves with work.

But this night even the pangs of greed have ceased to affect them: this night it is the pangs of hunger they feel and the deeper pangs of homesickness and loneliness and bewilderment. They are dressed, most of them, in their best clothes as though it was to some festival that they were setting out.

They fill the centre of the square. As night comes on they lie down to sleep, using bundles as pillows and tightening their coats and cloaks about their tired bodies. Many of them sleep heavily like hogs. But some of the old ones cannot forget easily enough to sleep, and they sit upon their gear gazing into the darkness stonily as the procession of the years goes by before their eyes.

Is it possible to measure all the grief that is expressed by this silent, drab company upon which the lights of the city fall so garishly?— the grief of the simple man who is the pawn in this game of war, of his womenfolk whom he has not learned to guide in these labyrinthine ways, and of his children who wound his spirit by their shrill complainings. If you come near to these folk you will discover new shapes and forms of grief: you will taste the exquisite vintage of mother's love as never before you have tasted: you will see this peasant woman of the broad, heavy face gather her children under her shawl to warm them and give her breast to the babe that clamours against it. Her self-sacrifice, so immediate and unconscious, will perhaps give you hope even in this darkest hour. You will hear the old women too, as the night deepens, crooning little songs to the children, and gathering those of them who are motherless into arms long since unskilled in mothercraft, yet never forgetful of the cunning of earlier days.

Around the square there are great lights blazing; the *cafés* have their doors and windows open and the shops are brightly illuminated. Around the square move in endless procession the women of the town and the men who make traffic with them. Vice has her marts open ever, even in this solemn hour. When you have tired listening to the sobbing of the frightened children and the crooning of the old women, you may come to the pavements and hear the laughter of these girls and their cavaliers. You may see rich dresses and gay faces—though the gaiety is more haggard than usual tonight—and catch sentences of conversation that has changed little, perhaps, in its tenor since men began to build cities and people them with the creatures of their pleasure.

It is a grim contrast this if you have an eye for the dramatic. It suggests, perhaps, a coffin surrounded by its lighted candles. Only the voice of the mourners do not mourn.

Let there be no misunderstanding. The sight of these refugees wrung the heart of the city and every effort was made to alleviate their distress. But the good citizens of Brussels were not upon the pavements of the city at this hour: at this hour they were abed or else preparing themselves for the exile that was so surely their portion. On the pavements were the riff-raff of the city that is like the riff-raff of all cities, of London, Paris and Berlin as well as of Brussels—a people without nationality and without home, whose city is the street, and whose devotion is toward the lusts it battens upon.

So the drama is played to its final act, and already the curtain begins to descend. These last were strange days indeed, even in this new world of the unforeseen and the incredible. Blow upon blow the evil news has fallen upon the city, every hour the harbinger of fresh calamity.

In these last days men have seen a whole nation driven like chaff under the fan. Roads have been thronged with a great tide of humanity surging to the frontiers of the land. All day and all night in steady torrent the life of the city has flowed away from it as a man's blood flows from a wound. Along the Antwerp road, which runs out between the station and the Palace Hôtel, motorcars and horse-cars and carts and carriages and bicycles and foot passengers have fled away from the doomed Brussels, and by every train they have gone, more and still more of them, fighting and scrambling with one another even to gain a place. I stood in the railway station and watched this exodus, and there was no end to it; from morning until night there was no end. Such an exodus Belgium had not seen, I thought, since the days when Napoleon bestrode Europe and the fear of his name went before him like a sword.

But some there are who do not join themselves to that human avalanche, who elect to stay and face the dark days in the strength of their own spirits. In a chamber of the Town Hall, panelled by dead hands and adorned with the ripest splendour of Flemish art, one man sits through these long hours for whom there is no door open whereby he may escape, one man upon whose acts and words will depend ten thousand lives and the safety of ten thousand homes. It is a cruel burden that he must carry, and his face is weary and haggard already at the knowledge of it. But he does not flinch. There are as brave men in Brussels this 19th day of August as went out three weeks before to the holding of Liège and the work in the lanes before Tirlemont and Louvain. Belgium is justified of her children. She has her Adolph Max and his devoted counsellors as yet against the dark days that are come upon her.

And she has imperishable memories. There is the memory of Leman of Liège, the Horatius of Belgium, who held the passage of the river while the Allies—France and England—were girding on their armour, and so perhaps saved Europe from shame and slavery. And there is the memory of the words of the king, spoken upon the eve of battle, and much more than justified.

Caesar said that the Belgians were the bravest of all the peoples of Gaul.

Leman and Max are lost to Belgium at this hour, but her king remains, surely the noblest leader ever vouchsafed by Heaven to a noble people. It is true what they said to me in the first days before the darkness:

Belgium has often been conquered: she has never been beaten. This people may be driven even to death, but who can doubt that this people will rise again from the dead?

CHAPTER 4

By the Way of the Hill

The Channel boat was about to sail; the Channel boat was half empty and the sea was like glass. In the delicious warmth of the August afternoon people seemed to forget to be in a hurry, or that all Europe and all the world was at that hour in the most desperate hurry of which history has any knowledge. The porters on the quay at Folkestone lounged idly against the trucks which they had unloaded, and the sailors on the packet waited, as idly, for the word of command to loosen away the ropes which bound the vessel to the pier. I stood on the deck of the boat watching the last of the few passengers come aboard.

The last of the civilian passengers was a very famous war correspondent whose name is known in most homes throughout England. He had forgotten to have his passport countersigned by the French consul, and so he was having an argument with some of the landing people which for a time looked rather ominous. Eventually, however, they shrugged their shoulders and let him go. He came down the gangway slowly, carrying his luggage, and there was disclosed, behind him, a little man in khaki uniform with the scarlet facings and the scarlet hat-band of the General Staff. The little man was smiling genially, and as he stepped on to the gangway said something to a friend who was with him which set that friend laughing heartily. The little man was Sir Horace Smith-Dorrien.

Then, the circumstance did not strike one greatly, but now, in the light of after-events, it seems full of strange meaning. Within a week what other scenes were the quiet, rather tired eyes of this little, oldish man to gaze upon—scenes of ruin, of carnage, of heroism and self-sacrifice which will remain emblazoned on the pages of our history while an Englishman lives to read of them and to glow with pride at the knowledge of them, scenes of terror which no pen can ever describe and no brush ever reproduce, scenes of dreadful anxiety that wrung men's hearts till young men grew old and old men were forsaken of knowledge and experience. How often in those days must this quiet sea have risen like a picture in that man's memory, comforting him perhaps with its suggestion of rest and peace! The steamer drew away swiftly across the blue spaces of the Channel. Folkestone and Dover, with their white cliffs, became a dim shadow in the evening sunlight; the other cliffs of Gris Nez rose up out of the sea, beckoning. The little man stood forward on the deck surrounded by officers; they talked earnestly among themselves . . . and beyond the cliffs, in the dim haze that rose like a cloud above the fields of France, lay sleeping a hundred towns and villages—Mons and Charleroi, St. Quentin, Le Cateau, Villiers Cotterets, Crepy en Valois, Senlis—tomorrow to be smitten into the dust and scattered to uncharitable winds.

At Boulogne a huge motorcar received the little man and spirited him away beyond the hills. The green hills above Boulogne where Napoleon camped his armies, have become, in these days, the barrier between the known and the unknown, between civilisation, what is left of it, and savagery; between life and death. But on that August night the terrible secrecy had scarce begun; the procession—the long, long procession, of fair youth which was to mount the yellow road by the old walled city, past the great cathedral, which stands like an image of love on the hill-top—had not yet set forth upon its pilgrimage, the beginning of which is rosy endeavour, and the end, so often, silence. It was still possible, if you wished it, to travel beyond the hills, amid the green fields of France, and talk with anxious men and women concerning their chances of salvation. Tomorrow the gates would be closed and the sentries posted: tomorrow and the next day and the next and the next, until the year will have grown old into winter and a new year come also to maturity. But the night remained.

A starlit night it was: still and quiet, because the sea had relinquished her moaning and the wind blew only softly amongst the trees. From the hill-tops you might look down upon the old town of Boulogne, and then, casting your eyes seaward, discern, far away, the lights that promised England and spoke of her confidence in this moment of all moments in her history; you might see the flat roof whereon Buonaparte walked with his marshals while yet the dream of Empire was a dream and discussed the fate of the vast expedition pulsing around him with eagerness and expectation. "The Army of England!"

And over yonder, standing out white and stark in the gloom like a wan spectre, is the column he builded to perpetuate the fame of this Army of England which was to wrest her trident from Britannia and put the yoke on the necks of her people.

It is like a dream, this eve of stupendous calamity, a dream in which the figures of warriors and heroes come again to their ancient battle-fields. You may see Julius Caesar going down the hill with his *legionaries* to make his crossing to the Isle of Mystery across the waves, and Henry V and his helmeted knights ascending over against the day of Crispin—for Agincourt is near at hand—Marlborough too passed this way, and Wellington. . . . You may see "the Little Man on the White Horse" riding away across the fields of France to his Empire and his downfall, to Austerlitz and Marengo and Wagram and Leipzig and Waterloo.

It is like a dream, because the smoke of the town goes up so lazily upon the still air and the sound of the town is like the tinkle of distant bells, a little music and some jarring and again a soft murmuring of sound. They are merry in the town because they have seen already the first regiments of a new army of England; and the girls are wearing the regimental badges pinned over their hearts; and the girls are wearing new little caps like *kepis*, and tartan skirts some of them for love of the "*anglais écossais*" because the swing of the kilt has already lit new ardours in the ardent heart of France. The streets and the *cafés* are filling with light, for it is near the dinner hour, and no matter what may be afoot in Paris, Boulogne has not yet changed her custom. The "*apéritif* hour" is still the gayest of all the day, let the shades that go up and down the hill, dream-wise, bode good or ill.

It is a dream surely—because on the full tide great ships are stealing into the harbour, one and then another and another, and far off, like an echo, comes to your ears the thrill of strong men cheering!

How slowly those ships creep in which bring the flower of England's fighting men to France. So slowly that it seems almost that they linger wilfully upon their coming, delaying, if it may, the hour of death by a little period. Great ships, well known on the long Eastern trail where the merciless sun blisters the paint on iron plates and makes the deck a grid for men to writhe on; ships that have sailed to the world's ports for the world's enriching and the glory of England, but never before to this little port between the sands over against the gateways of England.

The bridges of the ships loom up overhead through the dusk, and you see men, hands on wheel and telegraph, guiding the monsters to their berths. Men do not shout tonight as you have heard them shouting in the great ports in the peace days; they are still and quiet and they speak their orders shortly and sternly, with a curb on their voices all the time which thrills you to the marrow as all the shouting did not thrill you. And the men on the docks do not shout either, because the spell of this night is upon them also and has made them mute as they have perhaps never been mute before in their lives. And all the while a murmur of men's voices talking intently comes to you across the gangways and the strip of water which holds the ship off still from the dry land.

Men's voices, the men of England whom all Europe awaits with breathless anticipation, the men of England the hope of whose coming solaced Belgium in her hour of agony and still upholds her, whose fair, boy-faces have stirred the heart and the soul of France. You feel a great throbbing as you listen—and when your eyes discover them crowding the decks, a sea of faces moving in perpetual waves, you cannot speak the emotion that surges tumultuously in your breast. You too are dumb like the men upon the ship and the Frenchmen along the quays.

It is a spectacle strange and glorious beyond all the sights which an Englishman's eyes have ever looked upon, and in the retrospect melancholy so that your heart breaks to think of it.

Those boys whom we shall never see again, who will not come back adown the yellow road by the old walled town which their feet trod so gaily in those days before the reaping; those boys of the fair cheeks and the blue eyes, hard as a whip's lash, light-hearted as girls, merry and careless as the wind; those boys, the type and figure of the perfect soldier in joy of life, and fearlessness and experience and faith.

Beyond the yellow road and beyond the old walled town and beyond the green fields that stretch away from the hill-top towards the broad breast of France, they are waiting for them now as sick men wait for the dawn; there is a little work to do for each of them before the silence, and a little glory to win before the darkness, that the white fires of imperishable honour may be lighted again on the altars of England.

They are opening doorways in the sides of the ships, and into the doorways go the long planks that have been brought for this work. An officer is the first to step ashore, and as he passes along the quay you may see that he is still upon the threshold of his manhood. With an easy stride he passes, recalling somehow the stride of a panther in the wild. The Frenchman at your elbow, who knows the world, has marked him and exclaims with a touch of impatience in his voice, "But it is ridiculous, is it not? He tries to walk humbly and he walks as if he owned the universe." And that is the truth too, and worth recording because it is the truth.

Great flares are lighted along the quays and their light falls red and yellow upon the water. The soldiers come down the gangways stiffly because the voyage has cramped them in narrow limits; some of them begin to disembark the horses for the gun teams, and there are lively scenes when they prove difficult, as is the natural right of horses. The men warm to their work and you hear cheery imprecations being flung at the horses, and little, gay snatches of songs that men have remembered from their school-days or picked up a night or two ago in a London music-hall; and you hear beginning the sudden stream of chaff and banter which will last many of these lads to the presence of death on the parched fields that are awaiting them.

After the horses the guns; and so the great cranes on the dock wall are brought up and begin dipping their arms into the holds. Out of the holds come the chariots of war, short black boxes set upon heavy wheels and long guns with snouts that suggest a greedy animal of the baser sort. You learn that the guns are "Long Toms," and that, nevertheless, they are of the female sex and dearly beloved even as they are abundantly well known. You learn that a gun may have a soul even as a man has, and that the character of a gun is strange and capricious as the character of a girl. These things are revealed to you in the crisp language of the barrack-room which knows England as "Old Blighty" and pours its scorn upon the holder of the "couchy" job.

And there is revealed to you also the secret of the blazing devotion which in the days so near at hand will bind these same men to their guns as seamen in dire peril are oftentimes bound to their ship, a devotion that is more than the mere performing of duty, that has tender sentiment and fetishism—if you do not wish to call it religion—mingled inextricably in its composition.

When the men are gathered in the open beyond the dock sheds you are able to look at them at your leisure, and talk to them. But it is not so easy to talk because the little French girls are already in front of you, and already they are begging in those plaintive, haunting voices of theirs for "*souvenir, souvenir*"—and the soldiers are submitting with a smile to the theft of the regimental badges from shoulders and hats, which quick fingers perform ever so skilfully.

The soldiers are more interested in the little French girls than in any other thing, because this is the first time many of them have set foot on the shores of France, and the fame of the French girls is ubiquitous.

But when that novelty has been tasted they will talk to you merrily and you will learn their point of view concerning the tragedy in which they are destined to play so great a part. You will learn with wonder and the wonder will remain with you. For these men, most of them, do not know why they are here and do not care. They know that there is war—war with Germany—and they know that war is the life business upon which, some in haste, and some with deliberation, they have embarked. They are fighting men; and so they will fight, God helping them. And after that they will go home again and wait for a new campaigning. How should it be otherwise? And how should these know that they are going out, the vast majority, upon their last campaigning; that the old British Army with all its riches of custom and tradition is already in the melting-pot of destiny?

They stand, rank upon rank, boyish faces in the light of the yellow flares, stern at attention and perfect in their composure. The flares leap and diminish, casting long shadows. Behind are the masts of the great ships, and out, seaward, the lights of other ships stealing in with their burden of human souls. The city rears itself up, tier upon tier of light, across the harbour. The stars are overhead.

There is a sharp word of command.

The ranks begin to move forward towards the wooden bridge that leads to the city and the hills where the camps are.

The sound of marching feet is like the sound of deep, low thunder muttering along the plain.

Then above the thunder of the marching a strong voice thrills out the song that, by accident, has become the Soldier's Song of this year of tragedy.

It's a long way to Tipperary,
It's a long way to go;
It's a long way to Tipperary,
To the sweetest girl I know."

And all the marching men take up the song, swelling the singing of it to a mighty tide.

Goodbye, Piccadilly;

Farewell, Leicester Square.
It's a long, long way to Tipperary,
But my heart's right there.

The lilt of the singing comes back to you, wistfully, across the still night.

Who affects to despise that song with its mournful lilt and its sob-bing choruses? Not those who heard it during these August days and nights when brave men were going to death in battalions with its haunting foolishness upon their lips and ringing in their ears! Not those who lay awake through the stifling nights listening to it, hour after hour until the words became burned upon memory, and brain and body throbbed with its incessant cadences!

I speak for myself; so far as I am concerned *Tipperary* is sacred. As I heard it, it was the song of dying men; I think, of the best and bravest men this world ever saw; it was their song because they chose it and because it comforted them.

All night they sang it, thousands and tens of thousands, as they marched between the ships in the harbour and the camps on the hill, through the narrow, hot, smelly streets of the French town.

The sound awoke me and brought me to my bedroom window to watch them as they went. The long street was full of them, of them and their song, from end to end. In the dim morning light it was as though I stood upon the high bank of a great river and watched a torrent of swollen, muddy water covered with flecks of foam sweep by beneath my feet; the faces of the men were the foam upon the tor-rent's breast.... Then the sunlight welled up from behind the hill, her-alding the sun, and it seemed that a shower of living gold fell upon the moving throng, touching the boy faces with glory. The boys looked up into the sunlight and paused a moment in their singing to laugh for joy of it, and then again the throb of the chorus swelled and died through echoing streets.

Above the fishing village and the new town is the old town, the walled city of Boulogne which history knows; and above the walled city again the yellow road is divided; one branch of the road goes to Calais and the other branch to St. Omer and Lille.

They pitched the camps up here near the branching of the roads, and when you climbed the hill you came to a new city of white tents and waggons and tethered horses, and men moving about in their shirt-sleeves with the fag-ends of cigarettes in their mouths watching the horses and making preparation for the feeding of their comrades. A scene of abounding life it was which rejoiced the heart; a carnival of youth upon the threshold of mighty adventure. The great guns that protrude their snouts so formidably from between the wheels of the cars, and the huge pontoons, each like a lifeboat upon its carriage, and the artillery waggons, and the stamping, shifting mob of the horses and the tents and the ambulances, seemed like the playthings of giants heaped together for their entertaining.

You might walk where you chose along the grassy avenues between the tents and watch the life of the new city which yesterday was not, and which tomorrow would have vanished beyond the distant slopes. You might hear the merry talk, the jokes and laughter which were the cordial of this company; you might see the brawny cooks pouring soup from huge cauldrons which seemed to have been shaped for giants, or staggering under the weight of mighty rations which sent up a thin vapour of steam upon the sunny air. You might watch the barber at his work outside his tent and listen to the chatter of his customers while he shaved and clipped them, or you might visit the blacksmith at his forge and see in how deft a manner he performed his task.

There were young men and old men in this company; men who had had their salting on the Indian frontier and wore a strip of ribbon proudly over their hearts; men who fought through the grim days of South Africa and saw Buller ride into Ladysmith and Roberts go up to Paardeberg. And there were men who had never yet looked into the face of war, overgrown schoolboys from English villages, in Kipling's phrase "with the sap of good English beef in their cheeks "and the joy of England in their blood. The talk of all of them was of the war; but they talked of a war which has never been fought and never will be, of an adventure-war of glorious battles and great surprises and unending victory; a war like the great wars of old days, full of deeds and actions, wherein the happy warrior found at last the desire of his spirit; a short war too, of days or weeks, with a quick return and a long aftermath of rejoicing.

The officers knew better; and theirs were the only grave faces in this cheerful company. They moved about, quiet men busy with duties that had become a part of nature: they talked very little, and if you spoke to them they told you that they knew nothing at all. But occasionally you might see a wistful look in the eyes of some of them, especially the boys, which said much more than speech could have said—the look a man wears when he thinks of his home and of his mother whom he will not see again this side of the grave.

A sergeant, who had fought in the Boer War, with whom I talked a long while, bade me note the difference between the faces of the men and the faces of the officers. "It is education which makes the difference," he said, "because at heart they are the same men. But the educated man has a finer temper on him, that's all; he can see ahead and he can compare things and draw conclusions. Look at our boys now; they would hug the Germans to their hearts; they love them because they have put up a fight and given them this show. But wait a little. Wait till the Germans hurt them and get their blood stirred. Then you'll see what you will see. I have seen it all before, and I know. We can be an ugly crowd just as much as we can be a jolly crowd."

He was still speaking when a bunch of horses that were being brought up the hill from the watering took fright badly and bolted. They came up past us like the finish of a Newmarket gallop, and the boy who had charge of them nearly lost his seat half a dozen times in as many seconds. A chubby-faced, fair-haired lad he was with strong white teeth that you saw gleaming through his parted lips. When he realised that he couldn't stop the mad rush he did a bold and plucky thing very quickly. He swung himself from his seat to the ground and threw all his weight on the leading ropes that held his team together. For a moment he seemed to be tossed away by the flying hoofs like a cork on a rushing stream; but he stuck it gamely. And as he held on the pace of the horses slackened so that it was possible for him to regain his legs and pull backwards as he ran. A moment later the rush was checked and the horses stood still looking about them as if surprised that they could have behaved so foolishly. The boy led them back to where I stood, and as he passed I noticed an angry flush on his face, and an angry light in his eyes. The sergeant smiled and nodded.

"It will be just like that on a bigger scale presently," he said.

He had a shrewd knowledge, had that sergeant in the hill-camp above Boulogne.

At night they struck camp and went away beyond the green hills. They went silently in the dead of night so that no man saw them of all the men and women who had watched and welcomed their coming. Nor did any hear them, for there are few townspeople on that high plateau, and the townspeople go early to bed. It was strange, the manner of their going, and sinister because at that hour every heart quailed at the news that was coming to the town—the news of the agony of Brussels and of the avalanche that was sweeping southward towards France.

The merciless August sun rose up on white tents that were silent and empty and his first rays played sadly upon the dead embers of fires grown cold under the dew. The guns and the waggons and the great pontoons and the horses and the boy faces, that made you think 'twas a game they played, were all vanished away and only the muddied avenues between the tents and the footprints upon the grass remained to bear testimony to their passage. You gazed across the green distances and saw a smiling land waking serenely to the day's adventure; you heard, far away, the voices of the country, that make silence golden; but you heard no more the voices that yesterday rang so gaily in your ears, nor the tramp of marching feet, nor the rolling of the great wheels on the hard road.

The days of her darkness had come indeed upon this land of France.

Yet not all of those who had come were set out upon this terrible journey. A few remained who should escape this horror of the frontierland about Mons now brewing behind the sunny hills.

At the top of the hill stands a great, dark house, that was once the home of a religious sisterhood. In the days when France rose up against her religious orders the house on the hill fell upon bad times, and one night the mob came to it and took it by storm against the devoted women who were ready to give their lives in its defence. The mob broke into the old house and wreaked their savage anger upon it; they broke the windows and destroyed the rooms, and what they were unable to accomplish in the matter of destruction, the fire they called to their aid accomplished for them, so that the place became a ruin with grass-grown walls and empty courts and broken doors that beat dismally against their jambs when the night winds blew.

It was no man's business to rebuild the broken walls, and authority forbade the return of the dispossessed, so that the place stood a ruin for a long while awaiting the new destiny which Fate had ordained for it. The marching men who came up the hill from the ships saw it and looked up wonderingly at the gaping windows and blackened walls, and asked eager questions concerning the tragedy which had befallen it. The marching men passed on; but the doctors and the ambulance men who accompanied them lingered behind, because they saw that within these walls it would be possible to arrange a temporary hospital to accommodate early casualties that would in the ordinary course of events be brought down to them.

They were adaptable men these army doctors, and they soon got to work upon the ruin and brought some sort of order into its chaos. They found that there remained one wing of the building with a sound roof and a sound floor; and into this they brought beds and bedclothes and stoves and tables and cases of instruments and bottles of antiseptics and dressings, and the hundred and one things which go to make up a hospital equipment. They did the work very quickly, because there was no time to lose and because no man could say how soon, out of the mystery-country beyond the hills, the waggons with the red crosses would return loaded up with victims.

I saw their work on the day after the marching men went away. Good work it was, though necessarily a little rough and ready. They had some thirty beds in the hospital, I think, and some half-dozen doctors to look after it. The doctors lived in a tent which was pitched in the convent garden, and they had their food in another tent around which rose bushes were blooming. They gave me tea in this tent, and we talked about the war and about the tragedy of Belgium which I had witnessed. They told me that they did not know how long they might stay in the old house, nor whether it was proposed to make a great hospital base in Boulogne or not. They said that depended probably on the course of events at the front, of which already there was a total lack of news. Fine fellows they were, of the best stamp, ready to give their lives at any moment in the performance of duty.

But I think often how small that preparation was for the tremendous events which were to come and how it proved, in its way, that no man had envisaged the extent of this catastrophe. In other days I was to see a new hospital rise up under the shadow of those walls, and a whole city of hospitals stretched out below the hill by the sea, and then to learn that even that vast preparation could but touch the fringe of the agony and sorrow that flowed out like a broad river from the smoke and welter of war.

CHAPTER 5

The Catastrophe of Namur

The *cafés* of Boulogne, like the *cafés* of Brussels, were busy these days of waiting, but there was a difference that not even the dullest wit could fail to apprehend. The people of France are not like the people of Belgium, though they speak the same language and breathe the same air. The people of France are very old in the knowledge of war, and they have suffered grievous things in the acquiring of that knowledge. The bitter days of 1870 have left their indelible stamp upon this proud people, and the heart of France cherishes that memory as a man's heart conceals the knowledge of a wrong that may not be forgotten nor forgiven.

There were Frenchmen in these Boulogne *cafés* who remembered 1870; and there were men who with their own eyes had seen the terrors and humiliation of that calamity. These men were like a people apart and they held aloof, in their greater knowledge, from the mirth and hopefulness of the boys who wore their new uniforms so gaily. They had dim eyes that held a smouldering fire, and when they talked with you you saw their hands clench and their teeth set as the tide of memory carried them backwards. Their eyes blazed at a hundred grim recollections, and the deep note of passion made their voices strangely eloquent.

This man is a colonel of infantry, but *then* he was a private in the ranks. He tells the story of Sedan over again and the fearful days which followed that debacle. He recounts small intimate details that bring all a man's blood into his face for anger and shame. He speaks first in low tones that are like a whisper, and then huskily as his voice grows stronger, until at last he holds you by the very force of his words.

The Germans . . . they are not men, they are barbarians. I know as tomorrow you also will know, and all the world. Where they go there they pollute, and the blood of innocent victims is left to cry out for vengeance. The heart of France has been broken, but this day is the beginning of a new world for France. It is not revenge, it is retribution; we may suffer, we may die, but we shall triumph. France must triumph or she must pass for ever.

And then in softer tones you hear him add:

We have not nursed the spirit of revenge, God knows. We have worked for peace and lived for peace and hoped for peace. But Fate has willed. Today the bitterness and the shame of that year have come again from the graves wherein we laid them, and as we are men we must strike. . . .

There is a doctor in the company whose hair is white like silver. He is of the same view, though he speaks his thoughts differently.

There are forty years which when this war is ended we shall wipe away from the story of France. Yet we shall not forget them—the forty years of bitterness that were hidden beneath the mask of mirth. As a man remembers the hours of his weakness we shall know them, and France shall know them . . . for these hours the price is death. . . .

On the Sunday which followed the passing of the army they had a religious procession through the streets of the town. It was the old, old procession of Our Lady, whose kind spirit goes forth to the fisherfolk—those who depart to the fishing grounds of the North and those who wait and fear at home. In the days when they made war on the religious orders the procession was forbidden though the people hankered after it bitterly; but in these new days, when a man's life was measured only by moments and hours, and men and women besought in fierce anguish the mercy and comfort of God, there was no man who durst forbid or censure it.

So they held it as of old, and as of old the fisherfolk came in their best clothes and lined the narrow streets from the church under the walled city to the quays, where the boats lie, and back again by other streets to the church.

But not the fisherfolk alone. In the crowd were all manner of men of all manner of peoples. Shopkeepers were there, and wealthy merchants from the villas along the *digue*, and soldiers in their long blue overcoats with the ends buttoned up, and dashing cavalry men in sky-blue tunics, and here and there a sprinkling of our British khaki, where an ambulance man from the hospital on the hill stood to watch the spectacle. There were fashionably dressed women too who had come to Boulogne to play in the Casino or bathe on the beach before the war clouds gathered and who had lingered afterwards because of the fascination that held them; there were women of the town and a few women of the street come already from Paris in anticipation of gain, like vultures to a carcase. Also there were children in their summer frocks carrying pails and spades, and merry, without a care for all the sorrow that lay hid about them.

The procession came slowly along the streets, and it consisted chiefly of children and young women. The children and the women were dressed in white linen that fell to their feet in ample folds, and the women wore thin veils over their faces and carried, some of them nets and some fish baskets in token of the character of the procession. They moved slowly with rhythmic steps, and their faces were grave and sorrowful, as only the faces of the fisherfolk of Northern France can be. A few of them had red eyes, as though they had wept a little before setting out, and these, you might guess, had taken leave during the last days of father or brother or lover when the order of mobilisation was posted up through the land, in all the villages and hamlets. There were also some older women wearing the costume of the fisherfolk, which is beautiful in a barbaric sort of way and which depends for its effect chiefly upon the elaborate shawl that is bound over the shoulders.

Behind the long ranks of the women the clergy walked, bearing, under gaudy canopies, holy relics, at sight of which men bared their heads and women fell weeping and praying upon their knees. And after the relics the Blessed Sacrament, in a golden monstrance, was carried by the bishop himself arrayed in his vestments. There was sweet singing as the sacrament went by—an old chant that rose and fell in wonderful cadences—and the multitude in the streets grew still and silent and bent in deep reverence and adoration.

They carried the figure of the crucified Saviour too upon a great golden cross, that men might turn their gaze for a brief moment away from the spectacle of murder and bloodshed and behold the face of Everlasting Love.

Behind the hills they have already begun the work of death, but here in this seaport town men and women are waiting for news through long days that parch and scorch so that the very air seems

ENTRENCHING

French troops digging trenches in the north of France

to have become charged with fire. The veil of mystery which hangs above the hills is impenetrable now, and only rarely does a whisper reach the town of the fearful doings a dozen leagues away. The whispers are heard when the service motorcars come down, and at that time you may see men with anxious faces hurrying in and out of the Hôtel Bristol on the quays, where a handful of British staff officers have been quartered.

At first the whispers are reassuring, but very soon a new note is sounded that chills anticipation. The British Army is fighting, somewhere along the Belgian frontier; no man can say what the issue of the fight may be, but the hordes which the enemy is pouring down upon the borders of France are like the waves of an irresistible tide. "You may kill and kill—but after your hands are tired and your eyes grow dim there are new ranks in the places of the old ones, and new enemies coming against you as though you had not lifted hand in your defence."

So they talk on quay and *digue*, and so they relate in the *cafés* when the day's weary work is done. In the *cafés* they still argue as though war could be decided by talk, yet the strangers are going away silently and swiftly by every boat that leaves the pier, and by every train that runs to the southward. In the *cafés*, if you have patience to listen to them, they will tell you that Namur is a second Liège, and that it will hold the enemy in check for a fortnight at least, by which time the army of the Allies will have been able to consolidate its positions. "With Namur as a pivot our forces will sweep round upon Brussels and drive the German back upon the banks of his Rhine."

You may derive a little comfort from this talking, but your comfort will scarcely last you through the long hours of night, when a man sees the worst and not the best of things and makes coward provision against the incalculable chances of the morrow.

The news that comes with the midday boat from England is still the fullest and the most reliable, and so all the English folk and some Frenchmen as well gather on the pier to await the boat's coming. They gather an hour before the scheduled time, because it is impossible to rest in the hotels, where rumour has never done with her muttering. They claim the right of equal citizenship to introduce them one to the other, and there is the suggestion of boded ill in the way they crowd together upon the platforms where they are making ready the long train for Paris or in the *buffet* where the dinner tables are set out.

The talk is ever in the same strain, a weary repetition of terms newly culled from newspaper and strategy book; but because it is all that there is to talk about men and women alike devote themselves to it. You are reminded of the talk of doctors around the bed of a sick man when technical language is used to cover up dark forebodings or to make a pretence of obscuring the obvious.

Yet one hope remains, like a rock set among shoals. It is Namur. Namur is as strong as Liège, and Liège held out during many days. Namur is girdled with impregnable forts and armoured with guns that are of longer range than any field piece. A handful of men could hold this fortress against a great army, and already great armies are moving to its defence. So long as there is Namur there is good hope.

The ship glides in while the talk is still in full tide, and you are impelled by an irresistible curiosity towards her. As the passengers come down the gangways you begin to question them. You ask them all manner of questions which it is manifestly impossible that they can answer, but they do not resent this intrusion because they too are upon the rack of uncertainty. Today their faces are very grave and an atmosphere of gloom seems to hang over the white decks of the steamer on which they stand. You feel it already—the catastrophe which these have known of during many hours, and which within a few minutes you also will know. With hands that are unsteady you open the newspaper which has just been thrown to you across the deck rails.

"It is officially announced that Namur has fallen."

A quiet voice, which you recognise as that of a French officer who is always a member of the crowd upon the quay, discloses the meaning of this supreme catastrophe while you stand gazing dimly at the stream of passengers on the gangways. "If Namur has fallen," he says, "then the pivot of the whole operation is lost. The army must retreat or be outflanked." And as you pass up the hot street to your hotel you see again the vision of Brussels in her last days, when another army was retreating, and another people awaking to a knowledge that it had been left naked to its enemy.

Nor are you kept long in doubt as to the truth of the intelligence. On the way to the hotel you encounter one of the ambulances attached to the hospital on the hill rolling slowly down towards the quay. The ambulance is filled with beds and bedding and hospital equipment, and the men driving it wear ominous puzzled expressions that you have not seen before on the faces of British soldiers. The Hôtel Bristol too is packing, and reminds you of similar places in the Scottish Highlands at the end of the season. Only there is greater haste about this bundling together of furniture and effects.

What is the meaning of it? you ask, and are answered by the faces of the townspeople who are spectators of this abandonment:

"*C'est terrible ça, Monsieur: les Anglais vont partir,*" they tell you with the light of a great fear dawning in their eyes. They stand in little groups in the streets and talk quickly together as though time, even for talking, was short. . . . And the ambulances and waggons go by in a long procession that is mournful as a funeral *cortège*.

All that day and the next the process of going away continues, because there were, it appears, great stores of provisions and hospital equipment in the quay sheds, and these must not be left to the enemy should he care to come, in passing, to the "open town" (*ville ouverte*) of Boulogne. You may lie in bed and hear the rolling wheels through open windows that admit a little coolness in the stifling heat, and you may hear the crack of a whip and the occasional voices of men who talk together eagerly as they ride by. . . . In the morning you will see that yet another of the great transports has vanished from the harbour.

The fall of Namur was like the fall of Jericho. At the seventh blast of the trumpets it fell, and to this hour the why and the wherefore of that calamity are obscure.

"But this," as the French officer said, "is certain, the pivot of the Allied armies was destroyed in the fall, and the threat of envelopment to the armies made actual and imminent."

You will understand the position if you glance at the rough diagrams I have made of it. The heavy line is the line of the Allies on that memorable Saturday morning, August 22, when their army was stretched out in its long lines to meet the advance of the Germans from Brussels.

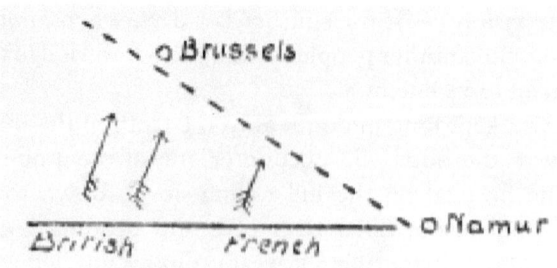

1. HOW THE ALLIES HOPED TO RELIEVE BRUSSELS

The dotted line drawn between Namur and Brussels shows the method in which it was proposed to sweep the Germans back again, using Namur as a pivot.

In the second diagram you may see at a single glance how the plan miscarried, how the fall of Namur spoiled the whole plan of the campaign and left the British Army hanging in the air and isolated upon the Belgian frontier.

Why did the calamity occur so suddenly and so unexpectedly? The answer is the old answer of history, which has explained almost all the catastrophes of which war keeps record. There was an enemy force where no enemy force was looked for; and the unlooked-for forces were stronger than those which had been expected.

The generals of the allied army expected to be attacked in front by an army coming due south from Brussels. They were so attacked; but they were also attacked in flank, on their right wing, by an army which had come straight down from Liège along the Meuse, using both banks of the river for its advance, and by another army coming from the east towards Namur. (Fig. 2.)

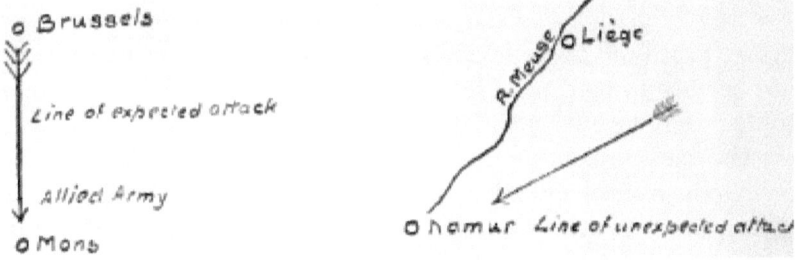

2. THE UNEXPECTED GERMAN ATTACK WHICH FRUSTRATED THE
ALLIES' PLAN.

The unexpected attacks overwhelmed the French force and, when Namur fell, drove it back; for the French force was in great danger of having its right flank turned and its lines of communication cut.

How near our armies were to extinction on that day is a thought which even yet may well chill the heart. When the French began to retreat on Saturday afternoon, August 22, they were not able, because the Intelligence Service had broken down, to inform their British allies of the fact, and so Sir John French held his ground against the attack which was delivered at him from the north until Sunday afternoon. He held his ground though he was outnumbered and out-classed so far as guns were concerned, and the story of his stand, there, amongst the canals and fields of Mons is one of the most splendid in our history. On Sunday afternoon news that the French had retired reached the British Commander. And then he knew that the British Army was alone with unprotected flanks amid hundreds of thousands of the enemy.

The British Army was all but surrounded, for already the German Armies, which had taken Namur and forced the retreat of the French, were advancing against it from the east: another German Army, the army of Von Kluck, faced it in the north, and attempts were being made to surround it on the west also. The British Army was in the jaws of a huge trap, and at any moment the jaws might close and seize it. And in that case the tragedy of Sedan would be repeated, for what could 70,000 men accomplish against the 200,000 coming against them.

Some of the men of our army were bathing when the first attack came upon them in the form of a charge by German cavalry. The Germans rode down upon the helpless men and thought to destroy them at their ease. But if there was no time to recover clothing there was time to grasp a rifle and shoot. Stark naked these men stood together to sell their lives by the shore of the little lake in which they had been enjoying themselves a few moments before, until help came to them and the enemy was driven off.

The battle which the British Army fought on that Sunday of the first German attack upon it ended not in defeat but in victory, and the victory saved the army. Because of the victory it was possible to retreat, when night fell, and so to get nearer to the French force already gone southwards. The victory was the starting-point of the terrific "Retreat from Mons," which, victoriously begun, was destined to reach again a victorious ending. No man, save those who fought and struggled and endured during those terrible days of heat and those terrible nights of hunger and suffering, saw all the course of this Retreat or has a first-hand knowledge of all its amazing incidents, and so a full description must be left to those—and they are terribly few—who survive to write it. But that small part of it which I did see I shall set forth fully, because the story of these days is amongst the greatest, the very greatest, of all our history.

Meantime, in the port of Boulogne the terror spread itself insidiously, so that, where one had known a hundred knew; where one had feared all were filled with dismay. In the middle of this anxiety there came one afternoon to the town the strangest body of troops which it has ever fallen to my lot to behold. They came in two long trains, the carriages of which were Belgian, though the engines were French. They crowded the train so that there seemed to be no space left in any of the compartments, and they sat upon the roofs of the carriages and upon the tenders of the engines. As the trains drew into the terminus they cheered and waved their hats and sang the Brabançonne and then the Marseillaise, and the townspeople flocked out across the bridges to gain a closer view of them and to learn who they were and why they had come.

The townspeople learned that they were the Belgian soldiers who had defended Namur and who had escaped from the fortress before the enemy took possession of it. They told strange stories of great shells that demolished whole streets in their bursting, and of war by air which completed the panic wrought by the shells; and they described the last awful days in the town when men and women came forth from their cellars with their children to flee from the coming terror and were engulfed, they and their children, in the roads and byways under the hail of death.

The Belgian soldiers cheered the townspeople with some of their stories, for they said that the Germans were defeated and had been driven back, and that all danger of an advance upon the coast was passed. They were full of splendid optimism, which, indeed, seems to be one of the birthrights of this race, and when they went away in these suffocating trains they left more happiness behind them than the town had known for many days. . . . But this happiness was not destined to endure.

Why the Germans did not take Boulogne and Calais and Dunkirk during these days is one of the mysteries of this astonishing period. I speak with knowledge when I say that half a dozen Uhlans could have taken Boulogne any day during nearly a fortnight—and the Uhlans had ridden as far west as St. Omer at one period—which is about thirty miles from the port. Boulogne was utterly unprotected, and every hour her citizens expected the enemy to ride into her streets. When men woke in the morning they looked first at the flag flying over the citadel to see whether it was still the Tricolour of France which flew there; and no man certainly would have been surprised if he had discovered the black and red and white of the enemy in the place of the red and white and blue. When one thinks of the awful price that was to be paid later in bitter attempts to reach the seaboard, that early failure to take it becomes more and more inexplicable. It seems indeed like one of the jests of a grim Fate which having opened the door of opportunity shuts it again before the promised land has been obtained.

A week after the going of the English Boulogne was a place of fear and silence. The hotels were empty, the *digue* deserted, the streets like the streets of a town stricken by some visitation of God. Not a uniform was to be seen where so many had been displayed, and the long rows of tables in the *cafés* stood forsaken and melancholy. Even the humble customs officers had discarded their long blue coats and their bayonets, and went about in plain clothes for safety, lest the conqueror should suppose that resistance was contemplated.... One night the craft in the harbour, the trawlers and fishing vessels and steamers moved out in a body to anchor beyond the sea wall, and that same night the cross-Channel steamer did not lie at her berth, but returned to Folkestone. In the dead of night they removed the last of the archives and valuables which it was deemed necessary to save from the coming disaster. . . . It is possible even that two Uhlans might have taken and occupied Boulogne.

The exodus from that Northern land was like the exodus of a whole world which flees into exile, counting all lost save only life itself. Once again within living memory the terror was come upon France. France has no need to be warned concerning the fate which would be meted out to her. The trains were very few, and those trains that did run were besieged as the ark may have been besieged when the floods began to rise upon the earth. Salvation lay along the railroads and in the trains; and when the trains had departed there was no salvation. Every station therefore became a battlefield in which men fought for their womenfolk and women for their children and babes. You could not help, and so you hid your eyes that you might not see and tried to shut your ears that you might not hear. . . .

I came to Amiens while the terror and the fleeing into exile were at their height. I came about midnight, and on the way was vouchsafed a glimpse of the pilgrimage of sorrow which on that day choked every road in Artois and overflowed into every field and meadow— the pilgrimage that was like the bleeding to death of a whole nation, so vast was it, and so long, and so sorrowful.

This was not the same spectacle which I saw in Brussels, when the peasants came to the city from the east country after the army had fallen back behind the forts of Antwerp. This catastrophe was a greater thing, as the light of the sun is greater than the light of a candle. This was a world which fell, and the sorrow of its fall went up to the skies because these people were without hope in their dark hour. These people believed, as we all of us came so very near believing, that the end had indeed been accomplished, that the armies had been smitten asunder, that the armies were reeling back, vanquished and broken, before the foe, and that the fair bosom of France lay defenceless, and at the mercy of the spoiler.

Easy it is now to speak of these fears as cowards' fears and to upbraid the craven spirit which harboured them. But that day smote courage out of the heart by the mere agony of the spectacle which it presented to casual eyes. On the roads of France leading into Amiens you saw a hundred sights, every one of which in other days would have wrung your heart and haunted your memory.

You saw a great mass of humanity moving in a phalanx the solidity of which was broken only by the vehicles which endeavoured to force a passage through it. You saw men supporting children who drooped with fatigue and women labouring under the weight of babes they had carried over miles of unsheltered roadway under a blazing sun. The faces of those poor people were terrible because a dull tragedy seemed to have become imprinted upon them; only their eyes held the wistfulness of animals being herded to slaughter. Sometimes the children whimpered a little because their feet were sore and blistered with walking, and sometimes they threw themselves down in sheer exhaustion. Then father or mother would attempt to drag them along or even to goad them by blows to a further effort; because this procession paused not day or night in its going; and to be left behind was to fall living into the hands of wrath.

You saw very old women who had ceased even to feel afraid in the dull agony of the march, and who toiled along as though under the influence of some benumbing drug, their faces wet with perspiration and caked with dust, and their white hair falling dishevelled on their shoulders; their clothing, the best clothing they possessed, was sadly torn and muddied. A few of them carried possessions with them in handkerchiefs, held tightly with a clasp that had become automatic: others had cast their possessions away because they proved too heavy and because the idea of saving anything out of their ruin appeared fantastic. So there were many of these little foolish bundles upon the. roadway, and men tripped upon them and cursed them as they passed. But women stooped to pick them up.

Some of the stronger members of the company wheeled hand-carts laden with their furniture. This had seemed a good plan in the cool of the early morning, but now it was torture scarcely to be endured. The carts dragged miserably, and the strength required to propel them was out of all proportion to the value of their freight. But a few of the men had thrown their furniture away and placed tired little boys and girls upon the carts, and so love had her abiding places even here in this army of the dispossessed. Once I saw an old woman in one of these carts with a child in her arms; a man and woman, evidently her son and daughter-in-law, pushed it.

A few had tried to drive away their cattle, and so you saw sheep and oxen mingling with the human stream, and you also saw many horses with strange riders perched on their backs. There were bullock-waggons in which the more fortunate rode in some comfort, and horse vehicles with farmers and their families who yesterday were prosperous people.

For the most part they were of the peasant and farming class these people; tall men and hard-featured women and pretty little children not yet fallen victims to the weariness of the peasant life. But sometimes you could distinguish other types—a priest, perhaps, walking sadly amongst his flock, trying to lighten their burdens and himself shouldering the burden of many with fine devotion (for these priests of Northern France my admiration will abide), or a soldier in khaki or in the long blue coat and *culottes rouges* of the French infantry, without his rifle, and with the look on his face which a man wears when he has no longer any care for life or death.

They pass, moving they scarce know whither, endlessly, like a flood. The skies above them are darkened with the coming of night, and the requiem of sunset is sung to the accompaniment of their dull feet. They do not look up; their eyes are downcast always upon the road that is their torment and their hope. If you stand quite close to them, they will not see you; the fierce hours of day have changed them, transmuting all the impulses of nature into baser causes. Like the wheels of a machine they grind the dust under their feet in their slow passing. . . . And the long road goes down to the river and up again to the hill.

But they are not alone upon the road. Cleaving through their ranks like great ships go the heavy vehicles of war—huge forage waggons and ammunition carts and ambulances full of wounded men. The hooting of the vehicles mingles harshly with the voices of the men and women—they who have to crowd together in the ditches to let them pass. They go by furiously, as is the way and necessity of war without reck of the misery surging around them. Sometimes a huge car, its sleek panels gleaming still through dust which covers them, sweeps along the road, baying in its passage like a great dog. In dim interiors you may catch a glimpse of uniformed men who lean back among the cushions, seeing nothing, hearing nothing. The game of war, when it is played with this intensity, takes small thought of the pawns. . . . They complain very little these people without a home and without joy; they go on in silence, into the night, amongst the shouting of the drivers and the baying of the motor-horns. . . . And Pity turns away her eyes that the funds of her grief may not be exhausted.

After Mons the Germans detached a "flying corps" to carry terror into the western provinces of North France and so prepare the way for the occupation of the seaboard, of Calais and Boulogne and Dieppe and Havre, after Paris should have fallen into their hands. The first objective of this body was necessarily Amiens, because Amiens is an important railway junction, and because the line of communication from the British front to the sea at Havre lay through Amiens. With Amiens in their hands the Germans could cut General French's Army from its supply columns and at the same time paralyse the resistance of the coast towns; Rouen would fall easily then, and Havre with its great dockyards and its command of the mouth of the Seine.

The flying column consisted of cavalry and motor sections, the dreaded Uhlans of 1870 and a new race of Uhlans still more terrible because their rate of movement had been multiplied tenfold and their power of inflicting damage increased in proportion. These raiders on horse and in motorcar swept down the roads of Artois towards the town of Amiens with terrible speed, driving the terrified inhabitants in front of them. They it was who were responsible for the procession of grief wending its weary way towards the town; they were the spur upon these jaded and sorry men and women, driving them on even when strength had become exhausted. The lively horror of their coming went with that company through every kilometre of its long journeying and wrought the silence which made of the exodus a spectacle strange and terrible.

But the exodus from Northern France was not only by road. It was not even chiefly by road. The railways bore the brunt of it, and their work will live in the memory of all who saw those stations and those trains and witnessed the scenes of anguish which were afforded by them. I stood all night on the platform of Amiens station and watched these refugee trains and the trains full of wounded men fresh from the battle-fields and the trains that hurried reinforcements to the front—French and British—the trains that came from Calais and Boulogne with cross-Channel passengers, whose first knowledge of the terror was gleaned from the sights they saw through the windows of the carriages. The sound of these trains was like the far-off rolling of thunder amongst the hills, and the spectacle which they presented was like the ruin of a whole people.

The very spirit of disaster seemed to be contained under the glass dome of the station, of disaster and confusion and dismay. The platforms were congested with all manner of types of people, refugees like those upon the roads, and soldiers who had lost their regiments, and well-to-do townsfolk hurrying away from the danger, and Americans rushing to Paris. There were a few British officers too, but these held aloof and viewed the scene with quiet patience, hiding their thoughts under a mask of indifference. No sort of attempt was made to stem this human flood, which grew fuller every hour, and no man seemed to know in what manner it would be disposed of. The whole railway system was disorganised; trains came and went, apparently uncontrolled. Those going to the south were besieged, taken by storm in the twinkling of an eye. People did not pause in that critical hour to differentiate between destinations, Havre or Paris or Dieppe, it was immaterial so long as the coast was reached or the way opened for further flight. . . . Far away you could hear the booming of the guns like an echo upon the calm air of night.

Your mind becomes dull and confused in all this endless confusion. There seems to be no established order in things, and all the values of life have been changed. The things which mattered yesterday are today nothing: only the stark facts of life and death remain in a world become suddenly fierce and hard and primitive.

Yet your apathy is swept away in a single instant when the first of the great trains of wounded from the battlefield creeps up to you along the platform of the station. At the sight of the men of Mons a new kindling of the spirit is wrought and a new edge given to pain.

The long train grinds into the station, slowly, serpentlike, and then stops in a series of short, sharp jerks. The train is composed of horse-waggons, and the waggons have no brakes, so that when the engine stops all the waggons clash together and pull back again at their chains and clash together again. . . . The clashing of the waggons is punctuated by the groans of wounded men who lie on the straw within them and whose wounds are opened and jostled by the brakeless waggons. . . . That is the first swift impression.

The train stops at last—you can hear the panting of the great *Nord* engine above the moaning of the sorely wounded men lying on the straw. The moaning of the wounded men, however, is continuous, and the sound of it frightens the women and children waiting on the platform. Some of the children shriek, and so a shrill crying is added to the deeper voice of suffering. Grief has many tongues in this station at Amiens.

You approach the waggon doors where the less severely wounded men are crowded together looking at you, but not speaking. They recognise that you are English and perhaps ask you for tobacco in curious level tones, almost indifferently.

Then a man speaks, to answer your unspoken question.

"Yes, it was hell . . . worse. . . ."

You will never forget those railway waggons of the early days of war, those brakeless waggons with their straw carpets and their dismal interiors; and you will hear long, long afterwards the pitiful moaning of the wounded men and their crying when the waggons jolted and jostled together. These were the lads who sang their way through the Boulogne streets so gaily only a short week ago, the lads who went away beyond the hills along the white roads of France. At last the curtain of doubt and secrecy is lifted up and they are back again, weary and broken, mangled in death, with pale cheeks that are blood-stained and mud-stained, and wistful eyes that beseech help when there is no help to give.

They are come again; and your heart is chill as you gaze upon this coming. This coming is terrible, as your worst fears did not picture it. Live rumour is already at work magnifying its terror, and the tale is told that these only have escaped from the maelstrom. The men speak; and though they would cheer you if they could, their words are full of darkness.

Terrible beyond anything you can think of: their guns are awful, and we have no guns to meet them. Our guns are no use against that hail of shells. We did our best, and we're better men than they are, but it's hell . . . hell.

So one man speaks. Another declares that in all his life he has never known such fury of battle.

Yet our men fought like demons, they fought till they could fight no more, and then they began all over again. There were three of them to every one of us, and they came on in waves just like the sea. They were as many as the waves of the sea. We stood our ground with our dead and dying around us till they fell back in the darkness, and then we marched and marched through the night, back and back. . . . In the morning we fought again that at night we might be able to retreat.

The faces of the men are very strange: like the faces of men who have suffered some great and sudden shock. I have seen the expression in the eyes of a patient recovering from the effects of a critical operation. It is a look at once wistful and bewildered and indifferent. These men, as yet, are separated from life by a barrier which is impenetrable as mist. They are divorced from all the interests of life. Now that the fierce effort is ended they fall into a kind of dream-state, a lethargy; they can talk and they can laugh, but their talk is disconnected and fragmentary, and their laughter is like the ghost of the good laughter that you heard when they went away across the hills.

So the tales these men tell you are not to be written down as the true story of the great encounter. They are not even to be considered seriously as representing the minds of those who tell them. To regard them in that way would be to fall into the mistake which was so common in these early days—the mistake of seeing the war in little bits. Mons and the retreat which began at Mons and ended at the Marne were terrible beyond anything which has as yet been written concerning them; but the Retreat from Mons was not, as events soon proved, a crowning disaster.

The truth of the retreat is simple and must be borne in mind if these pages are to be read intelligently. The retreat began because Namur, the pivot of the Allied line, had been lost. The loss of Namur meant the danger of being surrounded on the right wing. The retreat continued until that danger had been minimised and until opportunity for a counter-stroke presented itself.

The speed of the retreat is its most wonderful feature. Its speed, perhaps more than any other factor, turned the retreat into a victory. The heavy guns of the enemy were the cause of the fall of Namur; the heavy guns of the enemy were the terror of which all these wounded men in the trains in Amiens station spoke. It was because the enemy was so strong in heavy guns that it was found impossible to withstand his advance. The retreat saved the armies from the heavy guns and outran the guns. In their eager haste the Germans got in front of their main artillery, just as they had done at Liège; and when they came to fight the Battle of the Marne the "weight of metal" was more evenly distributed over the two opposing forces.

CHAPTER 6

In the Days of the Great Retreat

The action which bears the name of "The Retreat from Mons" lasted thirteen days—from Sunday, August 23rd, till Saturday, September 5th. It covered about 100 miles. Reduced to its simplest terms, it was an action of day fights and night retiring movements. The fighting by day made the retiring by night possible. The fighting was of the fiercest character and the retiring of the most strenuous, because often food and water were difficult to obtain, and always the chance of obtaining rest was infinitesimal.

Our men lay where they had fought for a brief space at evening, and then, shouldering their rifles, moved back again on the long trail southwards.

There were two events in the retreat that I must mention in passing, since the whole future of the struggle depended upon them. The first event was a battle fought on Tuesday night and Wednesday between the villages of Landrecies and Caudry, that is to say on a line about twenty miles south of Mons. This battle was the first real and serious attempt of the Germans to envelop and swallow up "General French's contemptible little army." The Germans had already engaged our army at Mons; they had pursued it during two days and two nights in its retreat southwards. Now was to come the *coup de grace* which would end Britain's part in the war on land and wipe out at a blow the force of the hated English.

The blow fell at night in a drizzle of rain when our tired men had thrown themselves down to snatch a short rest after their terrible struggle. The village of Landrecies, on the right of our line, was chosen for the first assault. The enemy threw himself in force against the village, believing that he had but to reach forth his hand to grasp the prize.

But our men slept lightly, and in a few seconds they were afoot again and at work. One of them said:

The Germans came on like mad through the dark streets, pouring their fire into us, and we had to form up as best we could and collect ourselves and make some sort of reply to them. God knows how we managed it. It was done so fast that I scarcely remember what happened. All I know is that I shot and shot into the darkness till at last the houses of the town began to catch fire under the shells, and then we saw them and were able to get at them.

The attack failed, but next day it was renewed all along the line with great fury. That day, Wednesday, August 26th, the fate of the British Army was decided. August 26th—called the Battle of Le Cateau—was a victory day because during its first hours Sir Horace Smith-Dorrien on the left and Sir Douglas Haig on the right held the mighty avalanche in check, so that during its later hours retreat on a great scale became possible once more.

Once on that day the cavalry of the Prussian Guard rode into the lines of the British Infantry, and once at least the hearts of brave and devoted leaders quailed for the issue of the combat. Of that day Sir John French wrote some time later that it was "the most critical day of all," and of Sir Horace Smith-Dorrien, whose splendid resistance on the British left wing did so much to save the day, he wrote:

The saving of the left wing of the army under my command on the morning of the 26th August could never have been accomplished unless a commander of rare and unusual coolness, intrepidity and determination had been present to personally conduct the operation.

When I read those words I thought again of the little man with whom I had crossed the Channel, the little man with the tired eyes and the kindly face.

The second event took place when the British Army was approaching the River Aisne from the northwards. It was the visit of General Joffre to General French's headquarters. That visit was made in order to explain to the British commander-in-chief that the retreat must continue, in spite of the fact that the rearguard action against the Germans had been, on the whole, successful. General Joffre spoke for the whole line, not for the British part of it—i.e. the extreme left. The centre of the line at Rheims was still being hard pressed, and it was essential that the wings should move back as the centre moved back, otherwise a hole might be driven into the long line. It was the German object to break the line and then "roll up "the two portions of the divided army separately.

Out of that meeting came the further retreat of the British force from the Aisne to the Marne.

How our men hated this retreating! Again and again I heard from their lips angry and amazed comments upon the action of their leaders. The men seemed to feel that they had a special grievance against leaders who each time that they "won a battle" ordered them to run away. But with characteristic *esprit de corps* they blamed the French commanders rather than their own. It was a French idea this retreating, they said, and it was a d——n bad idea. Their opinion of the French commanders went down to zero during these days, even as it was to leap up again in the great days after the Battle of the Marne. The ordinary soldier does not think strategically, and he always views war strictly from the personal point of view. The idea that the whole line must move in unison according to a wide plan does not seem to have occurred to him.

There remains, and will always remain, one commentary upon the great retreat which by reason of its very boldness is illuminating. It is the commentary of figures. In the thirteen days of the Retreat from Mons the British Army suffered 15,142 casualties, of which 276 were killed, 1223 wounded and 13,643 *missing*. . . . So that that sorrowful train-load in the station at Amiens, and the other train-loads which followed it, represented a mere fraction of the terrible penalty of retreat. The whole land of France, from the frontiers to the gates of Paris, was strewn with our dead and wounded, who had perforce to be left behind to the mercy of the advancing hosts of the foe.

They abandoned Amiens to the "flying column" of the enemy; the flying column, cavalry and artillery and armoured motorcars, took possession and made of the place its headquarters. From Amiens a campaign of terror was to be waged against the land west of Paris, the villages upon the Seine, Rouen and the ports of Dieppe and Havre. The Germans seized the public offices in Amiens and found there a plentiful supply of official note-paper and passport forms. They lost not an hour in equipping their "land pirates" with documents duly stamped and sealed which on presentation should gain them free passage along the roads of France.

It was an amazing thing this raid which began at Amiens and spread out like the strands of a spider's web over all the land to the sea. There is reason to suppose that no fewer than 400 armed motorcars took part in it. Each car carried four men, and these were dressed in the uniforms either of French or British officers. The cars sped away from Amiens at night and ran out into the surrounding districts. Their sole object was to spread terror. If they came to a village and were challenged they showed their papers, and if there was any trouble concerning these papers, they shot the sentry. When they got into the village street officers frequently fired with revolvers at the defenceless inhabitants.

They went into Senlis in this way and spread terror through the little town, thus preparing the way for the advance of the main army: they visited also a hundred little villages on the plateau above the Seine, and they even dared to thrust down as far as Havre.

The story of that astonishing dash has not, I think, been told in any detail. At the time some information concerning it did leak out but was generally disbelieved. The fact remains, however, that one day one of those cars attempted to get into the great French seaport and almost succeeded. On that day Havre was full of British soldiers and French Territorials, a great centre in its fullest activity; it must have been abundantly clear to the bandits that nothing but death could possibly await them in these crowded and well guarded streets. Yet so great was the presumption of the enemy at this time that not the least hesitation seems to have been shown. The car dashed towards the town by the low road along the river, and its way was not impeded. When it was challenged papers were immediately produced, duly signed and stamped, and the sentries saluted and let it go.

But just outside the town a sentry of a more inquisitive type ventured to ask questions of the bandits and to express doubts concerning their credentials. Instantly the car was set in motion. The sentry levelled his rifle, but before he could fire bullets were whizzing around his head and the car had dashed away along the flat, broad road.

The sentry continued to fire after the car, and the noise of his firing attracted the attention of a carter who was driving his heavy waggon into the town. He saw his chance and took it. He drew his waggon across the road in front of the advancing car. Next instant the car crashed into the waggon and reeled back from it a mass of broken and twisted metal. Two at least of the bandits lay dead in the road, and the other two were quickly made prisoners.

I have said that the story was generally disbelieved, yet in time exaggerated accounts of it did gain credence, and then accounts were added of similar doings in the country to northwards. So little by little the fear came down to Rouen and Havre as it had come to Brussels and Boulogne and Amiens, and once again the procession of the dispossessed began from these places. I came to Havre from Rouen just when the fear had begun to work, and so I saw all over again the scenes which I had come to regard as the inevitable concomitants of this struggle—the terror and the suffering, and the weary marching over the long dusty roads.

The railway journey from Amiens to Rouen was indeed a nightmare of discomfort and anxiety. The train was crowded so that not another human being could have been squeezed into its stifling compartments or granted a foothold upon the little verandahs which projected at either end of its carriages. The journey occupied fifteen hours, because every moment some new stoppage occurred and because the line was already congested with a huge body of traffic. All along the line you might see the signs of the coming panic; farmhouses sleeping among their ripe orchards, already in many instances abandoned and desolate; in others cases by twos and threes you could see the country folk beginning their pilgrimage. Fields lay ungarnered, trees unpicked, and sometimes when the train stopped men would run out of the carriages and pluck the fruit—apples and pears—no one hindering them.

At Rouen you saw a town already in the throes of great anxiety. They had begun to empty the huge cattle parks by the river banks under the wooded hills which are the familiar landmarks of this exquisite town. There were still great herds of cattle in the parks, sheep and oxen from Normandy and Brittany, and their lowing and bleating made strange music in the chill dawn before the sun had climbed up from behind the hills. There were also great barges upon the river moving down stream from Paris before the threat of occupation which every hour became more menacing. These were the barges which one usually sees along the river banks by the Quais under the Eiffel Tower. Through that dim morning light the white spires of the cathedral rose up clear and beautiful and delicate as lace, fingers pointing away from this clamour and moil to the things which are steadfast and unchangeable.

At the station at Rouen they were busy unloading a train of wounded from the battlefield of La Cateau, where Sir Horace Smith-Dorrien made his great fight. It was another of those goods trains improvised for the use of the Ambulance Corps, with straw on the

74

floors and a few rough wooden erections for swinging stretchers. You wondered as you looked at it why it was that whole men, civilians, might ride still in comparative luxury in first-class carriages, while broken and injured men must travel in these terrible brakeless waggons. But it was not possible to apportion blame, for this retreat had come upon a Medical Corps but little prepared to cope with it; the Medical Corps had done what it could with heroic disregard for its own safety or comfort. The fault lay not here in the field, but in the Government offices, where they had not envisaged the possibility of using better means—even though a lesson had been taught them years before in the case of the war in South Africa.

They brought a couple of Highland officers from the train and carried them across the platform to the waiting ambulances. One of these men I remember had a boy face that was as white as the paving-stones they laid him down upon. The soiled dressings, which had been applied on the battle-field two days before, had become loosened and had shifted, and there was revealed a great gash in that boy's side, the very sight of which brought the sweat out upon your brow. The boy was smiling nevertheless and attempting to speak through his parched lips. He was gay even while his eyes looked into the eyes of death.

You heard from some of these wounded men the cruel story of long days and nights spent in the goods waggons without food or water and without medical attendance. Medical attendance in these waggons was difficult or impossible, because there was no means of communication, and because the darkness and the dirt made any attempt to remove the caked and blood-befouled field-dressing a danger. Better it was to risk the blood-poisoning already developing in these wounds than to open the way to the dust and straw chopping which abounded on every side.

What journeys, what agonies these wounded men suffered in the days of the great Retreat! Here in this waggon are ten patients, four of them lying on the straw and six standing up by the doorway. Two of the four lying cases have shattered bones, and the other two are victims of terrible flesh wounds caused by great jagged pieces of shrapnel, which have torn the muscles asunder and impregnated the tissues with the foul, manured soil of this highly cultivated land. The wounds have been dressed but once, upon the battle-field, by an overwrought army surgeon whose splendid heroism alone has saved him from collapse. He could not wash and cleanse the wounds as he would have liked to do, there were too many wounds to attend to, and there was too little time in which to deal with them; the enemy pressed hotly upon our retiring ranks, and great shells rained down even upon this place of mercy.

So the wounded men went to the train with a rough dressing to dam up the bleeding from their wounds and to hold within the wounds the seeds of poison and death. In a few hours, as they lay uneasily upon the dusty straw, the germs of blood-poisoning began their work, and the wounds throbbed with the inflammation which was developing in them. A fierce thirst began to consume the sufferers as their temperatures mounted higher and the skin in the neighbourhood of the lacerations became most exquisitely tender. Then the train drew up sharply upon the line and the waggons clashed together and bumped to a standstill. Every bump was like driving a knife into the open wounds, and the men cried out in their agony for mercy, or bit their lips and caught their breaths so that the blood ebbed away from their cheeks and they fainted under the scourge of the pain.

The train lingered upon its journey because there were other trains in front of it, and because the railway system was disorganised. If the train had consisted of real hospital cars, that would have been the doctor's opportunity to move along the corridor and put fresh clean dressings on those inflamed wounds, or to wash them in some cleansing solution. But no doctor could come now, and so in darkness and stifling heat these gallant fellows writhed upon the straw praying, many of them, for death that they might achieve release from their torment.

Prolong this agony three, four, even five and six days and you will be able to measure the sum of it. And with the damp the state of many of the wounds grew worse, till at last gangrene in many cases set in and lock-jaw in a few. Realise that food and drink were often difficult to obtain in the case of men dangerously wounded, lying upon the straw. Count the number of the jolts and jars in a journey of one hundred miles occupying over two days. . . . The tale of suffering is terrible beyond words, so that your heart fails at thought of it. You begin to see all Europe as a torture chamber thronged with victims, and the sound of their anguish goes up day and night to a mute heaven. . . . Also, though you do not blame, you are filled with wonder that some other means of handling the wounded was not devised beforehand.

What has been done since those days might have been accomplished surely a little earlier. Had England forgotten the figure of the Lady with the Lamp, or the fact that in South Africa, towards the close, luxurious hospital trains brought the wounded down country to Cape Town? Did the organisers who sent out an army of 70,000 men with, for the most part, horse ambulances, imagine that that preparation would suffice against the greatest military power on earth? At that very hour England was stretching out eager hands to help and great physicians and surgeons had already offered their services to their country. There were a thousand problems to solve, the solution of which might have been carried out on an earlier day; there was a whole system to be built up, the building of which might have been begun in the days of peace.

These are strong words: they are true. The scenes of suffering I witnessed at Rouen and Havre, and a hundred places on the line, will remain with me as a terrible recollection—the more terrible that those workers who were on the spot laboured with entire devotion and unselfishness to mitigate the suffering around them. But they were too few and too ill-equipped to render effective service. This stream of wounded had falsified all expectations; where tens had been looked for, thousands had been encountered.

One may feel that the problems of a European war could not have been anticipated. That is true no doubt to some slight extent. Gangrene and lock-jaw were enemies that could not perhaps have been provided against. But even the Ulster Volunteers had supplied themselves with motor ambulances, and a hospital train might, one would have supposed, have been included in the equipment of the Expeditionary Force.

At Rouen there were hospital ships moored to the quays—ships from the Fishguard route with long yellow funnels and hulls painted white and marked with huge red crosses. There were more of these ships in the outer basin at Havre, and they brought the trains down to the dock wall and unloaded them directly into the steamers. There was infinite pathos in the spectacle of these boats' decks crowded with the lightly wounded men. In the good sunlight a little of the joy of life had come back again, but that little only served to accentuate the look of wistfulness on almost every face. These men were going back to England and safety, but the awful memory of the bloody days they had lived through haunted them.

They were not . . . they would never be again in all the world, the light-hearted lads who swung ashore only ten days earlier upon the soil of France. Age and care and sorrow were come upon them and the shadow of death had fallen upon every one. War was no longer a game: it had become a fiery trial. Some of these men would come back, but their return would be with bitterness, and with the deep anger of those who have a wrong kindled within their hearts. The spirit of the Frenchmen who fought in 1870 was entered already into their comrades in arms!

All day and all night the trains rolled down to the sea and at all hours the white ships with the blood-red crosses upon their plates went out upon the tide to England. Havre was the base now since Boulogne had been abandoned. But already the abandonment of Havre was in contemplation. The broad *digue* and the great *boulevard* were emptying with the flying hours, and the little boats that ply across the Seine to Trouville went out full of passengers—rich French people and their children whom they had brought in the July days to make holiday upon the shore.

Above the town upon the hill there were great camps as there had been in Boulogne. From the hill you might look out, across the long fields of the sea stretching to the horizon, or again you might behold the broad bosom of the river and see its first windings away inland, where it sweeps round into its proper estuary. You might also see the fleet that lay at anchor beyond the harbour mouth—the great transports which came so silently to Boulogne and slipped away again so silently when the danger fell upon the town.

Below you the town; and the noise and jangle of its streets rise up in cheerful monotony. You watch the long trains creeping in and out of the station like huge black caterpillars, and the motor-waggons lurching drunkenly along the roads and the street cars and the dense mass of the people in the central boulevard where the *cafés* are. Also you see the forest of masts and spars that indicates the docks and the shipping. . . . For Havre is the greatest of all the ports of France.

In the town the uneasiness grows more profound from hour to hour. Such news as has come down from the battlefield is bad news. The enemy advance on Paris continues, and the government has fled from the city. The population of Paris is fleeing by every road to the southward, to Chartres and Orleans and Bordeaux. The line between Paris and Rouen has been cut and the great viaduct at Pontoise on the Dieppe line has been blown up. "It is needful to have courage . . . but the worst . . . the worst may be expected."

And to confirm this evil report you see again the British ships drawing into the harbour to load up the goods and supplies which have already been disembarked. Havre, like Boulogne, is doomed to

THE EFFECTS OF BOMBARDMENT
A general view of the ruins of Baccarat

evacuation. You see the forage waggons rolling swiftly to the docks and the men from the camps marching off, company by company in the same direction—men who have never fired a shot in war, but who must go up to the fighting front by some other way than this one.

Yesterday your hotel was full of staff officers in red hats who talked merrily with you concerning the prospects of the campaign—of gallant boys and grizzled seniors vying with one another in their eagerness to "see the show." Today the tables are empty and the *salle à manger* strangely quiet, and the old lady in the *caisse* in the entrance hall has a furrowed brow and anxious, care-worn eyes. When you speak to her she asks you with pitiful eagerness, "*Les nouvelles sont-ils bonnes?*" and you must try to reassure her as best you can. At night in the *café* you find yourself once more counting the hours until this new act of the drama of war will have been ended.

Next day the tide of refugees flows into the town. But these are not the refugees of Brussels, nor yet of the roads and railways leading into Amiens. These refugees have boxes instead of bundles, and they came in first-class railway carriages and engage the best rooms at the best hotels, paying liberally, without care for all that they demand.

Nor are they refugees at all in the strict sense of the term, for they are homeward bound and are fleeing only from the scenes of their pleasures.

These are the American tourists who found themselves in Germany or Switzerland and France when the war cloud came, and who rushed to Paris, as is the instinct of Americans, in order to watch events from that safe vantage ground. But the day of the safety of Paris is ended. The army of the invader is already at the gates of the city: terrible visions of envelopment and siege have been conjured up: terrible visions of a fleeing population have been actually witnessed. There are dark days ahead for the gay city, perhaps starvation and punishment and death—and so the pleasure seekers have taken great fright and have begun to flee away also, back to the seaboard where they may embark for their own country.

A strange crowd they are and worth attention even in this hour. When you have recovered from the annoyance caused by the fact that to every cabman who drives them they give 20 *fr.* as a fare, and to every porter who carries their luggage 5 *fr.*—(which spoils both cabmen and porters for other people who are less generously-minded)—you will find that they can be very interesting. They will talk to you as much as you wish, for they have two days to spend in Havre before

La France, the great Transatlantic liner, sails from the port. They will tell you what *they* think of the war, and of the Germans who have made the war.

One of them—a woman—told me:

Paris is dead, but she is still beautiful. I mean the old Paris that we knew and loved and enjoyed. There is another Paris that we did not know—a hard, strong Paris, with the face of a woman and the heart of a hero. That is what I mean when I say she is still beautiful—she has the same face but her spirit is changed.

We sat in the big *café* in the square near the main *boulevard*. There were French officers and English officers and Belgians dining around us. My companion waved her hand towards them:

They are all fine men, but of course we admire you most. You are so like us and in a way we are proud of you: we expect you to win, and we believe you will win. . . . You always do win in the end . . . somehow. The Dutch (Germans)? . . . But they are dirty pigs.

It is the last scene of this drama of the Retreat, because tomorrow the tide will turn and a new world be brought to birth. It is a strange scene because there is no precedent for it in all our history. As I can never forget the agony of Brussels or the eyes of the men who came back from Mons, so I can never forget this swift revelation of brotherhood and kinship.

The scene is the outer basin of the great harbour, and the time is evening . . . the moment when the sun goes down the steeps of the West towards a golden sea, and the sky is painted crimson and vermilion and saffron for his couching. A great battleship lies in the harbour, her four funnels painted a dull slate-grey with white bands on them. The "Stars and Stripes" of the United States float lazily at her stern.

She is the American cruiser *Tennessee*, which has been sent to watch over the safety of the fleeing American tourists.

Suddenly on the quiet air is borne the sound of a British cheer—that strong, big, deep sound which grips the heart and sends a thrill tingling along every nerve.

The cheer is repeated and is drowned by a shriller cheering. The dock gates at the top of the basin are swung slowly open and there emerges one of the huge British transports, its decks thronged with soldiers in khaki.

The transport swings down where the *Tennessee* lies moored, and as she passes on her way dips her flag to the "Stars and Stripes"—the "Stars and Stripes" are dipped also in a profound silence as when two strong friends look into each other's eyes and shake one another by the hand in an hour of crisis. Then, softly at first, but growing strong and loud, there rises from the decks of the British ship that grand old sea chant of Britain that has cheered her warriors in many a day of ill-fortune:

When Britain first, at heaven's command,
Arose from out the azure main,
This was the charter of the land,
And guardian angels sang this strain.

The American sailors on the *Tennessee* crowd to the rails and wave their hats and then, as it were, impelled by an irresistible impulse, take up the rolling chorus, flinging it far across the sunny waters:

Rule, Britannia, Britannia rules the waves:
Britons never, never, never shall be slaves.

CHAPTER 7

The Scissors of General Joffre

It is possible that in years to come men will look back upon the Battle of the Marne and say of it that it was the greatest battle in European history. The Battle of the Marne decided the fate of Paris in 1914, but that was perhaps one of the least things which it decided. It decided also the fate of the British and French armies engaged outside of Paris, the armies which had come down from Mons and Namur in great retreat; it decided therefore the resistance in the West; it decided the result of the great German smashing blow that was to paralyse Western resistance and end the war in a few months; it made a winter campaign inevitable, or almost inevitable; it postponed the day of the attack upon Russia many months, and gave that nation time to gather together her resources for advance into the enemy's territory.

The Marne, too, taught Europe a lesson: it revealed the fact that with all her preparation, all her organisation, all her equipment Germany was not invincible, that her power lay chiefly in her mechanical engines of war, and that, man for man, she was an inferior people. It put new spirit into the allied nations, cemented the alliance and gave, like an early glimmer of dawn, the promise of victory in full sunshine.

Losing the Marne, the Entente would have lost Paris and all that Paris portends in equipment and in strength. It would have lost the whole of the North of France, and perhaps the whole of France as well. It would have lost a great army and a great treasure. It might have lost hope even and so have fallen before the fury of the conquering Germans.

The Battle of the Marne, at least the Western portion of it, is one of the simplest battles that ever was fought. You have only to think of a pair of scissors in order to understand it. The pivot of the blades of the scissors is the town of Meaux, just outside Paris to the north-east. Meaux stands on the River Marne somewhat to the west of a point where the River Ourcq flows into it. The Marne comes from the east to Meaux, but at Meaux it turns southwards to flow down into the Seine at Paris. So at Meaux the river makes a bend like an elbow, with the point of the elbow directed to the north-east. The Ourcq River at first runs parallel to the Marne to the north of it, and then also makes an elbow turn to the south and runs due south to flow into the Marne.

The Germans wheeled down over the Marne, leaving Paris on their right, in order to attack the Allied Army, which lay to the east of Paris, and which is represented by the lower blade of the scissors. At that moment the scissors had no upper blade at all. But when the enemy had come down far enough General Joffre supplied the upper blade from his reserves in Paris. . . . And the scissors were shut!

That, in the fewest possible words, is the story of the battle. But there are two points that must be made quite clear, because so much discussion has taken place in reference to them. The first of these is the reason why the Germans moved to the eastward to meet the Allied Army and did not advance directly upon Paris.

That question has troubled many people, and continues to trouble them. I have heard it discussed all over the Western front by people of all types, from Russians to British journalists. The usual way of discussing it is to ask mysteriously what secret reason impelled the enemy to relinquish the prize, Paris, which he held in his hand and then mysteriously to hint at knowledge. "The Crown Prince failed to join his army to the army of von Kluck, and von Kluck had to swing to the east to get in contact with him." "The Germans felt it would be easier to surprise the city by an attack from the east than from the north," and so on.

Now this mystery is manifestly absurd when the true reason is so abundantly obvious. The true reason why the Germans swung to the east away from Paris was that in that direction lay the unbroken army of the enemy. The retreat from Mons had not been a rout; the French Army was still an army and capable of fighting. The French Army had to be fought before the spoils of victory could be obtained, just as you must catch your hare before you cook it.

To attack Paris while an unbeaten army lay in wait close at hand would have been madness: no sane general would even consider such an idea. If the Germans had done that they would have written them-

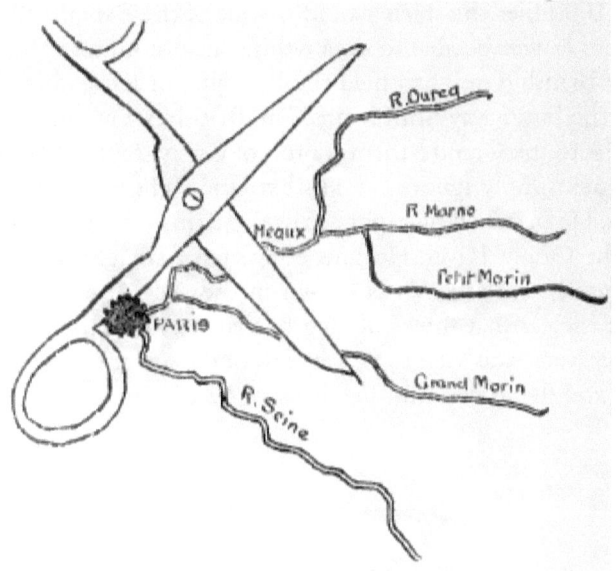

3. THE BATTLE OF THE MARNE

The lower blade of the scissors represents the position of the Allies at the beginning of the battle. At this time the upper blade did not exist. It had still to be supplied.

selves down not as victors but as imbeciles. On the other hand, the defeat of the Allied Army meant the immediate fall of Paris. This is clear the moment it is realised that the siege of a great city is a vast undertaking requiring absolute and unhampered freedom of action. It is a great undertaking no matter how feeble, relatively, the defence may be. The whole object of the enemy was to crush his opponent's army, not to leave it to recover itself and to attack him while he knocked down houses or made breaches in defence works.

The second point is a much more difficult one, for it concerns the strategy of the battle. Now there are two great features in the strategy of the Battle of the Marne that must never be lost sight of. The one feature is the mistake which von Kluck made in supposing that the British Army was too demoralised to fight, and the other feature is the "taxicab army," or upper blade of Joffre's scissors.

Von Kluck had driven the British Army 100 miles from Mons to the gates of Paris. He had about 10,000 prisoners, wounded and unwounded. He had seen the khaki coats melting away in front of him night after night as soon as the darkness fell. He assumed that at the end of 100 miles the spirit would be out of these men and that they would no longer be able to do anything against him.

The British Army had held the left wing or left end of the Allied line all the bitter way from Mons. The British Army came down over the rivers to the Grand Morin (Forest of Crécy) on the left of the line. Von Kluck simply ignored it. His extreme right lay on Senlis, north of Paris. He marched his right across the British front so as to bring it along the Ourcq River. He thus converted a straight line into a line representing the letter V (as shown in the accompanying diagrams). Now it is clear that the upper leg of that letter V—the leg along the Ourcq River—was vital to the success of the lower leg. Break the upper leg and the lower must flee back or be cut off.

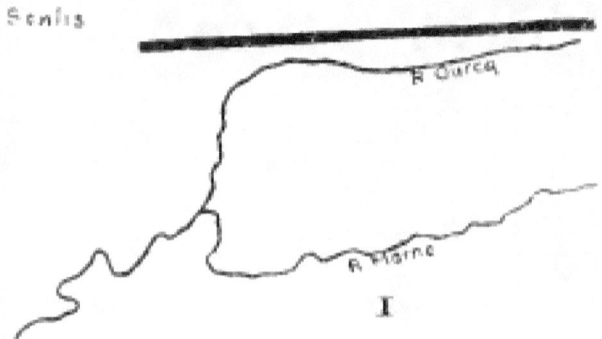

4. 1) VON KLUCK'S POSITION BEFORE HE MARCHED TO THE MARNE.

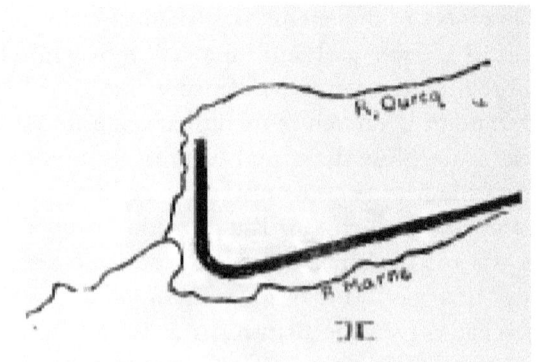

4. 2) HOW VON KLUCK EXPOSED HIS FLANK ON THE OURQ.

So long as the enemy in front of you is demoralised and has no reserves that upper leg of the V is safe. If he is not demoralised, if on the contrary he is full of eagerness and has reserves ready to throw upon your flank, you are in deadly danger.

Von Kluck miscalculated; and when von Kluck performed that wheeling movement he put his army in great peril for the sake of driving down quickly upon the Allies and forcing a decision. (Because to have advanced the whole line would have meant the bringing of the right wing within range of the guns of Paris. The whole line had either to stand still and wait for an enemy counter offensive or rush on with a rolled-in flank.)

It was this upper leg of the V which rendered the upper blade of the scissors of General Joffre a possibility. The only question was from what quarter was this upper blade to come, seeing that the Allied Army had already retreated far to the south and represented already the lower blade.

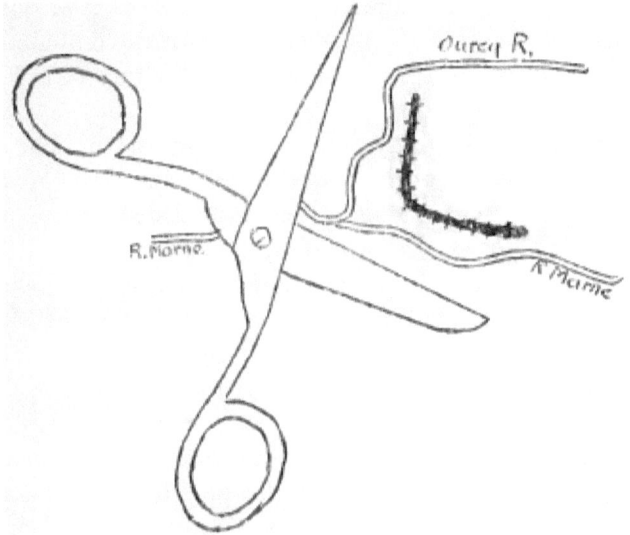

5. THE UPPER BLADE OF THE SCISSORS.

The answer to this question lay in Paris—and the fact that the answer existed made von Kluck's mistake in exposing his right flank absolutely fatal. The answer to the question can be expressed tersely as half a million of fresh French troops.

So the battle began with a little gentle pressure by the lower blade of the scissors and a fierce and sudden thrust by the upper blade, the very existence of which had scarcely been suspected. The half-million men who were the force driving that "upper blade "reached the battle-field surely in the strangest manner that ever yet an army had come to a great movement. They came, these reserves, in the Paris taxicabs and motor-cars which had been gathered together in readiness for the purpose. And that is why they still speak of the "taxicab army."

The taxicab army, the 6th French Army, decided the Battle of the Marne, because it was there when wanted, and because it was not expected to be there so soon. It was the upper blade of the scissors which had seemed to von Kluck to be a-wanting, but which Joffre had held in reserve during all those long days. In order that that upper blade might be used it was essential to fall back right down to the walls of Paris, because it was essential that the Paris fortifications should cause the enemy to roll up his flank and make the V formation. The prescience and sagacity of Joffre won their splendid and well-deserved reward.

And that thrust of the upper blade of the scissors, how quickly it set the German Army fleeing back in order that its communications might not be endangered. At the very first sign of the "taxicab army" the German staff began to tremble. A little more, they saw, and the army which was fighting away to the east and south would be cut off. Only by flight could safety be secured. The German Army must at all costs be got out from the radius of the scissor blades.

And so in the space of a fortnight history repeated itself. The Allied Army retreated from Mons to save its right flank from being surrounded from the east: the German Army retreated from the Marne to save its right flank from being surrounded from the west.

The Germans came to the Marne and to the scissors of General Joffre flushed with the good wine of success. Everything had seemed to fall before them, and the splendour of this new achievement justified the wildest hopes. Compared to this progress 1870 was a mere snail's crawl. Within ten days of reaching Brussels they were at the walls of Paris, and could even see, far off, the spires of the coveted city and the outline of the Eiffel Tower.

The German horsemen, the Uhlans, rode ahead of the army and found it in their hearts to be gay at the prospect of easy victory which opened before them. In the villages they even behaved well on occasion, toasting the new citizens of the German Empire, whom they declared they saw around them in the shape of a sullen and terrified peasantry. At Chantilly, the Newmarket of France, they behaved so well that an English jockey who stayed out the visitation gave them a good character when I saw him a few days later, he declared:

> They behaved like gentlemen. When they rode into the town and I heard their horses in the street I thought they were some of our own people, or the French, and so I went out to look at them. Then I saw who they were. But they didn't molest me. They rode to the mayor's house and told him to keep order and no harm would be done. Then they came to my stable and asked for a horse. I had no horses except a two-year-old, and I told them it was not strong enough to do cavalry work. They were quite polite about it, but they said they must have the horse as one of their own had been wounded in the nose. So they took my horse and left the wounded one behind to die.

The tobacconists in Chantilly, however, had another tale to tell, because the Germans helped themselves in the tobacconists' shops, and what they left behind was scarcely worth carrying away. They looted some of the chateaux too, and made the palace by the river their head-quarters, bivouacking in the beautiful grounds. Visitors who go to Chantilly race-course in after years will perhaps be told that it was here that the vanguard of the victorious host lay on the nights before the great defeat. As a matter of fact, however, Chantilly was taken only by a company or two of Uhlans. The main army turned aside before it reached Chantilly.

From Chantilly the road falls downwards to a delicious vale and passes under old trees that cast long shadows. Then the road rises again and mounts a hill, and from the hill-top you can see the little village of Senlis, with its cathedral, sleeping in the afternoon sun. But today Senlis is stirred fearfully in its sleep, and the streets are empty and the windows barred and bolted against the terror that walks abroad. Senlis has heard the dull boom of the guns through long hours and the news of the approaching avalanche has reached the quiet streets. The French and British who were in the town have fallen back, and very many of the inhabitants have fled away to join the host of the refugees pouring out through Paris to the southward.

Outside of the town, on the hill, a party of French *chasseurs* are hidden in a little wood. They are only a little company but they are fulfilling their duty, the duty of harassing the advance of the foe. Presently as they wait they can hear hard hoofs on the dry road, and presently they see a small company of the hated Uhlans riding merrily towards them.

The Uhlans are going to Senlis to join in the debauchery soon to take place in that town. They ride easily, talking and laughing as they go. Suddenly a sharp word of command is heard ringing out among the trees of the wood. Blue-clad figures superbly mounted dash out upon the confounded troopers. With a yell of bitter execration the Frenchmen hurl themselves upon these despoilers and profaners of France. Bright swords, thirsty for blood, gleam in the sunlight. The Germans reel back, wildly attempting to control their startled horses. The good blades leap to their task, plunging through the bodies of the foe. Saddle after saddle is emptied; man after man rolls in his death agony upon the white country road, beneath the trees and under the great sky that is the benediction of all men. Then the enemy breaks and flees, dashing away down the hill for his life, with the French chasseurs pursuing after him.

They buried the dead men by the roadside, but for some days the horses were left unburied. In the sun their bodies swelled up terribly and became gross and hideous. Clouds of flies gathered upon them and the taint of their decay spoiled the fresh wind. So it was over all this sweet land of France where the foul hands of war were laid upon men's life and upon the good fields—death and pollution and the dreadful stench of decomposition like a blasphemy carried upon all winds.

Senlis awaited the Germans in resentful mood, for already the little town had tasted the gall of their fierce methods. One of the armoured motor-cars which ran out of Amiens had come to the town. A sentry who ventured to challenge it had been shot down at his post. The car had rushed through the long village street to the accompaniment of the revolver shots of its occupants. And men who witnessed that outrage swore a solemn and bitter vengeance.

They had not long to wait for it. The enemy came to the town a few days later in some force. That was the fifth of September, one of the splendid days of that glorious autumn. As usual they betook themselves to the house of the mayor and issued their threat. "Let a shot be fired and we raze the place to the ground." They selected the mayor and some of the citizens as hostages.

But the bitterness of the people overcame their fear and their discretion. The bullies swaggered through the streets and molested the people. The houses, all houses, were open to them; and a man's honour was as nothing. Wives were sorely afraid, and with good reason, in those days, and men's hearts quailed as they waited, suffering all things, for the sake of their beloved.

But there was one man at least who could not brook this insolence—a tobacconist in a by-street whose goods had been commandeered by the conquerors. One day in fierce exasperation he broke out upon the German soldiery in his shop while they stood heaping insults upon him. "I serve men, not bullies," he declared. And he followed up his words with action. He struck one of the bullies, throwing him out of the shop door.

It was a brave act, but fatally indiscreet. The bully picked himself up from the gutter and began to bellow to his comrades to come to his assistance. Half a dozen soldiers hurried up and they dragged the wretched tobacconist out of his shop into the roadway. His wife saw them at their work and she rushed out of the shop and threw herself upon the men, begging them, as they were husbands and fathers, to forgive and show mercy.

A German soldier show mercy!

Two shots rang out. Man and wife lay in their blood at the door of the tobacconist's shop.

They heard the shots in the houses over the street, and heads appeared at the windows. Men gasped with the rage that consumed them. A few of the windows were thrown open that the dead faces, which were the faces of friends, might be the better seen. Then a shot was fired, it is said from the direction of one of the opened windows. A soldier fell, wounded (that is the German version of it!) A moment later all the windows in the street were shuttered and barred.

But death awaited already without the shuttered windows. The infuriated soldiery marched at once to the house of the mayor, their hostage. They entered his house and seized him, telling him that the inhabitants had fired upon them—that men had dared to defend their houses against the brute-beasts who came to defile them. They forced the mayor to go with them and they marched him at once to the military headquarters on the hill, where he was imprisoned for the night.

Next day they tried the Mayor of Senlis by court-martial and found him guilty. They marched him out from the court to the place of execution. They shot him there and he died fearlessly before them, a brave Frenchman, a very gallant gentleman, whose name will be held in honour by all righteous men when the names of his murderers are forgotten as obscene things are forgotten.

But the bloody repast was only just spread. There was still the sack-

91

ing of Senlis to be carried out for a memorial. Great guns were turned upon the town and huge shells crashed into it. House after house fell in ruins upon terrified inmates. Women and children died horribly in the street. Those who had cellars crowded down in them waiting for death, others ran in the ways of the town, knowing not where they went if only they might escape from the agony of their fears. A prosperous place became a desert wilderness. The railway station fell in utter ruin; a great mansion house was battered to destruction; the humble dwellings of poor people were razed to the street; even the church suffered, and there are shell marks upon its beautiful tower at this moment. The murderers came to the town to complete the work of their guns. A little boy pointed a wooden gun at them. They shot him. Men and women were the fuel for the flames of their blood-lust. Senlis the beautiful became a place of carnage and death; the moon rose upon it and it lay under the moon naked and ravished. A great silence fell upon its pleasant ways.

I heard these things myself in Senlis in the same week that the Germans were driven forth from the town.

And Senlis is but one little town: there were hundreds of other towns to which the same damnation was meted out. Nothing, no one was sacred. In Senlis they stabled their horses in a church, leaving the befouled straw upon the floor and even up against the altar steps for a proof. I saw it there. In other places they left the like memorials. And they smote Rheims and mutilated it, the city of a hundred kings.

CHAPTER 8

Waiting for the Dawn

So the Germans came to their undoing at the Marne River. At the Marne River they had planned for themselves the greatest success of all, which was to afford a "decision" by cutting the Allied Army in two somewhere to the east of Paris. One half of the army was to be driven in confusion into the city, the other half was to be surrounded and destroyed in the open.

The scene of this battle is almost an island if you consider that the Marne River flows half round it to the north and that the Seine performs a similar function to the south. The land between the rivers is cut across by two smaller rivers, the Petit Morin and the Grand Morin, which run from east to west and flow into the Marne. Between the rivers is higher ground covered with woods, then glorious in their early autumn foliage. And near the Marne River, to the eastward, are the marshes of St. Gond, around which Napoleon fought his last battles upon French soil in 1814.

The Germans came down across the rivers. They crossed the Marne at a dozen different places because, though the bridges had been destroyed by the retiring army, there was little or no opposition. They crossed the Petit Morin, they crossed the Grand Morin. They came to Provins and Sézanne. And at Provins they found the French and British drawn up and ready to give battle. That was September 5th, a Saturday.

I was behind the lines, to the south of Provins. I had come up from Havre by a long way, through Trouville the gay, and Orleans the ever serious. Days and nights I had travelled without intermission, happy if I succeeded in accomplishing twenty miles within the twenty-four hours. For all the railways of France were disorganised, and the trains stood during hours upon the line waiting until some chance made it possible to go on.

How changed was Trouville in these days! A strange silence hung over the great watering-place: the broad sands were empty, the booths along the sands where in other days they sold you post cards and iced drinks and cigarettes stood solitary and dismal. A few nursemaids with children passed in melancholy procession along the beach, but even the children seemed to feel the atmosphere of oppression. The Casino, like all the other casinos of France, had become a hospital. You could see the black faces of wounded Turcos grinning over the balustrade, or the weary features of soldier men from the far-flung line between Paris and Belfort. These wounded men were too shortly separated from their ordeal to have recovered their spirit, and they were melancholy also as the beach and the sea and town itself were melancholy.

At night from the beach you could see the lights of the great ships lying off Havre across the estuary of the Seine, and you could see the lights of the town itself, and the lights of the few camps which remained above the town on the high cliffs. But Trouville was dark and lonely; once again the little fishing village of old times; and the gay world of its heyday had been blotted out as if it had never been.

I came from Trouville to Mantes and then to Chartres and Orleans. All along the railway line you saw the black hands of war laid upon men's lives. You saw great troop trains stopped at the stations, the men bivouacked on the platforms eating their rations gaily enough and talking hopefully of the future. But their officers had grave faces, and they talked little, even among themselves. For these French officers saw visions of another catastrophe for France, and the old anxiety of 1870 gnawed at their hearts. Evil reports of the great retreat had already come to them, and they knew that already the French Government had been moved to the south. The German avalanche seemed to have swept all opposition before it.

There is no finer man and no finer soldier than the French officer. He is brave as a lion and kindly as a mother towards his men. But the great shadow of '70 lay upon France; it lay upon the hearts of all Frenchmen. No Frenchman could shake it off, try as he would. The superstition of Prussian invincibleness was a dread superstition: even in their strongest hours it went with these men, haunting them.

So the French officers smiled sadly often when you spoke with them, and sometimes they shook their heads. "If France must die," one of them said to me, "at least she will die with the sword in her hand. We will die, all of us—with France." Others were more hopeful, and a few had good hopes, for they said General Joffre played with his enemy and had led him thus swiftly into the heart of France that he might punish him the more severely.

At the stations too you saw men and women who had left their homes, waiting with the dull patience of country folk for the trains that should take them to places of safety. Sometimes one of these refugee trains would go past, and you might see with how great courage the common people of France faced their tribulation. How they found it in their hearts to smile even at their ill fate, and how their chief care was not for themselves but for the children or old people they took with them, and also for the gallant soldiers they saw at the stations as they went by,

"*Nos vaillants soldats*," they cried, and waved their hands, and scattered flowers they had gathered by the side of the line when the train stopped.

How many flowers were cast upon these troop trains of France and upon the men who thronged the carriages and leaned out to wave *au revoir* to the villagers at the halting-places! You saw great laurel wreaths hung on the brass handles of the carriage doors, and wreaths of chrysanthemums and roses. There were festoons of roses around the windows of some of the compartments, and long chains of them binding the carriages together; and the engines had whole bushes of flowering shrubs tied to them for good fortune. Also the doors and windows of the carriages bore significant inscriptions: "To Berlin." "The *Kaiser* is an old pig." "*Revanche.*" "Remember 1870." "Remember Alsace-Lorraine."

"To Berlin," shouted the soldiers in the carriage doorways as the long trains—how long those trains were!—crept away from the station. "To Berlin and a safe return," responded the people gathered on the platform. The train became a speck upon the plain, the people in the station resumed their vigil. The autumn leaves fell, one by one, and were blown across the concrete pavement with a short crackling sound until they dropped on the railway line. The old priest, sitting under the shelter, continued his prayers.

I came to Orleans late at night, after so many stoppages that I lost count of them. The great station when I reached it presented a strange sight. It was no longer chiefly a station; it had become an asylum for the homeless. The broad area of platform between the lines and the exit was converted into a huge dormitory, where lay all manner of men under the dim light of the electric arcs. They slept so soundly these tired men that nothing disturbed them. The arrival or the going of trains passed unheard; the marching of troops, even the roll of heavy wheels as supplies were dragged through the station.

Some of them slept upon the bare flags; others had mattresses, supplied I know not by whom; others had taken off their coats and rolled them tightly to serve as pillows. A few slept upon the bar of the cloak-room, and their legs dangled from the bar like the necks of fowls in a poulterer's window. Another bar where luggage is checked was similarly adorned.

They were of all types those people, from the well-dressed merchant and professional man to the farm labourer. But they slept cosily side by side in the strange brotherhood of adversity. Even the hard stone could not break their slumber, though you might see them rolling painfully upon it if you watched. A station official stood guard over them like a shepherd watching his sleeping flock, and sometimes as he watched you could see him smile to himself at the strangeness and incongruity of the spectacle.

Outside the station, in the streets, there seemed to be no sign of life at all. The streets were empty except for an occasional *gendarme* and a few people carrying baggage who were searching for lodgings. If you asked them they told you that lodgings were difficult, if not impossible, to find in Orleans on this night because Orleans is on the direct route between Paris and Bordeaux, and half the fleeing population of the capital had broken its journey here to await developments.

And soon enough you discovered for yourself that these travellers spoke the truth. Half of the hotels had a written notice attached to the bell handle: "It is useless to ring, we have no room." The other hotels which had neglected to post up any notice were besieged and soon learned of their folly. When you rang a head appeared at an upstairs window and you heard the phrase again and again, "*Il n'y a plus.*" In every street of the city it was the same phrase you heard, until the sound of it became menacing and terrible.

So when I could not obtain lodgings I walked the streets instead and saw how the war had come to this sweet old city and transformed it in a few hours into a vast hostel for well-to-do refugees. I wandered first into the great square where Jeanne d'Arc, the Maid of Orleans, on her great charger holds aloft the Standard of France and of honour. The huge statue rose up black and gaunt in the moonlight, but the moon fell graciously upon it, nevertheless, as though granting benediction to this memorial of the splendid courage and hope which are the heritage of the French people. I drew near to the statue and marked the wreaths which devoted hands had hung upon the plinth in this new hour of France's calamity. "*Pour la patrie*," they had written on one of the cards attached to the wreaths, and on another, "*Ora pro nobis.*"

Beneath the statue two women, in deep mourning, knelt praying for France and for the men who had gone out to sell their lives for her.

The moon hung clear and steady above the great black horse and its girl rider with her brandished sword.

On the other side of the town, by the edge of a wood, I found a great camp. These were French regiments which were encamped here, and the number of them seemed to be very great. There were rows upon rows of field kitchens with fires glowing and men busily at work around them. You might see huge ovens in which hundreds of loaves of bread were being baked, the bakers standing near by ready for the work of taking the loaves from the fire when the exact moment should arrive. In the moonlight the ovens glowed like lamps, red against the pure white, and the figures of the men had a strange, barbaric appearance.

Near the ovens were tents with sentries posted, and you could hear the rattle of weapons as the sentries moved upon their beats and then presented arms. The tents seemed very white and very quiet. But the cattle penned near at hand were lowing now and then, and the horses too neighed occasionally, softly, as though enquiring what all this work was about. There seemed to be hundreds upon hundreds of horses tied up amongst the trees.

While I waited a great convoy of motor waggons came to the camp and to the kitchens and was loaded up with bread. The convoy moved away as soon as it was loaded. Was this bread for the regiments stationed near at hand or was it food for the great armies engaged with the enemy away to the northward?

Paris had come to Orleans overnight so to speak, and Orleans was therefore a deeply interesting town. In Orleans you saw a chastened edition of the crowd which walks so gaily in the boulevards of a Sunday afternoon. It was the same crowd, but it did not look the same. It looked worn and anxious and mirthless. The women of the town too were here, rather draggled and rather hungry. . . . All eyes were upon Paris.

When you sat in the *cafés* you heard what Paris had thought yesterday about the war and what no doubt Paris, as much of the city as remained there, was still thinking today. You heard that Paris had made up its mind to a siege—a siege more terrible than the Siege of '70. Paris had not, apparently, taken into account the fact that the French Army was still unbeaten, and that the army must be beaten before the city could be captured. True to her woman instinct, Paris saw herself the prize and discounted the chances of salvation.

Yet how brave Paris was. These people had not been greatly afraid for themselves: most of them had left the city for the sake of children or old people who could not well bear a siege with its attendant horrors. They had left their all in a worldly sense, and few, if any of them, had hope of saving their goods from the ruins. Some were about to return to the city nevertheless to do what they could. They did not complain. The wonderful, the glorious patriotism of the French people was aflame in their hearts. They no longer lived for themselves: they lived, they thought, they spoke, they acted only for France.

That, you learned, was the mood of Paris in this hour of her suffering. Like a mother, she thought of her children; she became, as she had always been in hours of crises, the spiritual embodiment of the whole land; she became France, a microcosm of the nation; a storehouse of all the national ideals; a figure representative of all the national yearnings. Paris lived then in the heart of every Frenchman just as the heart of every Frenchman had an abiding sanctuary within the walls of Paris.

From Orleans I came to Malesherbes, a little town on the outskirts of the forest of Fontainebleau, and from Malesherbes right through the forest. What an experience that was upon the outskirts of the greatest battle of all time. It was again a clear night with a moon, so that you could see far into the forest ways, under the great trees, and could but dimly mark in the sky, like long pencils of silver, the searchlights over Paris. What memories crowded upon you: what thoughts. Here while you lived from moment to moment they were remaking the world. In all years to come men must look to this day, must speak of it as a crisis day in man's history, must wonder how the men who were privileged to see it lived through its breathless hours and what they did and what they said.

Yet the forest preserved its ancient stillness when the fate of Europe literally trembled in the balance. "The forest of Fontainebleau, is it not the last refuge of lost causes," a Frenchman said bitterly to me on that night, and added: "You know, of course, that these trees witnessed the downfall and agony of Napoleon." I knew. But on this night, somehow, the sombre forest did not whisper of defeat and agony. There was a new consolation in its wide spaces and its great trees. That very day I had seen many troop trains go up towards the east full of the youth of this France, a youth blazing with enthusiasm and devotion. I had heard the singing of these young men as they went by, and their cheers and their laughter, and had caught the infection of the new courage which was surely come to France in her darkest hour. France again had dared to believe in herself, in her destiny; the old spirit of her greatness was come upon her.

And so the forest brought great comfort on this eve of battle and of fate, and you might view the astounding spectacle presented by the forest without apprehension. You might even find in the spectacle a new assurance of victory.

What a spectacle it was! Into the forest of Fontainebleau had passed the whole population of one of the richest areas in France, the area between the rivers, from Eperney and Rheims in the north to Moret-sur-Sables and Troyes in the south, from the Aisne to the Marne and the Seine. They had fled before the vanguard of the foe, and amongst the ranks of the retreating armies of France and Britain. They had fled just as the Belgians and the inhabitants of Artois fled, in fear and haste, taking with them only the few necessaries they could carry over against the uncertainty and hardships of the future.

Most of them though were small farmers with a team of oxen and a few head of cattle and sheep or goats, perhaps with a horse or two and a cart to pack the household goods in. They drove the oxen before them, yoked together as for the plough, and they had their children on the carts with the old folk and the furniture and a coop or two of chickens. The sheep and the goats were tended by the boys of the family who, as boys will, viewed this pilgrimage as a great adventure and rejoiced in it.

The pilgrimage came to the forest because the forest promised shelter. Here among the great trees there would be safety from the prowling Uhlans, and no army could deploy here, be the decision good or be it evil. Moreover, the dispossessed could await here in peace the news of the battle their eyes had seen in course of preparation, and if the good God heard the prayers of France it would be possible to go back easily from this place to the homesteads they had left behind them.

So they came to the forest and hid themselves in it, encamping in the darkest glades and gathering their small possessions around them after the fashion of nomads in the desert.

The forest is bright with a thousand camp fires glowing softly amongst the trees. Around the fires you may see the families gathered at their evening meal, like gipsies on the shores of some Highland loch. The faces are illuminated by the glow, and you may recognise the hard, honest faces of the French peasant class, the old women with their seamed cheeks and the young women beautiful in a rude, healthy fashion. The children are already asleep, wrapped in all manner of strange garments. They have been laid upon the soft sward of the forest, and the cool night winds are their lullaby. Further out, almost beyond the golden circle of the firelight, the cattle lie with raised heads, solemnly chewing the cud and now and then turning their great eyes towards the glowing embers as though in mute questionings. The sheep and goats browse quietly beside them.

So has it ever been with mankind in the days of war. One hour and all the ways and means of civilisation are palsied; one hour and the stark primitive emerges from the trappings of modern life. The great trees are the roofs of this people, and the heavens are a light to them. In the requiem of falling leaves they have their peace and their comfort.

And all the forest waits for the morrow as they wait who attend a great decision. On the morrow it will be life or death: the dawn or the destruction of hope. In the vast stillness you may hear the boom, far away, of the guns which are now the arbiters of destiny; you may see also, up above, the slim pencils of light which perpetually search the skies. You may catch now and then the deep red glow in the eastern sky which marks the scene of the conflict—and which marks also the burning and pillaging of the hamlets and towns that have fallen into the hands of these terrible invaders.

It is morning in the forest and the day of battle is come, the day they will speak of through all ages as the greatest day in the world's annals. The camp fires that grew cold overnight are lit again now, and the womenfolk are busy with their preparations for the morning's meal. Apart the men are standing together to talk of the future and to glean what comfort they can from an exchange of news.

They know, these peasants, that great doings are afoot, but like the whole world, they are ignorant as yet concerning the precise events that may be expected. They know that Joffre has turned and will make a stand here, beyond the eastern borders of the forest, against the German host. But they cannot envisage the nature of that stand, nor yet in what manner the battle will be developed.

And while they talk together the roar of the guns comes to them across the morning sunshine, telling that the dice are being rattled in the box for the throw.

CHAPTER 9

"The Battle without a Morrow"

From Fontainebleau Forest to Moret is but a little way; from Moret you cross the great bridge over the Seine and come to Montereau, and thence there is a short line of railway that runs close by the river towards Troyes. There is also a branch line going up to Provins and so to the edge of the Battle of the Marne.

That was the course I followed, and it brought me nearer to the battlefield than I had any hope of being able to come.

The day was warm and sunny, as had been all these days of the retreat through northern France. When the sun had been up an hour or two the atmosphere became hot almost to the point of suffocation. Northward of where I stood, a mile or two, heavy clouds, however, hung over the plain marking the place of battle. The sky in that quarter was dark and lowering, with strange veins of reddish gold running across it, as though some painter had tried with crude brush to improve a sombre theme.

Under the reddish gold of the sky the guns were booming—the guns of the Marne, whose thunders will resound down all the ages so long as a man is left to tell of them.

The first act in the battle was played upon the plain about the town of Provins. The Germans had reached this plain in their hasty advance to the south which was to split the Allied Army. Their advanced guards, the usual cavalry screen, had orders to push on at all costs and discover the positions of the enemy. The advanced guards found the enemy, the British, near the wood of Crecy on the Grand Morin, and there the battle was joined.

What a battle line it was upon that Sunday morning, September 6th—von Kluck's Army on the west, von Buelow to the east of him by the marshes of St. Gond, von Hausen's Saxons east of von Buelow, and then farther to the east again the Duke of Würtemberg and the Crown Prince and the Bavarian Crown Prince. And facing those armies the armies of Joffre with the British Army.

Here are the orders of the day as issued to the soldiers of the three nations by their generals.

General Joffre wrote:

At the moment when a battle on which the welfare of the country depends is about to begin, I feel it my duty to remind you that it is no longer the time to look behind. We have but one business on hand—to attack and repel the enemy. An army which can no longer advance will at all costs hold the ground it has won and allow itself to be slain where it stands rather than give way. This is no time for faltering, and it will not be suffered.

General French wrote:

I call upon the British Army in France to show now to the enemy its power and to push on rigorously to the attack beside the 6th French Army.

I am sure I shall not call upon them in vain, but that, on the contrary, by another manifestation of the magnificent spirit which they have shown in the past fortnight they will fall on the enemy's flank with all their strength and in unison with their Allies drive him back.

And thus spoke the German:

The object of our long and arduous marches has been achieved. ...The great decision is undoubtedly at hand. Tomorrow, therefore, the whole strength of the German Army, as well as that of all our Army Corps, is bound to be engaged along the whole line from Paris to Verdun. To save the welfare and honour of Germany I expect every officer and man, notwithstanding the hard and fierce fight of the last few days, to do his duty unswervingly and to the last breath. Everything depends on the result of tomorrow.

And so the "Battle without a morrow" was joined.

The 6th French Army, the "taxicab" army, came up on that Sunday to the line of the Ourcq and began its struggles with the German outposts in the village to the west of the river. And the big guns of the enemy poured a storm of shells across the river back upon the heads of these devoted Frenchmen.

Also the British force, away to the south behind the Grand Morin River, crept out of its cover in the woods and threw itself against the enemy lines near the place where they registered their most southerly progress. The coming of the British was like the coming of a thunder-bolt among these German troops, for had not the Army of General French been destroyed at Mons and Landrecies and Le Cateau? Von Kluck knew, in that hour, that he had erred greatly when he swung his flank round into the line of the Ourcq River. The scissors of General Joffre were completed, lower blade and upper blade, for the chastening of this foolishness.

They bivouacked that night, the Germans on the eastern bank of the Ourcq and on the southern bank of the Grand Morin, the French and British in closest contact with them. And already the bat-tlefield gave up its wounded to the ambulances and trains awaiting near at hand. The trains from the south of the line moved down to-wards Montereau, running slowly through the cool night with their grievous burden.

At the wayside stations they stopped awhile, and you might speak with these gallant men and hear from their lips the first tales of the first day of the struggle.

Strange tales they sounded from the lips of men who lay often grievously ill, panting upon the straw in the railway waggons:

The enemy were not far from us, with the river behind them (it is idle to ask what river, because these are men from the south and they do not know); we charged across the open meadow-land after our guns and their guns had been hammering at one another for a long time. How gay we were: what a spirit our men showed. (*Quel élan!*) You felt that France was irresistible in that moment, as though nothing in all the world could stop us. I have heard my father speak of the terrible depression of '70, and how the men had no heart or stomach for the fight. It was no longer like that. The men burned to attack: they could scarcely be held in restraint. Their faces were aglow and their eyes flamed.

When we had done shooting and came to close quarters the enemy broke and fled before us. Then you might hear terrible words shouted into the ears of these fleeing men—'Louvain' and 'Tirlemont,' as the bayonets drove home, and 'Remember Belgium.'

Others told in similar language the stories of detailed fighting upon other parts of the long line, how the enemy was surprised in his triumphant advance while yet he was overtired with rapid marching and while he had so far outstripped his big guns and his commissariat as to be rendered an easier prey. They told how stubborn nevertheless, and how arrogant, had been his defiance, even after it became clear that he had been out-classed and out-manoeuvred.

Some of these trains were a very sad spectacle even in the midst of this early glory of victory. And sometimes the chill hand of death was outstretched at these wayside stations.

I saw one poor fellow, wounded about the head, die in the arms of a village priest who had come to the station to meet the train and give what consolation he could to the sufferers. The man was quite young and he had still the expression of boyhood upon his face; but his face was drawn and very pale, and his breath came in short, sharp gasps that were terrible to listen to. The good father prayed with him and, so far as was possible in that place, administered the last rites of the Church, while the other wounded men stood by with bared heads and sad faces. A woman, a nurse, in the little crowd on the platform wept softly while she went about her work, trying to make the dying boy's last moments comfortable. He died with joy in his face, and the priest told her that his last words were of France, his France for which he gave life and youth so cheerfully. When he was dead the priest covered his face and they took the body to a van at the end of the train that was used as a mortuary car.

The French priests are noble fellows, and they responded nobly to the great call upon their services which these days made. Day and night they remained at their posts in the wayside stations, working with the nurses at the food stalls and helping to carry comforts and dressings to the wounded men. All might command their services, and there was no thought of self in their free giving. Many a dying man had his last hours made easy for him by the good old men, and many a youth who had cared little for the ministrations of the Church in the days of strength turned to the wayside priest with appealing eyes during these long nights under the September moon.

The younger priesthood of France fought side by side in the trenches with their lay brethren, sharing all the hardships of the campaign and all its dangers with them, nor asking any preferential treatment; the older men set the same great example in other spheres. So that even amongst this hell of death and destruction the peace of God might be whispered in dying ears and the emblem of Salvation exalted before eyes already grown dim with suffering the only end of which could be death.

On Monday the seventh of September the battle was joined again with renewed fury from the Ourcq in the north to the Grand Morin in the south, and thence away eastward by Sézanne to the sources of the Petit Morin, the marshes of St. Gond, the Argonne forests, Verdun and the Vosges. On this day the pressure of the 6th French Army, the "taxicab "army, under General Maunoury, became more pronounced across the river Ourcq. This army was attacking the upper limb of the V which General von Kluck had created in defiance of the rules of cautious warfare. Von Kluck's flank, the upper limb of the V, rested upon the Ourcq river, and so long as it could prevent the 6th French Army from crossing was safe. But the 6th Army, the upper blade of the scissors, showed the most determined courage, and by nightfall had driven the enemy entirely from the western bank of the river and had begun to prepare for the crossing on the morrow.

Meanwhile to the south the British were pushing northward, as a glance at the sketch will show. The position occupied by the British troops was of immense importance. The British attacked the German line just where it ceased to run north and south and began to sweep away to the east. They attacked thus between the big effort on the Ourcq river and the still bigger forward thrust on the Grand Morin, towards the Seine.

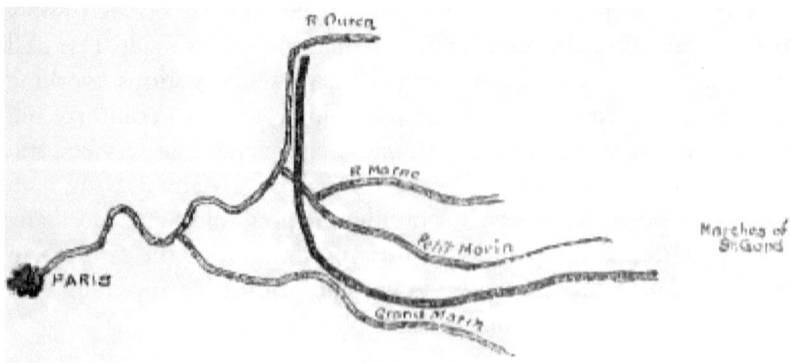

6. The Battle of the Marne (second day)

The Germans had meant to hold the Ourcq while they thrust down on the main French Army. This great thrusting movement was their big card, the card that was to win Paris. It will be seen that the British Army literally took that great thrust in flank—its right flank—and rendered it a dangerous instead of a safe manoeuvre.

So here was another miscalculation of General von Kluck. He had not realised that General Joffre could bring the "taxicab" army so quickly from Paris to the Ourcq, nor yet how strong and efficient the "taxicab" army was. Again, he had not realised that the "contemptible little army of General French" was awaiting him, hid in the woods of Crecy by the Grand Morin River, upon the very pivot of the scissors. And he had refused to believe that the British Army had any fighting strength left.

The British Army took the great southward thrust in flank; it also, to some extent, threatened the left flank of von Kluck's defence on the Ourcq. Von Kluck found himself suddenly, upon this Tuesday, fighting upon two fronts. He was well within the blades of the scissors of Joffre. And between the blades, as their pivot, stood the British Army.

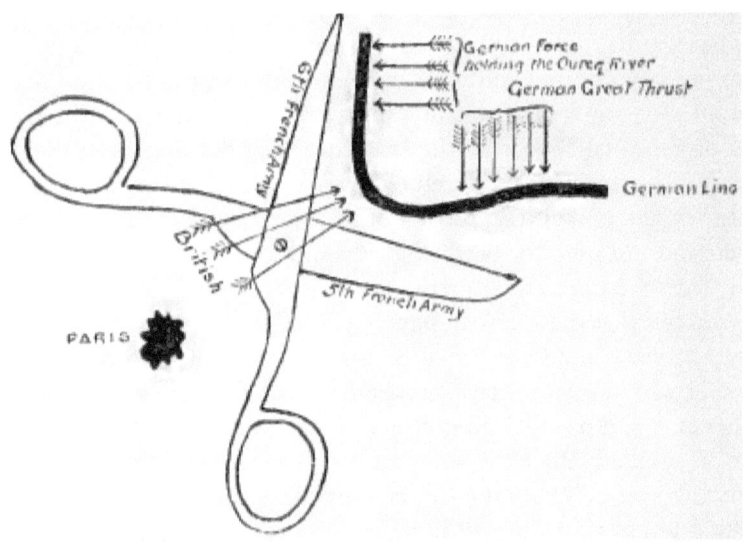

7. How the British Army held the pivot of the scissors.

I stood not far from these great events and watched the first train-load of "unwounded prisoners" going back into the heart of the France they would have ravished had they been able. Grimy fellows they looked, with the heavy jowls and fat cheeks which one associates with the German of the cartoons and is continually surprised to see exemplified in the man himself. All the men wore the green field uniform—which looked very drab and dirty now. Some of them were hungry and asked for food, saying that they had not tasted cooked meat for a week. Others declared quite frankly that they had lived on beetroot plucked from the fields through which they marched. The private soldiers were amiable enough now that they had fallen into the hands of the enemy: but the officers almost without exception seemed surly and defiant. They sat bolt upright in the carriages looking neither to right nor left, and they pulled down the blinds in the windows in the face of the open-mouthed crowds at the stations.

I think I speak without prejudice—difficult as that is to do in these days—when I say that the aspect, the demeanour of these prisoners from the Battle of the Marne was distinctly repellent. They were weary, of course, with much fighting and with long marching, and their clothes were dirtied and dishevelled, and they had uncropped heads and moustaches and dirty faces—but these externals can be discounted. It was not their dirt nor their misery which repelled—one could perhaps sympathise a little with these misfortunes. It was the bearing of the men themselves. They reminded you of dogs who have just been beaten and who cringe to beg forgiveness: their smiles had an oily, ingratiating quality, such as you encounter in the smile of a professional beggar by the roadside. They did not hesitate to say that they were glad to be taken prisoner—doubtless they were!—and that they had always disapproved of this war, but were forced to fight. There did not seem to be that sturdy and uncompromising anger in their faces which, to their credit, the officers wore almost to a man.

You felt that the German people are indeed a nation of slaves, not after all very careful who shall be their master. You realised also that the German officer is a slave-master and a patrician, cold and hard and unbending and proud. I do not suggest, of course, that this impression is to be applied generally. Many of the German soldiers have proved themselves to be brave men in face of danger, and our own soldiers speak often in warm terms of the enemy's qualities. I give merely my own idea. Afterwards I saw other batches of prisoners who conformed more nearly to the standard of the officers without, however, showing the evil temper most of the officers displayed so conspicuously.

A Frenchman to whom I expressed the views I have just set forth told me that his own impression coincided with mine. "Our fellows," he said, "compare well with these men, though we must make

108

all allowances for conditions. I cannot see Frenchmen smiling from the train windows upon the crowds at wayside stations in Germany, though I suppose all nations have their share of weaklings. Captivity kills a Frenchman because it divorces him from France and lowers the pride that burns in all our breasts, the pride that is pride of France. Our psychology is so profoundly different from the psychology of these fellows. They belong to the race that has peopled the whole world with waiters and flunkeys. It is, after all, the flunkey's instinct to kiss the hand that beats him."

It was from these long train-loads of prisoners that you gathered first of all the extent of this victory—for no man of course in those days had seen or even known of a hundredth part of the great struggle. You realised that this was not only a reverse to the enemy, but that it was salvation to the Allied cause. You began to see a new dawn rising amid the darkness, over the stricken fields of death—the dawn, very early but very sure, of a new era in the world, purchased by the blood of patriots and by the sorrow and pain of half the world. In those hours, when the first hopes of victory materialised, men and women held their breath in devotion and thankfulness to the good God who, once again, as in old time, had heard the prayers of France, had strengthened her arm, and had beamed his benediction upon the just cause of liberty and righteousness.

On that second night of the battle there was indeed good hope in the Allied lines. The great decision was not yet, but the hour was at hand and the preparation for the hour had been well speeded. The army on the Ourcq rested that night upon the bank of the river facing the Germans, who still held the other bank, and they rested, knowing that good work had been accomplished. What fighting this upper blade of the scissors, this army that came by taxicab, had accomplished! Men who fought in the battle to reach the Ourcq tell of the great shells that drove huge holes in the ground and sent up their black clouds of oily smoke to drift across the orchards and harvest fields; they tell of the fearful explosives that seemed to rend the air and the ground, and that froze in death whole companies of men so that in death they seemed to be alive, sitting ready to the word of command; and they tell of ravished villages blazing through the long night and haystacks aflame and farmhouses crashing to the ground with dreadful rattling sound.

A sugar refinery, one story goes, was set on fire, and the Germans within it had to jump from the blazing windows under the fire of their foes. Away to the south too the pretty town of Meaux on the Marne, where that river turns to the southward, was lying almost in ruins, with the great shells lashing their hail of destruction upon its roofs and gardens.

The green fields and the orchards near the river bank, where the fighting was fierce all day, are still at evening, but the orchards are strewn with dead, German dead and French dead lying side by side under the sky, their faces lit up by the far glow of the burning villages.

What a scene truly of horror and wonder! The long antennae of light "feeling" the sky from the heart of Paris; the solemn woods upon which the winds play mournfully as of old time; the deep glow, reaching to the clouds, of the burning and blazing houses; the voice of the guns not yet silenced in the darkness and the lurid flashes, red and green, where the shells are bursting fitfully over the opposing armies—the long flares of light that sweep the whole sky to reveal to the silent watchers the enemy's movement—that on this night of nights is the battle-field of the Ourcq.

But the Ourcq is but the end of the long line. Mile upon mile, over the wooded river lands of the Marne and its tributaries, over the downs to the eastward of the broad rivers; over the dreary plains of the Champagne-Pouilleuse; over the dark forest-land of the Argonne, away to the heights of the Vosges the fires are burning and the flares making night vivid with their lightnings; the guns are booming that are the menace of this fair land of France, and likewise the guns that are her comforters. Truly the battle of all battles this; the struggle of giants not for a city only, nor a kingdom, but for all the ways and all the bounty of a world.

But there is another light in the sky along the Ourcq Valley and on the plain above the Marne River: a fierce and sinister light which the eyes of men have not viewed before in this Western world of civilisation. It is the light of the German funeral pyres which they have builded to cremate their dead. By the glow of the burning villages they have gathered the dead and brought them together in piles, heaped up under the pure sky.

Man upon man they are heaping them, youth upon youth, bodies that yesterday went forth with young life in them and today are offal upon the face of the earth. Great pyramids they build with these dead, that loom up dark and horrid in the night and already cast their taint upon the winds. Around the piles of dead they build wooden pyres and over them pour barrelfuls of paraffin and then cast straw upon them that the work lack nothing in its effectiveness. . . . And the strong fire leaps upon the dead men, curling about their faces and picking out for the last time beloved features which it seems to caress before devouring.

Oh wives and mothers and little children, that they should perform this thing amid the orchard trees and under the stars!

On this night the British Army lay along the Grand Morin on both sides of that river. It had been a great day for our soldiers, this Monday, 7th of September, when they drove the foe before them as they had dreamed of driving him during the pitiful heat and moil of the Retreat. At 4 a.m., when the chill dawn woke over the tree-tops of the woods of Crécy, and the long eastern skies above the Champagne-Pouilleuse were spread with the grey mantle of an autumn morning our camps were astir. The great guns roared their challenge then along all the vale of the Morin River and were answered by shrieking shells from the enemy guns which, bursting, filled the morning with their pollution.

The guns spoke and were still, and then our infantry went forward as they had gone forward on the stricken fields of Mons and Le Cateau. They came from the woodland to the river, and rushing on with splendid courage, singing even in that chill dawn that presaged yet another scorching morn, they drove into the town of Coulommiers on the Grand Morin River.

That was a fight to rank with the great stand at Landrecies. It was not only a fight of infantry but also of horsemen, the flower of our cavalry against the flower of the Germans, our forty-five squadrons against their seventy-two. The 9th Lancers and the 18th Hussars won immortal laurels that day by the bridge over the Grand Morin at Coulommiers, over which the stubborn fire of our footmen had driven the enemy in confusion.

The long line of the battle is spread out before the town of Coulommiers in the golden sunlight that seems to fall in showers upon the meadowlands. An incessant thunder fills all the valley and you can mark the fierce flame where the shrapnel bursts, lashing the ground with its venomous whips of fire, and the white clouds that betray the heavy shells. You can mark also the extended line of the infantry creeping forward from cover towards the river under the massed fire of the enemy on the north bank of the river. You can see the cavalry gathered in the woodland, restive horses and eager riders with the stray shafts of sunlight gleaming on bit and spur; you may even hear the faint, delicious jingle of the bridle chains. And overhead, like a swarm of angry wasps buzzing, the aeroplanes of friend and foe searching with keen eyes the positions of troops and signalling to the guns where to cast their fire.

'Tis a scene of wonder and fury amid the cool day-coming, but there are fiercer moments in store. There is the charge of the infantry over the bridge across the Grand Morin, and there is the combat of cavalry which shall decide the fate of the German stand and its undoing. There is the crossing of the river and the pursuit of the foe along all the roads and byways leading out of the town to the northward.

In these late hours under the full sun our men may see the terrible work which our guns have wrought upon the enemy, whole batteries torn to pieces and everywhere the dead and the dying, broken bodies of men that lie in every attitude of pain and agony.

It was this fight at Coulommiers on the Grand Morin that ended at point-blank range, so to speak, the main downward thrust of the German Army. The fight at Coulommiers turned the flank of that part of von Kluck's Army which was engaging the 6th French Army under General d'Esperey, which we have chosen to call the lower blade of the scissors of Joffre. When the Germans retreated from Coulommiers they must needs retreat also along the whole length of the Grand Morin River. So that the 8th French Army which had fought a frontal fight all day could advance also at night across the river at La Ferté Gauche and Esternay.

That is why, as I have said, there was good heart and good hope in the British bivouacs on this Monday night.

Next day, Tuesday, the form of Victory emerged clearly from the mists of circumstance. The great downward thrust of von Kluck's Army upon the 5th Army had failed. The British Army was driving the flank of this thrusting force before it in confusion from the Grand Morin River; and the Army of the Ourcq, the upper blade of the scissors, was about to fight its way across that river and so threaten seriously the greater flank of the whole German line. Today therefore the field of battle has narrowed as the blades of the scissors approach more closely together. In the north it is still the Valley of the Ourcq, a river between steep banks, which is the *mise en scène*; but farther south the Grand Morin has been crossed and the battle rages upon the plateau, eight miles broad, between the Grand Morin and the Petit Morin to the north of it.

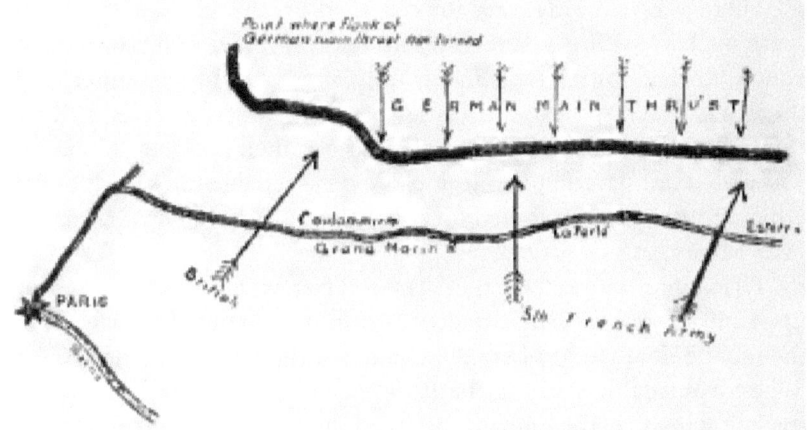

8. The situation on Monday night, September 7th, after the British victory at Coulommiers.

This plateau is a beautiful orchard land, but today the trees are torn and uprooted by great shells as the advancing British and French guns pour a continual fire upon the retreating Germans; there are piles of dead men too lying among the orchards, and broken gun-carriages and accoutrements and munitions of all sorts which could not be gathered up to be carried away because of the implacable foe which pressed behind.

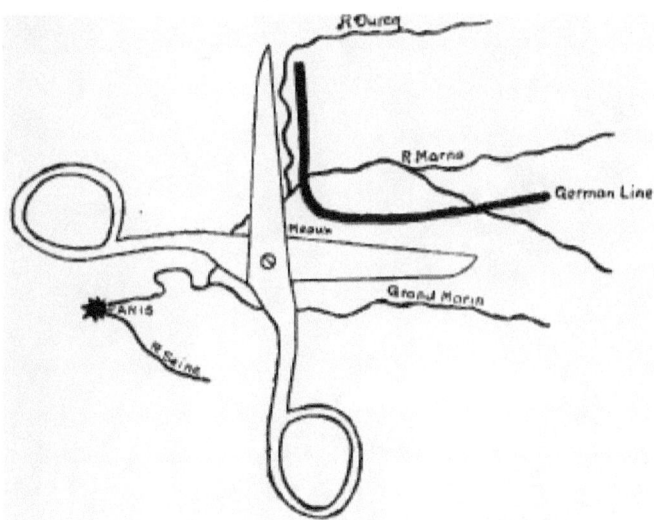

9. The battle on Tuesday, September 8th. The lower blade of the scissors has begun to sweep upwards.

113

There was fierce fighting for our men on this day, and they still speak of La Metoire where the First Corps, under Haig, drove the enemy forth from his lodgements only after a fierce encounter; and there was much spoil too, because the enemy counter-attacked in a vain effort to shake off his pursuers. But our men had their blood up and would not stay; despite great loss under a terrible sun which burnt where it beamed, they forced on across the ridge to the new river, the Petit Morin, and victory.

That night we reached the Marne River where the Petit Morin flows into it, and we held the Petit Morin in its whole length even as the night before we had held the Grand Morin. The 5th French Army joined hands with us along the Petit Morin, having come also across the belt where are the orchards between the rivers; and the 6th French Army holding the Ourcq joined hands with us where the Ourcq River flows down to the Marne.

CHAPTER 10

The Closing of the Scissors

On that day, Tuesday, our men went out from their sleeping places whistling tunes and singing as is the custom of the British soldier. They sang their old marching song "Tipperary," and they whistled the latest choruses from the London music-halls, because they were gay and light of heart with the good work which they had accomplished already across the rivers.

But on that day they came, among the orchards, to a new vision and a new revelation of war, and the songs were hushed in their throats and the merry whistling upon their lips was stilled. In the morning they were as boys who go out to new adventure; but in the evening they were grown men who have looked upon all the terror of lust and cruelty and have turned from it with the light of passion and hatred in their eyes.

It is one thing to hear of war, another thing to see it. In the days of the Retreat, when the crowds of refugees mingled with the columns of the French and British Armies, men saw how sorrowful was this exodus which is the accompaniment of war. But that burden could be borne and it could be brightened. History will not tell how many of these French peasants, men and women and children too, blessed the sturdy lads from our English countryside for a helping hand and for rations loyally shared, though the prospects of another meal were remote almost to the verge of the ludicrous. History has greater matters to deal with. But having heard from the lips of these people the stories of some of these good gifts, I am able to set them down. Our men, tired and war worn, yet found enough strength to carry children sometimes and sometimes to help a terrified family along the weary road by giving a pull at the farm cart or by a distribution of bread or a draught of precious water.

So this sorrow, though it was big enough to melt any heart, did not take the songs from British lips. The "long way to Tipperary," with its gay lilt, might cheer the French wayfarer perhaps even as it cheered his British brother, and it could bring back the dimples to children's faces that had almost forgotten the way to smile. They sang all the way, and forgot the sorrow in their singing, and made others, whose sorrow perhaps was greater than theirs, forget it likewise.

But this new sorrow which they found in the orchards, among the trees, could not be lightened by any singing. It was the sorrow of death, which is eternal, of violation, and rapine, and murder, where a man's eyes are dark and the brute beast that is within the spirit of man awakes and walks abroad. In the orchard they found the dwellings of poor peasant folk, like the peasant folk of the Yorkshire dales and of the sweet Devon country, thrashed asunder and torn and burned, and they saw the bodies of women and the bodies of children, and they could guess as they passed by, shuddering, what doings had been afoot in this orchard land a few days before when the Hun held rule here and the sanctities and mysteries of life were the material of his blasphemy.

. . . So they sang no more, these gallant boys, as they went on across the orchard land between the rivers.

And if the British soldier from beyond the sea had his song killed upon his lips by this first revelation of the actual horror of war (of this war, for the bestiality of the Hun is not, thank God, the measure of all men who go out to fight), what of the Frenchmen who saw their own land, their dear France, thus ravished and profaned.

I have seen the eyes of Frenchmen as they gazed upon these spectacles, and were I a German I should tremble greatly at the recollection. For the eyes of Frenchmen in these hours are like the eyes of Fate herself—they hold things unspeakable, yet things surely, as God's justice itself is sure, to be accomplished to the last tittle.

They say that the soldiers of the 5th Army as they won across the orchard land between the rivers and saw for the first time the spectacle of ruin and death, were as men maddened by a great wrong. Avengers of blood they were, and their fierce rage was a new strength like the strength of gods. Before this consuming fire the armies of the alien melted as snow. . . . And the end of that rage is not yet, for it burns deeply, far down in the living heart of France for requital when the day of requital and recompense shall be accomplished.

But while these doings were afoot the battle raged without intermission literally to the frontiers of Switzerland. Next to the Army of von Kluck there was, as we have seen, the Army of von Buelow and then the Army of von Hausen, and the Army of the Imperial Crown Prince and the Army of the Crown Prince of Bavaria.

On this 8th of September General Foch with his 9th French Army had faced the armies of von Buelow and von Hausen. He faced them across the extreme tributaries of the Petit Morin River where that river rises in the famous Marshes of St. Gond. In the morning the Germans lay to the north of Sézanne, which is built upon the Grand Morin, and also Fère Champenoise, which lies to the eastward of Sézanne. But by the evening they had been driven to the northward over the Petit Morin (as a glance at the plan will show). The 5th French Army, as we have seen, held the line of the Petit Morin along with the British Army. The 9th French Army therefore joined hands with the 5th along this river course just as the Army of von Buelow joined hands with the Army of von Kluck.

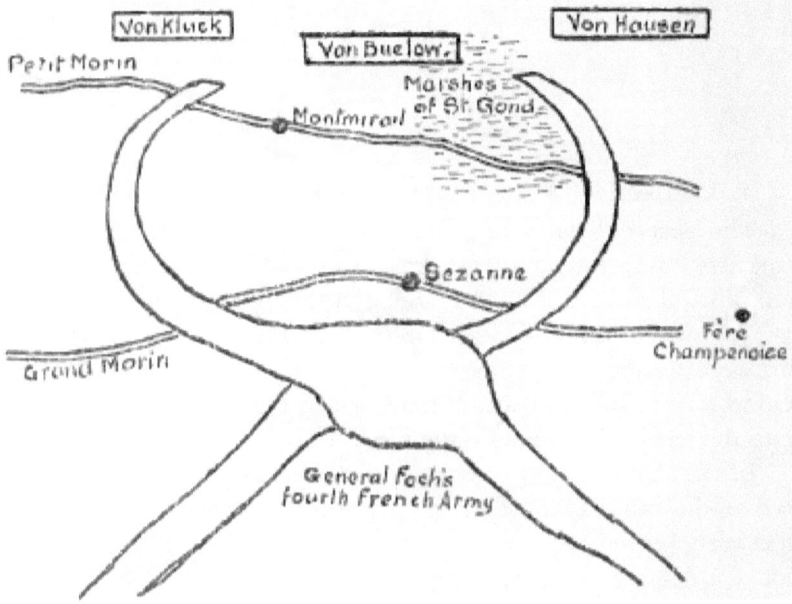

10. THE PINCERS OF GENERAL FOCH.

But the Petit Morin River has its origin in a great swamp—called the Marshes of St. Gond. So that von Buelow's Army was retiring over very dangerous ground, more especially should the weather happen to break and the marshes become flooded.

To General Foch, one of the world's greatest strategists, the presence of the marshes suggested a great *coup* whereby the army of von Buelow might be rolled up on either flank and driven headlong into the marshes.

Fortune gave to the French general the first trump in the game in the shape of the village of Montmirail on the Petit Morin, to which his impetuous advance carried him on Tuesday night. Montmirail was at that moment actually in the very flank of von Buelow's Army and the troops which held it—Foch's troops—had actually separated the one German force from the other, von Buelow's from von Kluck, and had turned the right flank of von Buelow's Army. This night in the darkness Foch thrust his pincer points further up between the forces of von Buelow and von Kluck. Meanwhile he had heard that there existed a gap between von Buelow's Army and von Hansen's—a gap this time readymade by German carelessness.

11. HOW GENERAL FOCH INSERTED ONE POINT OF HIS PINCERS AT MONTMIRAIL.

The beautiful starry night had become clouded over and great darkness was spread across the skies. Rain had begun to fall, the first rain since the night of Landrecies. Soon the light downpour became a great torrent, which flooded the rivers and made the meadow land impassable—above all which caused the drains in the Marshes of St. Gond to overflow and which transformed the well-drained ground into the terrible quagmire of the old times.

In the darkness and through the rain Foch pushed forward his right—the other limb of the pincers—into the opening which he had been warned by his airmen existed between von Buelow and von Hansen. All night long he pushed while the Germans lay bivouacked and the guns spoke and steady rain, falling in sheets, soaked down into the dry earth that was greedy for its coming.

So the morning of Wednesday came, which was the supreme day of the conflict—the day that sealed for all time the fate of France and of Europe—perhaps the fate of the world. A fierce morning that was, as I well remember, with a screeching wind and long whips of rain that drove mercilessly through the chill air. The battle-field, with its heaps of dead and its moving regiments and its vast transport, was transformed into a quagmire, and the men who fled and the men who followed plodded across soaking fields, under dismal skies, themselves soaked to the skin. On that Wednesday three tremendous events occurred almost simultaneously.

The 6th French Army, the "taxicab" army, won the Ourcq finally, and when the Germans tried to come back across the river on their pontoon bridges the French artillery threw great shells upon the bridges so that they were lashed to pieces and their living freight was hurled into the turbid waters of the river between its high banks. You saw the wretched men struggle there a moment before they were swept away, and the river was full of them. . . . The river swallowed them up.

The second event was the mighty struggles of the British to seize the crossings of the Marne at La Ferté-Sous-Jouarre and Changis. That struggle culminated in success. The British left won the Marne, and the British right which the evening before had held the Petit Morin crossed that stream and came also to the Marne River at Chateau Thierry, driving the enemy across the flood and drowning him in great numbers in its waters. The 5th French Army meanwhile which had resisted the great German thrust on our right, had won through also to the Marne at Château-Thierry by nightfall. So far indeed had it come that the Army of von Kluck was driven back from its junction with the Army of von Buelow and the task of the pincers of General Foch rendered more sure and more easy (see diagram).

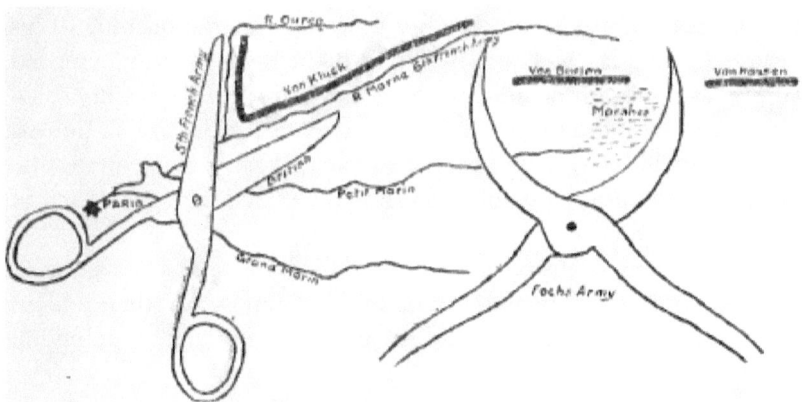

12. THE SCISSORS AND PINCERS AT WORK. WEDNESDAY, SEPTEMBER 9TH.

The third momentous event was the work of Foch's pincers. The full story of that work has still to be written. But the facts are plain. On the Wednesday night Foch drove his wedge between von Hausen and von Buelow and then, holding von Buelow's Army in the grip of his pincers, applied them to it. The right wing of von Buelow's Army was driven down into the Marshes of St. Gond, where men and guns and horses were lost in numbers—though von Buelow succeeded in saving the greater part of his force. The left wing was forced to flee back to the Marne at Epernay, while von Hansen's Saxons were also driven back to Châlons, where they lost terribly at the hands of the pursuing French.

So the battle was won and France was saved from her enemies. Only the task of pursuit now remained. The scissors of Joffre had accomplished their work.

Fierce indeed was that pursuit over the rivers, over the Marne and the Ourcq, to the Aisne on Thursday and on Friday and on Saturday. It was the pursuit not of a rout but of a retiring movement quickened at places so as almost to resemble a rout. The Germans blew up the bridges behind them as they went, and so our engineers had to build new bridges and our infantrymen had to cross them under a bitter fire. Our cavalry too hung doggedly upon the heels of the foe, harassing his retreat along the wet roads and over the sodden fields.

All day and all night and again all day and all night the pursuit went forward. In the night the valley of the Marne blazed anew with shells and flares, and the thunder of the guns rolled along the steep banks of the river. The glow of the funeral pyres was no longer upon the sky, because the enemy had no time now for the burning of his dead, and they lay where they fell with their white faces upturned among the grass, thousands of them, the flower of the mighty force that was to have dealt the smashing blow that should shake all Europe and the world. They lay till they grew bloated and terrible under the hot suns, and until the whole land should be filled with the stench of their corruption.

But the glow of the burning villages filled the night again along all the river, and Frenchmen saw it and in the darkness paid their solemn vows to God that this day should not go unremembered until the full penalty of its bitterness should be paid.

. . . Away to the southward the searchlights of Paris pierced the darkness like sword blades of fine steel.

And this France that had found a new hope and a new life in these awful days, how did she bear the triumph hours that were come to her as from the hand of God? France is ever the land of high emprise, the land of real romance. But on this day she is more than that: on this day in her new strength she is also the land of splendid and terrible renunciation. On this day when the bulletins tell her that the foe has been turned from her gates she gives way to no transports and no vain glorying. Her face, rather, is set towards the future, towards the greater day when her fair fields shall be cleansed of the invader and her sons shall return to the mother for whom they have poured out their blood. General d'Esperey, the commander of the glorious 5th Army, wrote from his headquarters at Montmirail on September 9t:

> Soldiers, upon the memorable fields of Montmirail, of Van-champs, of Champaubert, which a century ago witnessed the victories of our ancestors over Blücher's Prussians, your vigorous offensive has triumphed over the resistance of the Germans. Held in his flanks, his resistance broken, the enemy is now retreating towards east and north by forced marches. The most renowned army corps of Old Prussia, the contingents of Westphalia, of Hanover, of Brandenburg, have retired in haste before you.
> This first success is more than a prelude. The enemy is shaken but not yet decisively beaten. You have still to undergo severe hardships, to make long marches, to fight hard battles.
> May the image of our country, soiled by barbarians, always remain before your eyes. Never was it more necessary to sacrifice all for her.
> Saluting the heroes who have fallen in the fighting of the last few days, my thoughts turn towards you—the victors in the next battle.
> Forward, soldiers, for France.

It is indeed a new France that I find myself in this September morning when they are passing the long convoys of the prisoners to the rear and hastening up reinforcements to the front. There are new lights in men's eyes, and a new tone is in their voices. A troop of the chasseurs rides past me, the splendid coats of their horses gleaming in the morning sun, their bits and spurs jingling deliciously. They laugh and sing as they go by, the little snatches of song that are the French soldier's most cherished characteristics, at once gay and alluring and sorrowful.

121

And the peasant girls who have heard the great news throw flowers at the horsemen—flowers gathered from little gardens that have only just escaped the feet of the spoiler—roses and chrysanthemums and even little wreaths woven cunningly of laurels.

At another place I heard far away that splendid ringing sound that no Briton has ever listened to unmoved—the sound of a British cheer rising in strong *crescendo*. A moment later a great troop train swings along the line, the soldiers hanging from the carriage windows to salute the new land they are come to. On the train are huge pontoons like the pontoons that they brought to Boulogne before the retreat. They are going up to the rivers these lads to the harassing and pursuit of the enemy. Another great cheer and they are gone, and you see the train far away a vanishing speck upon the wide plain.

At the station a French troop train stands *vis-à-vis* with a train of German prisoners. The prisoners are quite composed, and they are engaged in the strange work of bartering their spiked helmets for money and luxuries. The Frenchmen are eager buyers and so are a group of Englishmen upon the platform. Fifteen *francs* for a helmet, or fourteen *francs* and a packet of tobacco—and in this hour the crowd forgets that it is war and laughs and applauds while the sale goes merrily on. For they are brother men after all, when the unspeakable thing is taken away and banished from them.

This then is the story of the Battle of the Marne, which I have called the Battle of all Battles. From the Marne the Germans fled to the Aisne, and the long warfare of trenches was begun with its new battles and its new crises. Along these old plains of France there will yet be fought great battles which shall decide great destinies. But the Marne battle will stand alone even when it has been eclipsed in point of mere magnitude. Never again will there be fought, in this war at any rate, a battle to decide the fate of all mankind and to determine not only the allegiance but the thought, the lives, and even the salvation of civilised men.

At the Marne system and discipline and oppression—the machine man—met the nobler and the truer discipline of liberty. . . . And the iron fetters were broken that had been made ready for the enslaving of the world.

CHAPTER 11

Paris

It was night when I came to Paris, one of the nights after the battle, when the news of victory was spread abroad in the city. The city had gone to sleep, with the news in its mind and with a prayer upon its lips—a prayer of thanks to the good God because once more He had saved France from the hands of her enemies. I drove through empty streets, which were quite dark, like the streets of a remote village. There was no one abroad except an occasional *gendarme*. Could this indeed be Paris, the Paris of Austerlitz and Marengo and Jena, even of the early days of '70? For all these victories were as nothing to this victory, and those others she celebrated with mad rejoicings. From Montmartre to the river, from the river to the heights of the Latin Quarter, the city kept her vast silence, a watchful silence perhaps, but a silence deep and strange and wonderful.

I was in Paris in May before the war cloud had begun to gather in the skies and when the trees in the Champs Elysées and the Bois had just dressed themselves once again in their delicious greens. I stood in the Etoile and watched the motor-cars and carriages, I remember; and then looked up at the great Arc and wondered if France had at last forgotten—if she had resigned herself to a showy cosmopolitanism and relinquished the heritage of nationality in the grand and narrow sense, if she was content to be called the second country of all men, the "home from home" amongst the nations, and her Paris the city without a memory because memory held only bitterness and grief?

But walking home in the clear twilight across the Concord, with the huge bulk of the Louvre rising up before me, I knew that it could not be so, and that this nation, under its mask of merriment, hid a sad and a shamed heart. I knew that Frenchmen could not waver in their glorious allegiance to France, which has remained one of the miracles of all the ages.

And then I came to a statue which was draped in black—a veiled statue.

It was the statue of Strassburg, the lost city, in the lost Province.

And five months later I am in the Paris of the Great War, the Paris of the Battle of the Marne, of Joffre and the 5th Army, of Galliéni. To-day the Etoile is empty; today these few passers-by who come to the great star-square look with new eyes upon Napoleon's mighty arch by which came Moltke and his Prussians in the days of darkness. They see that scene no more now, but other scenes when the little man of their dreams came home to his capital which he had raised to be the capital of the world. There are smiles upon the lips of the men and women who look this day upon the Arc de Triomph de l'Etoile. . . . And in the Concord they have torn away the veil from the Strassburg statue, hanging wreaths of flowers upon it.

Paris is empty as she has not been empty these forty years. The Grand Boulevards are empty, the Rue Royal is empty, there are no longer children at play behind the railings in the Tuileries Gardens, the fountains do not play any more, and the birds, the sparrows of Paris, go unfed. This emptiness seems to be everywhere like a presence. You cannot escape from it. If you wander by the quays it will find you there in the shape of barges moored idle by the walls and uninhabited; if you cross the Pont Neuf to the Cité and in the square before Notre Dame again it will come upon you. The great cathedral is silent today and the winged monster on its roof gazes out over a deserted city; there is something strange and terrible in this silence before the Cathedral of Notre Dame, where usually the *voiteurs* are gathered and the American tourists crowd together vociferously. Even the Latin Quarter has no life or joy left to it. . . . And in the great square of the Place Vendôme the figure of Napoleon looks down upon empty streets . . . the Rue de la Paix shuttered and empty!

Paris has gone, fled away to Bordeaux and Orleans; or Paris is at home indoors. The city is safe and knows itself safe: but the Spirit of the city is calm and stern, like the Spirit of the Army which is the Spirit of all France.

But at the *aperitif* hour you will still find a few wayfarers, and in the *cafés* you will meet with soldiers who have already returned for a tiny space from the battlefield to the city.

This *café* is like the Brussels *café* (of which I have written) on the night after the news of Liège. It is full of men in black coats, elderly men, who are of the merchant class or who have come to hear the news from the soldiers because the newspapers no longer tell anything which men want to hear. These black-coated men are getting a little merry over their wine, and so they are talking quickly, volubly, explaining their views about the battle and the strategy of the battle, while the soldiers, who have spoken already, listen to them in some amusement, but tolerantly as parents listen to the prattle of their children. There are a few women in the company, but these are women of strict propriety from suburban homes probably. The other women are not here: they are no longer in Paris at all, thanks to the forethought of a paternal administration.

The women are much more interested in the soldiers than in the black-coated men who, no doubt, are their husbands or fathers. You may see how their eyes dwell upon the faces of the soldiers—upon the lean-faced artilleryman with the clean-cut features who bears a faint resemblance to the pictures of the young Napoleon—upon the dashing *cuirassier* with his big moustache and his grand manner.

The artilleryman begins presently to tell some of his experiences, and the men in the black coats are silent immediately.

I was on the left, on the Ourcq. *Mon Dieu*, but it was hot, there, on the left. . . . (He spreads out his hands, thin and white like those of a woman who sits next to him. . . .) We counted our lives as from one minute to the next, while the 75's were working, barking and biting; they are good children our 75's.

"It is wonderful," a woman says; and her face is aglow with a devotion like that which must have blazed in the face of Joan of Arc. Every Frenchwoman at this table, you think every Frenchwoman in this city of Paris—is a Joan of Arc tonight. And you learn quite suddenly, so that you are almost startled by the discovery, all that women mean and signify in the life of Paris and of France. You learn that the story of Joan of Arc is the story of France in all the ages. . . .

"Our Joffre," the caressing voice of another woman exclaims. "... To have been the mother of that man!"

They close the *café* at 9 o'clock and after that there is only the street. It is useless to walk in the direction of Montmartre tonight, unless you wish to view the sepulchre of those other days. There is no *Bal* for the Englishman who demands that for his five pounds paid to a tourist agency he shall see Paris naughty—or something like it. The Moulin Rouge is shut. Even the Paris of night which the Englishman

GERMAN SNIPERS CONCEALED BEHIND A BUSH IN FLANDERS

on cheap tour does not see is to be seen no longer. The Germans have gone, taking their womenfolk and their shop-window vices away with them. Paris tonight is the Capital of France, a French city. The French are a grave people—did you not know it?—and a people of sober life.

A Frenchman who walked those dark streets with me that night said, I remember:

> For years your fellow-countrymen have come to Paris to be regaled with sin made in Germany. We are tolerant, and so you misunderstood. . . . Now it will be otherwise.

We stood at the closed and shuttered doors of "Olympia." He laughed a little, then his voice grew hard and stern.

> We have waited for this day all our lives. This day France is reborn. You will never see the old France or the old Paris again.

It is so dark in the Grand Boulevards that you cannot even read the names over the shop doors. Opposite the Madeleine you pause a moment to realise if you can all the strangeness of this night of gloom, of silence. Half-past nine and Paris sleeps! Above the dark avenues over the housetops are the stars, which men did not see in these city ways until yesterday. It is a great cleansing surely which has been wrought by the hands of war—cleansing of the tinsel of life, leaving behind the essential things; laying bare a nation's heart in its strength and its devotion.

In all your knowledge of Paris you dreamed not of this Paris. Yet the new vision neither surprises nor disquiets. Somehow, in some unexplained manner, you have known a long time that it is of this material that French hearts are made—you have known that when the hour struck the soul of France would awake. France fights on this night for her life and for her place among the peoples; she fights silently with the quiet courage of a desperation that knows no respite. . . . It is terrible, this quiet and this darkness that cover the face of the city.

And on the morrow the streets are still quiet under a glorious sun that showers its arrows upon a hundred towers and minarets. Sacré Coeur gleams from the heights, white as a temple of Greece; above the bend of the river the Trocadero recalls happy memories graciously; the golden dome of the Invalides is burnished anew, and there is beauty even in the gaunt shape of the Eiffel tower thrust up into the ambient light. You may hear children at play, a few children of the poor class, in the gardens of the Tuileries, and they are playing the war game here under the Strassburg statue, as their fathers are playing it a few miles away where they pile up the bodies of the dead to make a buttress against the enemies of France.

The social order is reversed and such life as remains to the capital is to be seen at midday, before the hour of *déjeuner*. Officers walk at this time in the *boulevards* talking earnestly together; they are old men for the most part, grizzled, with stern expressions which, however, are belied by kindly eyes. They will lunch at Maxim's, at the end of the Rue Royal, which has become French once more and a great meeting-place of officers, and there too you will discover Englishmen from the Aisne, and Belgians, with a sprinkling of lesser political and diplomatic people, and, of course, the cheerful and ubiquitous journalist. . . . The talk is all of the battle, for already men begin to realise how great a salvation has been accomplished. The legend of the invincible Prussian is broken; France feels again the warm blood of her strength rushing in her veins. The bitterness of death is past. France will not die; she has risen from the dead.

It is the very reverse of the feeling which was manifested in the *cafés* of Brussels. There the numbing influence of doubt and apprehension chilled the spirit; here, on the contrary, hope is made young that men may be in love with her. It is as though a plague has been stayed; as though the world comes again to honour and truth and liberty.

As the days pass you learn, in Paris, exactly what the Retreat from Mons and the Battle of the Marne have meant. In the fierce days of retreat this lesson could not be learned, because men's minds were racked with anxiety and foreboding. But now in this calm clear air of benevolent autumn it is possible to secure a little perspective. You see how great a triumph Joffre accomplished when he sacrificed acres to men and saved the army at the expense of some of the most valuable territory in France. That choice and that decision must have been bitter indeed. Yet how fully justified by events! For men saved are a guarantee of future salvation. So in later days were the Russians to defeat the smashing blow delivered against them—by yielding territory and saving men until the force of the blow should be exhausted.

They made excursions from Paris in those days to the deserted fields of the Marne, where white corpses still lay unburied and the accoutrements of war were scattered across green fields. And they brought back to the city souvenirs gathered from the battle-ground, helmets of dead soldiers bearing the dreaded motto "*Mitt Gott für*

König und Vaterland," and great pieces of shells with jagged edges and time fuses battered and broken. There were strange wicker baskets too, in which the shells had been carried, and long copper tubes that were their cartridge covers, and rifles and broken bayonets. And these were the remnants of the army which was to have conquered the world, the army of blood and of iron, the devourers of Belgium, the ravishers of France. Women played with the relics in the *cafés*, handling them casually, even without curiosity. To such a pass of indifference has this debauchery brought our world!

The battlefield—but there is no battle-field, believe me, any longer. Autumn leaves are falling softly upon the dead faces as the good God spreads his pall of forgetfulness over this horror—great chestnut fans yellow in the sunlight and small beech leaves and oak leaves that rustle gently under the wind. The dead sink back upon a gracious sward and the weapons of war are cold under pure skies. To-morrow the plough and the oxen of the plough will pass by this way effacing . . . effacing. . . . And that yonder is Meaux the town of fire and blood. You may gaze upon the white ruins, the shell holes and the broken roofs and the windows without panes. Tomorrow they will rebuild as men rebuild after a storm, in great confidence that the two hands of a man are potent against all anger and all hatred.

On this day a crowd has gathered in the great square before the Invalides. The crowd has gathered to watch the soldiers parading, these new soldiers of France upon the holy ground of the French Army and the French people, almost within earshot (as they say wistfully) of the little man who sleeps under the dome, and who used to parade his soldiers upon this place when the name of France was terrible among all nations. This crowd is not large; it is not familiar, because in Paris in the old days one did not see Frenchmen and Frenchwomen as one may see them now. The mask of those days, the affluence, the insouciance, the gaiety, where is it? These people are very calm—unlike your conventional French folk; they are stern even and they have a quiet ease of manner which is altogether delightful.

The women are dressed in very sombre clothes and there are many widows among their number. When they look at the soldiers you may see their eyes soften and then, if you watch carefully, grow bright with pride. The women of France have not forsaken her traditions: the women of France are her strong defence. Up at the Etoile they are sitting even now knitting comforts for the men, and in the hospitals they are labouring night and day without respite. There is no woman in France who has not made this war her sacred cause, whose spirit is not aglow with love and pride and hope.

And the soldiers. . . . These are boys of the new class only just come to man's estate. Today the estate of a Frenchman is a defender of France. They step so proudly, with that knowledge in their hearts; their boy faces are lit with it so that they have a holy light in them under the golden sky and under the shadow of the great dead. Their new uniforms are sacred already, and already they have made, one and all, the great renunciation.

Has England realised this passion of devotion which has swept the French race like a strong fire? Has England guessed how deep were the wounds to French pride inflicted by the defeat of '70; how cruel the sorrow; how unbearable the pain? Englishmen were deceived by that surface mirth that hid the torment—for France is terrible in her sensitiveness; they knew the gaiety but the tragedy they did not know, and the lips of France were sealed. . . .

The band has played the *Marseillaise*, not once but many times; the Marseillaise is the music of France, which no other people can hope to imitate. It is France; it speaks her splendid and troubled spirit; it reveals her joy and her long, long sorrow. France is the child spirit of the nations; all things have come to her; all things have been known of her; the cups of joy and sorrow, of defeat and victory, of shame and triumph—all of these she has drained to the dregs. And she lives still a child, fervent, generous, beautiful.

You may learn all this upon the great square before the Invalides this September day after the Battle of the Marne.

But there is yet another lesson to be learnt. For suddenly upon the peace breaks a great terror that flies swiftly, affording no warning. You hear the first thrill of it from the crowd itself. . . . "Taube!" And then the angry buzzing of the propeller comes shortly with the alternating breeze. You gaze up following the universal instinct. It is yet a long way off, a speck like a great bird seen clearly above the turrets of Sacre Coeur.

There is a sound of guns firing, and the women in the crowd utter little short exclamations which are not fear but only excitement and curiosity. The crowd does not move; it does not even thin out, though the booming of the guns is become loud and menacing, and the vulture-bird is sweeping towards the place with terrible swiftness.

The women smiled with brave lips; and once there was a sound of light laughter which rang out musically in the stillness.

Then the aeroplane threw bombs, and you could hear the crashing reverberation of them among the streets in the neighbourhood of the Lazare Station. The people laughed again; they did not pause in their watching. The aeroplane swerved to the eastward, and then it was seen that there were two of them, perhaps more. You could not catch any murmur of fear. A moment later the danger was ended amid the crashing of bombs which fell upon the roof of Notre Dame de Paris.

The soldiers continued their drilling.

The women are knitting at the Etoile in the gardens—the women who have remained in Paris. They do not pause in their work except when an ambulance goes by to one of the hospitals in the Champs Elysées. They look up and sigh for the brave men who have given strength and hope for France. The women will not forget in France, and their memory will include Englishmen as well as Frenchmen; for France is tender always to those who have succoured her, no matter what disputes may arise by the way. In the Champs Elysees are many hospitals, and indeed in all Paris, for the Marne has left behind a terrible toll of suffering and mutilation; and it is only now, days after the battle, that they are gathering the wounded and bringing them to the capital.

France and England have reason to remember the kindness of America during this sad period. When there were few hospitals and many wounded, when danger threatened and helpers were difficult to recruit, when France and England had their hands full with the great retreat and the great battle, then came America to the rescue, offering, as she called it, her "gift to humanity."

A noble gift, nobly conceived—a great hospital, fully equipped, staffed, with a transport service of its own, ready to receive the poor wrecks from the shambles beside the rivers. They planned it in the American Embassy, and they placed it in a great new school at Neuilly, just beyond the gates of the city. Americans of all classes thronged to help in the work. The concierge was a famous artist; a famous sculptor assisted him. In the wards most eminent physicians and surgeons gave time and money liberally. Women whose names are famous in two continents wore the uniforms of nurses. The ambulance convoy went out into the by-ways of the battle and brought back wounded soldiers in hundreds. Frenchmen and Britons and even Germans; and these were laid side by side in the long sweet wards and taught to believe again that there is kindness and love and beauty in the world.

Linger in this ward and realise all the horror and all the madness of war. That man is a French peasant from the south country, where they till the vineyards on the slopes of the Pyrenees and where peaceful ploughmen follow great white oxen through the long days of spring. He is grievously wounded and the soul of him seems to hover, doubtingly in his wide eyes. His mute eyes are full of wonder that this thing should have been done upon the fair earth. Next to him a German lies, a cropped-headed fellow with rather heavy features. He is a Saxon and he will tell you that he has a wife and family there, in his own country, who write kind letters to him and are proud of him because they believe that he is fighting his country's battles. His wife and children, he says, are dreadfully apprehensive as to his safety; they do not cease to think about him, and his children love him very dearly because he has always been a just and good father to them. Yes, he will certainly be very grateful if steps are taken to make it known that he is alive and likely to recover. . . . He is weak and so he allows a tear or two to roll down his cheek.

A Hun—(he was amongst those who swept down through Belgium and France)—but now not "Hunnish."

What is this then that has converted a good father into a despoiler of the women and children of other men?

And not far off a big Highlander with the soft accent of the West of Scotland lies uneasily, in great suffering. This man kept a road once upon a time up in the clean moorlands of Argyllshire, where the peace of Heaven is not broken through all the seasons. In his delirium he has returned to that beloved work and wanders now by the sunrise lochs of his native land, where the black pine trees whisper together at the dawn.

At Versailles they have another hospital, where friend and foe lie side by side in quiet wards. Under the Palace of the Kings this hospital is set, upon the ancient Courts of Chivalry where every stone wears a memory. But these simple folks who have been brought hither to do battle with one another know little of that great tradition. What is it to them that the Sun King wandered here in the days of his glory, or that here the Invader wore for the first time his Imperial crown, trampling the form of France beneath his feet? They are simple folk; devout folk for the most part in spite of their rough and boyish freedom of speech. I met a man here who was a railwayman in a Fifeshire village; another who minded cattle in Devon, a third who belonged to the quiet, hard people of the Fen country; and I met Saxons and Bavarians here also, and even a few Prussians from the dead lands near the Polish frontier.

It was Sunday evening, and while I spoke to them an army chaplain, a mere boy, with a pink face and very nervous in his manner, came into the ward to conduct evensong. He spoke a word or two and the Scotsmen and Englishmen and the Saxons and Bavarians and Prussians had no longer any memory of their bitterness. They prayed with him, each in his own tongue, whispering as men whisper who have much eagerness to be heard and very much to ask for. And later I heard them sing a hymn together—for I had gone out into the gardens of the palace under the stars, where once the knights and dames of France were wont to wander. The familiar tune was like a benediction, though the singing lacked almost everything of harmony.

CHAPTER 12

The River of Death

The Battle of the Aisne will go down to history as one of the world's "fights without a finish." The more so because it succeeded so closely upon the Marne, in which, by reason of the fact that victory was plucked from the very jaws of defeat, the Western Powers will ever see the promise of their salvation. Yet this view of the Aisne is not quite accurate and should be tempered by at least one momentous consideration. *It was upon the banks of the Aisne that the redemption of France and the safety of England were sealed.*

Consider what was the position when this fearful struggle was joined. The German host had been surprised and thrust back, Paris had been saved, the Allies had taken new heart and three nations had lifted up their heads again. But the enemy, likewise, had saved himself. He had turned his defeat to account in that he had preserved his forces from annihilation. He was defeated; he was not routed. His losses, great as they were, were not so great as to render him less able to carry on the offensive movement upon which his final hopes of success depended. . . . And the autumn weather remained ideal for his purpose. . . . The winter was as yet far off.

The Aisne, then, from the German point of view, was a halting-place, no more. It was a rest-station where exhausted forces might be rallied and tentative efforts which had failed might be reorganised. The very strength of the place secured it, so they thought, against assault. Here on the cliffs above the river they might hold the forces of the Allies until such time as they should be able to renew the offensive movement and sweep down, a second time, upon the plains of Paris.

But these considerations were of little account to the Allied forces which came to the river bank on Saturday, September 12. The Allied forces were very strong now, with the new strength of victory. A great joy and a great pride filled the breast of every soldier. Had they not defeated the great onslaught; had they not turned back the "invincible army which cannot be beaten "; had they not seen the vaunted Prussian soldiers fleeing in surprise before them? Throughout France and England hopes beat very high; the Aisne, men said, should be the ending of the great punishment begun upon the Marne; this battle would resolve itself, surely, into another defeat for the foe, who must then fall back along his whole line, leaving France and Belgium free once more to their rightful owners. "*We shall winter upon the Rhine,*" was the universal prophecy, and there were few who cared or dared to dispute it.

The time was Saturday evening. The German Army had retreated some sixty kilometres across the richest plains of France, across the broad Marne and the lands of Champagne so lately the scene of their debauchery. Rheims, the city of a hundred kings, was "uncovered"; Soissons and Compiegne were vacated; but the River Aisne itself was held as yet, and the great guns had been mounted in the quarries above Soissons to command the crossing-ways.

He who would understand this battle must fix his mind upon these quarries above the river at Soissons. They are the keys which unlock the door of the mystery of this battle, the mystery of a battle that was won and yet lost by France and England, and that even now, as I write, has not been decided finally.

The quarries of Soissons have a history, as I learned one night from an agent in a Secret Service which knows no superior.

They belong to the little accidents of history which are so big when one looks at them in the retrospect—like the little horse-shoe nail which decided the battle. These quarries—why, there were other days when great farm carts used to go up to them across the bridge— or so I have heard—laden with manure for the mushroom beds. They grew mushrooms in the quarries once upon a time. It was a company which owned that business. And can you believe it, the company was floated in Germany! But the good people of the Aisne Valley are not suspicious. They did not inquire too closely what it was that these manure carts carried so industriously to the quarries upon the hill. Manure no doubt, manure for the mushrooms. Until the Battle of the Marne was fought and the guns began to speak from the mushroom beds in the quarries.

My informant smiled as he added:

> The country folk were indeed very unsuspecting, for during the days of the great Retreat they drove their herds into the quarries for safety, so that when the enemy fell back upon them he found them ready victualled for his comfort.

The Germans prepared for a great effort upon the north bank of the Aisne, upon the heights which overlook the river. Here he must hold his foe or yield up the major portion of his conquest. If the Allies should succeed in driving him back across the plateau by Leon and the Forest of the Eagle all that had been won so hardly at Mons and Landrecies and Le Cateau would be lost irretrievably.

On Sunday morning, therefore, when the hosts faced each other, desperate men faced desperate men. "Hold the Aisne or die" was the order of the day along the whole enemy front: "Win the river at all costs" was the Allied watchword. And the river, swollen by the recent rains, rushed turbid and swift between its high banks at their feet.

The battle began with an artillery duel across the valley, for only when the terrible guns in the quarries had been silenced was an assault upon the main enemy position possible. The valley became soon an inferno. The air was shrill with the passage of the huge shells, and great clouds of smoke marked the places where the high explosives burst. A dreadful booming echoed between the river banks and was carried upon the wind even to the gates of Paris, so that men and women knew that the great struggle for France and for the world was joined once more. The German guns were the bigger and they were better mounted, there in the quarries, than were those of the Allies upon the southern bank. But the gunners who had won the crossing-ways of the Marne knew how to face this superior fire with a superior courage and so to triumph against it.

And while the guns thundered along the heights what scenes were being enacted in the valley, across the river meadows that stretch out upon either side from the waters of the river itself! Here, upon the meadows men were fighting out, inch by inch, the possession of the valley and of the heights beyond the valley, of the fair lands to north and south, of France, of the world.

At Soissons a broken girder of a bridge still stands, and that is footing enough for desperate men to go forward into the jaws of death. There are other crossing places that have not even this shadow-semblance of a bridge. At Fontenoy, at Vic-sur-Aisne and close to Amblenz there are other crossing places if you have boats to cross in or men who will build bridges for you under a rain of shells and bullets. . . . The engineers are at work by the river side as you have seen them working by quiet rivers in England, when the leaves drooped to the water of a summer's afternoon and the shy kingfisher hid him beneath delicious foliage. The Royal Engineers on this day are building much more than bridges, though as yet they have not guessed it.

How quietly they go about this work which in all history has not been equalled for danger and terror. That man with the boy face who binds together those uprights near the bank . . . do you see how he has paled suddenly in the noonday sunlight and how he reels and falls backward on a kindly sward with a little froth of red blood upon his lips? Mark that his unfinished work scarcely suffers from this event. There is already another in his place and already the quick rope is plied deftly about the planks.

Watch that soldier in the boat as he works his way along the half-constructed piers examining and suggesting. Already his life is lost a hundred times a minute and saved as by the Grace of God. Yet he does not pause in his work. Time is so short here upon the river of death, and there is so much to be accomplished before the darkness.

In the camp above the hill at Boulogne they had great pontoons upon waggons, and the pontoons looked like the "property" of some entertainment, like the green boats which sail so easily upon the jocund streams of a Christmas pantomime. . . . There again are the green boats, being dragged down to the Aisne River on this September Sunday when men and women in England are sitting around their midday meal . . . the pantomime effect has been lost somehow. . . .

The engineers labour doggedly under a fire which eats into their numbers. Slowly and sternly they pursue the slow stern work of dragging their pantomime ships to the river's edge and launching them upon the swift water.

But the guns upon the height have already been trained upon the frail bridge that has been woven and girded by hands already cold in death. Across the valley breaks out a dreadful cannonade with shrieking shell and exploding bomb. The bridge is burst asunder as it swings in the swift current of the river, and the green ships are hurled madly against the banks where they beat themselves to destruction. But at Neuizel there was a road bridge which was still capable of being repaired. A pontoon bridge was built near it, and so in spite of the guns that continue to thunder their menace from the wooded heights above the river the hour of the footmen draws near and men gird themselves to face the ordeal that lies before them—the ordeal of the bridge and the fiercer ordeal of the heights that stretch beyond it.

...And the day grows old under the green banks and the sound of the wind amongst the trees is mournful and bitter. . . .

> *Throb of a thousand feet,*
> *Hear the brave beating!*
> *Over the sweet low grass,*
> *Over the babbling ford by the brooks' meeting*
> *Where the oxen pass—*
> *Up to the hell-night's lowering face.*
> *Where Death hath hidden her bridal place,*
> *And young Death faints in young Life's embrace.*

In the hour of sunset a chill wind sweeps the heights bearing rain in short, sharp whips. They struggle across the bridges, who still live in that hell of fire; they sweep the meadow lands with their bullets; they rush forward, bayonets fixed and faces flushed. They struggle upon the heights with a foe whom they scarce can see in the darkness. . . . And the panting of strong men who struggle for life and the moaning of men who die is mingled under the darkness beneath the forest trees of the Eagle.

And so the heights are won for this day at any rate, and the enemy thrown back. And not at one place only, but at many places. The river no longer divides friend from foe. Good augury here, surely, for the days that are to come.

I have passed through a smiling land to a land wearing the mask of death; through harvest fields rich with great stacks snugly builded against the winter to the fields of a braver harvest; by jocund villages where there is no break in the ebb and flow of everyday life to villages and towns that despoiling hands have shattered in ruins. And I have passed up this Via Dolorosa towards the very harvesting itself—where under level skies the river flows red with the blood of youth and courage and hope.

Above the river is the plain, and beyond, set in the plain, a height, the *massif* of Leon, where the enemy gathered himself a week ago for the assault which should sweep back those insolent English from the northern bank. What a theatre this for great battling. There away to eastward is the Champagne country with Rheims rising splendid among her hills, and there westward the Oise flows tranquil through delicious meadows that are tender as yet with the caresses of summer.

I know of heroic work along these plains of France that will live while men speak of the great things which men have wrought; but the tale of them is too long to be told. I know of fierce attacks the thought of which is like strong wine in a man's blood, and I have heard how the columns went down again and again to the blazing death in the valley, and how men worked building and girding with hands that gripped, as it were, upon the throat of death, winning moments that in death they might know the accomplishment of their purpose. Here is an extract from a letter written upon the banks of the river:

> We lay together, my friend and I . . . the order came to fire. We shot and shot till our rifles burned. Still they swarmed on towards us. We took careful aim all the while. But at last I grew tired. I turned to him—my friend—and as I turned there came a thud like the thud of a spade upon newly turned earth. He rolled over slowly so that I saw the face of him. ... I think that my aim was not less good afterwards. . . .

"It was queerly quiet in the night," said another of the men who crossed that day by a pontoon bridge over the Aisne River.

The Aisne was a frontal battle; it was a siege. It was during these early days of the Battle of the Aisne that Europe got its first intimation of what the long months to come had in store—of the weary trench warfare that was to make of Europe a vast fortification builded around the Central States. The hopes, that beat so high, while memory of the Marne remained fresh, met on this terrible river their quenching. The days went by and the toll of death mounted up, and yet there was no decision. Men said, "Tomorrow it will end; they cannot last much longer." But the morrow ever falsified prediction while good soldiers gave their lives for the bitter heights that were so near, and the autumn leaves sailed down to earth in the forest lands to north and south. The line from Paris to the Aisne is the line which runs from Crepy en Valois and Villiers Cotterets—though you may travel also by another route.

What a journey that was in these days of the battle before the knowledge of the weary days had dawned upon men's understanding! You came from a city in the young glow of enthusiasm by pleasant orchard lands where the fruit hung ripe and golden in the sunlight. Mile upon mile the good country of France unrolled itself before you, a land of peace and great quiet, so it seemed. When the train stopped and you put your head out of the carriage window the delicious stillness of this world was a solace. Here had not the foot of the enemy been placed. These fields lay unviolated under the skies, the rich fields, ripe to the harvest. You marked the little villages each with its church rising above the roofs of the houses, and its church tower that may be seen far away as one sees the towers of the churches in the fen country eastward of Lincoln and Ely. A wind that blew softly brought the voices of the country graciously to your ears. . . .

"How little after all war alters things," was the thought in your mind, and perhaps in your face also, when, suddenly, as though a long-pent flood had broken its bonds, the Frenchman, your travelling companion, broke in upon your reflection.

"*Monsieur* sees," he declared, "what this enemy has accomplished. Is it not terrible?"

You had not seen. You dared not confess it. You allowed him to tell you his grief and his anger.

"Listen," he cried, raising his voice in his excitement. "Ah, you hear nothing . . . only the voice of the land which is the voice of birds and cattle. The voice of man, but it is no longer to be heard in these villages from which my people have been driven away."

He rose and pointed north-westward towards a low upland that rolled like a wave in the plain. "There is Senlis, behind those tree-tops, and in a few minutes you will see what they have accomplished even here."

You had already seen the martyrdom of Senlis and could tell him so, he cried:

Senlis it is a name written for ever upon our history . . . and upon our hearts. Shall we forget those names? Shall we forget the things that have been perpetrated upon us, upon our women and our children? Listen, I am an old man, I have lived. But this day I pray God that I may live just a little longer that I may see these dogs brought to the judgment. That I may see the coming of justice once again into the world.

"Ah, you mean the battle now being fought." He shook his head then, because he knew more than you knew.

Monsieur, I am too old to believe that. They are not killed with a cane, these vipers. It will not be this battle, nor the battle of tomorrow, even, that will end them. . . . But the days will bring judgment and justice just the same.

In Paris on the day war was declared against Germany a funeral passed through a mean street, and the *gamins* stopped their play to stare at it. One of the boys shrugged his shoulders when the funeral had gone past. He said:

"*Monsieur n'est pas curieux.*"

Perhaps you recalled that incident when your travelling companion said that he prayed God that he might live just a little longer to see "these dogs" brought to justice.

And then the train began to move again, and suddenly you beheld the scars of war upon the face of this smiling land. You saw a farmhouse set in its orchard; the roof of the house was rent with great holes and the windows had been ripped out like the torn pockets of an old coat. There were dead things lying in the orchard, heaped, huddled. You would not have speculated as to what they might be had not your companion insisted in words that seemed to hiss as he uttered them. . . . In the orchard it seemed there had been a bitter encounter of small units. And this is a station into which the train creeps so carefully, as if mindful of its safety. That huge battered drum of iron that is like a beacon washed ashore after a great storm, that was a water-tank in the old days where the engines might replenish. It is rolled now upon the top of the waiting-room, and both have gone together to ruin. Behind the station, in the roadway, there are piles of bricks and mud and planks that were once rafters . . . the station-master's house.

And farther along the line, standing alone by the roadside, you saw a sight that very nearly brought the tears to your eyes even in these days of stern reality. It was a London omnibus. . . . You saw that a shell had carried away one wheel so that the omnibus leaned over giddily on its side like a drunken man who has come to a standstill after a supreme effort. The old thing was painted a slate-grey, but you could still see the advertisements glooming out through the paint. The windows were broken and the weather had already begun its work. The omnibus was "huddling up" like the things in the orchard; but its front, you noticed, was towards the battle. . . . There happened to be a bend in the line at this place so that you were able to keep the omnibus in sight a long while, until, in fact, it had become little more than a black speck against the level green of the fields.

The train stopped at Crepy en Valois, and so you had to descend and wait upon the station platform. Crepy en Valois is a little place of village street and villas. The villas stand in gardens, and they are built like the villas at Uxbridge with red tiles on their roofs. Most of the red tiles had been ripped away, showing the wooden rafters. And the walls of the gardens were broken down. In the fields beyond the gardens were more of the huddled things, and there was a horse or two amongst them. Men were moving about in the fields with spades burying away the horror from the eyes of men. They had little white crosses too, but they used them sparingly because there were not near-ly enough of them to go round.

On the platform of the station your travelling companion, the Frenchman, made a discovery and took you into his confidence about it. You had noticed him picking up little things from the iron flooring of the platform and then rubbing these things between his fingers. He gave you some of them to examine, and his face was flushed and his eyes glowed with a light that might have been excitement or anger.

"Look, *Monsieur*, at the confetti which I have found."

The little things were square and thin like small pieces of black cardboard. They were very small—as may be seen from the illustra-tion. When you rubbed thembetween finger and thumb the black coating came off upon your fingers, which it marked in a shiny way like blacklead. The little discs were then seen to be made of a clear substance like celluloid, which bent very easily.

13. Discs of nitro-cellulose
carried by German soldiers for firing houses.

"It is the confetti of hell," said the Frenchman. But you did not un-derstand: you had not yet fathomed all the possibilities of this enemy. He grew impatient with your obtuseness. He took a match-box from his pocket and set light to one of the little black squares.

In a moment there burst forth an intense flame that hissed and sizzled as it spread.

The Frenchman replaced his match-box in his pocket:

> Every soldier in the German Army carries a little bag slung to
> his waist-belt. In the bag are many hundreds of these little discs.
> And when he leaves a town he spreads them behind him so that
> the shell fire of his guns will not lack for fuel. It is the confetti
> of hell, *Monsieur*, is it not?

You came from Crepy en Valois by Villiers Cotterets through the
sweet autumn woods. It was a strange and memorable experience. All
along the route death and destruction—dead men, dead horses, villages in ruins, railways torn to pieces, telegraph wires scattered over the
bare fields, here a transport waggon, abandoned, leaning giddily over
the bodies of the brave men who failed to save and refused to leave
it, farther on a reaping machine, its work half accomplished, beside
the decomposing carcases of its team. The long road winds on inter-
minably through the woods to the battle-field. The long road grinds
under the wheels of vast transport trains and ammunition waggons;
it is gay with song, the strange songs of marching infantry that are so
grotesque when you write them down in cold blood, but so charged
with magic when they come to you through woods and to the sound
of marching; it is gay too with the jingle of bits and spurs as the cavalry
regiments trot past towards the lines.

What sights this white road has discovered in these last days when
the German host was fleeing northward to its sanctuary and the Allied
Army drew swiftly upon its heels.

And so you came to the river about evening when the guns were
grown hoarse and the rifle shots sounded fitfully along the bank. It
was the hour of relaxation, which even in war they have begun to
recognise and call sacred. In the long, long silence you could scarce
believe that here were the very lists of death, and that here through
many days and nights the flower of Europe's manhood has been withered like grass beneath a hot sun.

And then as you waited under the cold stars the storm burst again,
grandly, along the valley. The flares threw up their sheeted flames,
which were like lightnings over against the thunder of the guns. The
roll of the thunder made the earth shake and tremble, and along the
wind the fumes of "sulphur smoke "were carried hatefully. Also you
heard the singing of bullets, which is a sound that sets a man's teeth
on edge when he knows the cause of it. "*Ping-g-g-g-g,*" and you saw
the nervous eyes of the searchlights seeking amongst the trees for their

prey. And in the outer darkness among the trees fellow-men laboured unceasingly in the horrible work of death, selling good life against good life for the sake of home and country, for the impalpable things which make up the faith of a man.

And so it has been during a whole week upon the banks of the river of death.

CHAPTER 13

A Race with Destiny

In Paris they are waiting and in Calais and Boulogne and Dunkirk. Day after day the vigil is kept,—the vigil of a people that waits in feverish anxiety to learn its destiny. In Paris they say that the banks of the Aisne are a sure defence—though they say it less confidently as the days go by; but in the ports of the north they speak with no assurance at all—for the gates of Calais and of Boulogne are open and there is no protector army betwixt these gates and the foe.

The Channel ports indeed are helpless at this hour as a sheep in the hands of butchers. Only because the butchers are too busy to attend to this business is the sheep spared. Tomorrow it will be otherwise. News of the Marne has indeed come to the ports, but it has echoed feebly because the old terror is still very live and actual. And every blow of the German against the Allied line along the Aisne banks echoes here with sinister reverberation.

The Battle of the Aisne grows old and yet there is no decision: the line to Paris is cut and the great *trains rapides* no longer draw out of the maritime station at Boulogne: the English boats come and go delicately—as though timid of their own boldness. The streets are deserted; the hotels empty; the roads without guards.

You may hire a motorcar and travel—as I did travel—along miles of the coastline of Northern France, and there will scarcely be a village policeman to question your going. You may travel if you like inland as far as Lille and see for yourself the utter desolation of this stricken country—for the days of the darkness have not yet fallen upon that great city.

You are within four hours' journey of London in one of the richest provinces of the world. You stand upon the very holy places of civilisation (as also of war) and lo! it is desolation that surrounds you. The villages are largely deserted, though some hardy and determined men and women have clung to house and home against all the terrors and the threats. The roadways lie empty under the grey skies of autumn. A spirit of mourning, deeper than words can ever express, broods upon the fields and woodlands—as though inanimate things were sharers in this horror of the world of men.

At night upon the shore, usually so gay, you hear no sound save the falling of the waves, and perhaps the scream of a seabird. The town rises up blacker than a black sky; strange; lifeless; afraid. . . . The long wind mourns upon its ancient pathways.

And in the south the cities keep watch and the foemen fall back exhausted from the banks of the river of blood that none may hold. The Battle of the Aisne is fought and finished: the Battle of the Aisne is proved a no-man's battle; the dead lie upon the river's banks, young men and old men, piled high and heaped together, and it is said of them that their death has saved the world but not yet vanquished the enemy.

How mournful now this river of a thousand hopes—now, beneath the grey sky and the wind. In spite of the rain and the wind there are airmen still hovering over the carnage, as they say vultures hover. Only these vultures look for the living, not the dead. They scout ever above the heights and then, greatly daring, skim swiftly over the forest lands to the northward. The artillery thunders dully along miles and miles of front, shells bursting with monotonous regularity, each to reap its little sickleful of death. In the valley, along the marsh land beside the river, troops are being moved from place to place, moved over the dead men who are heroes and patriots no longer and who sleep stiffly with hard faces upon the meadows, where they came to death so gallantly.

Death . . . death . . . dead men, dead leaves, dead hopes . . . dead enthusiasms . . . the dead of three nations. . . . There are broken machine-guns, broken accoutrements, wasted material, shattered weapons. . . . And now the measure of the quarries is taken, and the measure of the men who hold them. This battle is all according to the plan—to the plan formed in secret while yet men loved one another and were just and generous. Somewhere near by the river is a little valley protected by a wooded hill. Through the valley passes a roadway leading towards the heights. From the heights one looks across the river to the entrenchments of the enemy. In order to direct an accurate fire from across the river on to the little path (by which come supplies and foodstuffs) it would be necessary to have a signaller upon the hill.

Yet there was no signaller upon the hill when the shells were tearing the little pathway to tatters. . . . In days past the enemy had actually surveyed all the ground, even to the little pathway, against the chances of this day. As a Frenchman said to me concerning another question, "*M'sieur*, it is a matter of elementary mathematics."

And these peasants, too, who were so friendly in the early days, and who used to come to our lines with milk and eggs? This old man, who dropped a coin behind yonder gun position and stooped twice to pick it up—how came it that as soon as he was gone away the guns in the quarries opened fire upon that position and destroyed it? This woman with the pretty white neckerchief—what is she doing gathering fire-wood so near to the line of trenches? And why does that airman dip so suddenly above the little wood where the artillery are lying hid?

But the battle which still goes on fitfully is ended as the end of a battle is reckoned. The decision that is no decision, has been come by. The Allies know now that this position of the enemy above the river cannot be taken by frontal attack. The grand sweep that was begun upon the lands south of the Marne has been checked. The army of the *Kaiser* is once again menacing and dangerous.

In Paris they speak the news sadly as men who have lost a good hope. The *cafés* of Paris are opening again upon the *boulevards*, and men are thronging them of an evening to discuss this battle which has come to no proper ending. You may see all manner of men in these *cafés* and listen to all manner of opinions. You may see strange inhabitants of the Latin Quarter mixing with soldiers who were their boon companions, and journalists, and politicians—of the lesser order—and men of business who have come to sell to the fighting nations all the necessities of war, from boots to barbed wire.

In this *café*, which you have visited a hundred times in the old days, you will hear tonight what is the view of the capital concerning the battle and concerning the progress of the battle. And if you are discreet, and have friends, you may receive a hint concerning the next move in the great game of war which they are playing so near at hand under the autumn skies. It is a hint which will set your pulses throbbing, and open your eyes to vast new possibilities.

Your informant whispers:

Remember Antwerp. There are good troops there and the strength of the place is a proverb. What a thorn that in the Prussian side? I know that your Government will send troops to Antwerp to help hold the place. Then it will be to the north-ward that the battle will go. We shall rush up to the northward and surround them. Because of Antwerp they will not dare to extend their line to the sea.

A young fellow with a muddied uniform and the weariness of bat-tle in his face joins you and accepts a cigarette. He too knows of the great plan, though he will not speak much about it. "Your people," he says, "are on the move again."

"Where?"

"Ah, *M'sieur*, how should I know? We soldiers know only our little portion. But it is permitted to think. And you know the rule—turn the enemy's flank if possible. The German Army has only one flank and that rests tonight upon the Oise. . . ."

There is much life in the *café* in spite of the gloom of the hour. The air raids have whetted men's nerves and set the women laughing. It is easier to laugh lightly if there has been a spice of danger. So the glasses are clinked very pleasantly and the wine flows and tongues are loosed to recount deeds that already seem almost tame because one has heard them again and again with only the places and the names altered. . . .

There is, sitting just opposite, a heavy man with a gross face and small bright eyes that seem to see everything yet to keep themselves unseen. They are eyes which hide themselves in much fat, seem-ing to recede behind bloated lids which roll up bibulously in many folds. This fat man is a *litterateur* whose heart has spared him from the trenches—for it is a bad heart physically as well as morally. And now he is pouring his scorn upon the conduct of the campaign in terse sentences that have a flavour of many cups. He speaks quietly though, so that only his admirers who surround him may hear—for it is not safe to be very critical of the army in these latter days.

And while he speaks a young lieutenant with a baby face and a big sword enters the *café*. His face is pink with self-consciousness, and his sword clanks bravely on the pavement beyond the door and makes a good sound on the wood floor, so that the self-consciousness of the boy is quickened with each step. A woman at a little table looks up approvingly and smiles and the boy blushes as he passes her. Other women from other parts of the room cast quiet smiles in his direction because they have noticed how handsome he is and how clean and boyish. But the fat man who criticises armies has seen him too, and has coined a phrase which seems to him so good that even his natural caution is intrigued by it. The phrase is spoken and Fate has made a silence for it, as Fate will do now and then when ill words are spoken in crowded places.

You mark the boy stop and grow stiff suddenly like a beast which is wounded. You see the very hot blood surge under his fair skin. You see the swift glance which measures his critic and also assesses the effect of the criticism upon the company. You note the boyish hesitation which is altogether charming, and the boyish reluctance to become the object of public attention.

The boy passes on: the critic mops his brow upon which the perspiration seems to have come quite suddenly.

And then an older man, in the uniform of the cavalry who has been watching and listening intently, rises and follows the boy and speaks to him in a low voice. The boy flushes and turns and strides back with the gleam of quick and nervous resolution in his eyes to the table where the critic is sitting.

"What did *monsieur* say of me? I challenge him to repeat it!"

The critic of armies is pale now, and flabby and ugly.

"I did not say anything," he declares.

The boy steps back and fumbles with his pocket a moment. He has a card-case full of white, new cards. He throws a card down upon the table in front of the fat, flabby man of letters.

The critic shrugs his shoulders: he does not accept the card. The people in the *café* have already scented trouble and are gathering round the couple with very eager faces. For most of them know the man of letters well—and detest him. The women too are drawing close and are encouraging the boy with remarks which cannot be pleasant hearing for the critic.

"You will not take my card," cries the boy, his voice growing rather shrill.

"No, I will not. I am not a fighting man."

"Then you shall have that, dirty coward—"

And the boy strikes the critic across the mouth with his hand.

There is a scene then in the real sense of that word, a scene in which men and women, soldiers and civilians, appear to become mingled together inextricably. The boy's voice rises above the other voice and it is saying ugly things, because the boy has lost his head a little, as shy boys will when they are embroiled in public demonstration. The women shriek their anger and contempt. They wave their arms and point at the literary man and laugh loudly and discordantly.

To deceive the Aerial Scouts

British soldiers getting a dummy gun into position

When the fray has passed you do not see the literary man any more.

But the boy is cooling down at one of the tables.

And the women are looking at him.

It is an incident, nothing more. But it reveals perhaps a trend which may achieve a destiny. France and her army are at one again, as they have not been at one since her army followed Napoleon into all the European capitals. Paris thinks in battalions once again as she thought during the magic years of her conquests.

And in the pleasant valleys of the north the army of France is defending her once more upon the ancient battle-grounds.

The Battle of the Aisne is ended. The "battle of the left flank"—or if you are thinking of the enemy's forces, of the right flank—is about to begin. The "race for the coast" is about to begin. Three armies are about to play the great game of attempting to outflank each other over one hundred miles of hill and dale and flat. History is about to witness the completion of a barrier of human flesh which when complete shall stretch from the North Sea to the Alps.

This is the last "move" of the Western Front up till the time when these words are written (December, 1915). It is the last development of the campaign. The last thrilling episode before the game shall become fixed and formulated. The last link with the wars of other days when armies were not great enough to span whole continents.

The race-course, if you will permit the metaphor, is spread from the banks of the Aisne at Compiegne away northward across the green valleys of France by Albert and Amiens and Arras, through the "black country" round about La Bassée and Lille to the bogs and fens of Flanders at Ypres, and thence by the Yser Canal, "the canal of blood," to Dixmude and the Yser River. The end of the race shall be run along the Yser river banks under the willow trees and amongst drear marshes until the red roofs of Nieuport on the sea and the spires of its fair Flemish church come into view and men halt or turn at bay upon the yellow sands of the North Sea, among the bathing pavilions of happier days.

A race this of the giants, the prize of which is the world, it may be. . . A race like no other in all the history of war and of warfaring . . . by the side of which the greatest achievements of antiquity are grown small and meagre.

Understand the measure of it or you will fail to appreciate its significance. Here are two armies facing one another upon the two sides

151

of a river. They have fought for many days with the most extreme desperation; they have lost many men; they have exhausted all the meagre possibilities of strategy. The truth, that neither side can win this battle, has been forced upon them.

Both the armies have one flank protected and one flank exposed. The German Army has its right flank exposed, the Allied Army its left. It has occurred to both sides simultaneously that he who can turn his opponent's flank may win this drawn battle. The reward for the enemy if he shall turn the Allied flank is Paris and the sea coast from Ostend to Havre—Dunkirk and Calais and Boulogne, and so the Channel and the coast of England. The reward for the Allies, if they shall turn the German flank, is a broken offensive and a liberated France; and after that the freedom of Belgium and a campaign, perhaps, upon the banks of the Rhine. Big stakes these if ever there were big stakes in the world. He who wins this race will win such a victory as history holds no record of; he who loses may well lose all that he holds dear. Can you wonder that every nerve was strained and every effort exhausted in the mighty task, or that men accomplished that which man's judgment would have pronounced impossible in the days when the call of freedom was but a little voice?

The race began towards the end of September, and on October 8th General Foch was near Amiens. To General Foch had been given the command of all the armies of this northern flanking arm. Sir John French was in the north too with his army, which had been fetched from its positions on the Aisne River with a speed which is surely a record in the story of rapid movements of men. How that movement was accomplished is too long a story to tell here, but some day the full account will be written for the satisfying of British hearts. It was a movement of a night, swift and silent and very sure. It was a movement by rail and by road, excellently well planned, excellently well accomplished. In it the London street omnibus played a leading part. Men who saw it have told me that it was strangely thrilling, so silent, so swift, so expeditious was it.

In the dead of a dark night the great vehicles rolled and pounded along quiet roads under trees already growing bare towards the winter. The men sat silent inside and outside, strange passengers upon a strange enterprise; you could hear only the rhythm of the engine and the gritting of the wheels upon the road. The villages when you came to them slept, and there were

152

no lights in the cottage windows. But sometimes a dark figure would be seen standing in the street to watch this midnight race of armies.

How exhilarating too in the darkness, with lights out, this rushing to win a world and this knowledge that even as you were rushing to win so also was he, your enemy: that it was a real race you were engaging in, fraught with real destiny, and determined by the most urgent need.

But if we would consider this mighty race in detail we must first take account of the battles that were fought in the days of its beginning—for the race, as has been said, arose in the first instance because two great armies were endeavouring to turn each the other's flank.

Let me express it in another way and by a simple figure. Two streams of water running in opposite directions meet one another. They bring each other to a standstill. The force of this impact causes them to overflow to the side and so a resultant stream flows away at right angles to the original streams. Or we may regard it as it is shown in the accompanying diagram—as a series of battles accompanied by a series of rushes to reach the next battlefield before your opponent.

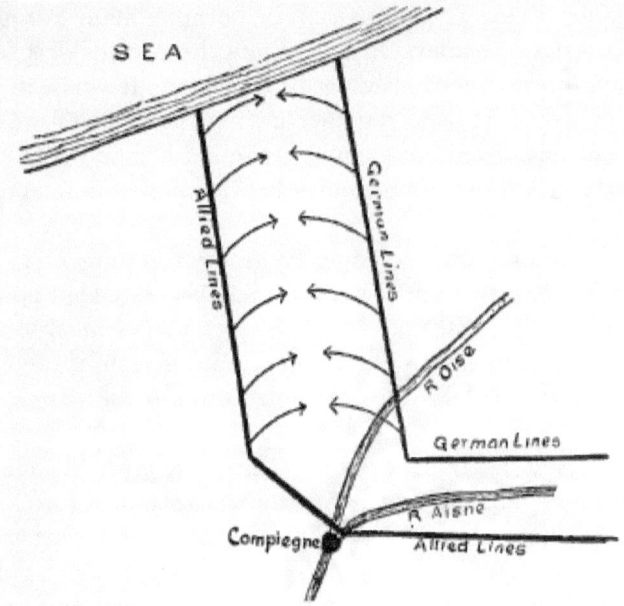

14. How the opposing armies raced one another to the sea.

The first battle, then, was joined on the flats between the Oise River and the Somme River. The date was approximately September 21. The French were under General de Castelnau, and they succeeded at first in taking the town of Noyon.

Then they advanced against von Kluck's right, across this long stretch of country, which is the birth-region of four of the greatest rivers of northern France—the Oise running south to meet its tributary, the Aisne, and to fall into the Seine below Paris; the Somme running westwards to Amiens and the sea at Abbeville; the Scheldt, to the north, running northward to Belgium and Antwerp; and the Sambre, to the east, running eastward to Namur and the Meuse.

There was a three-days' battle here, the object of which was of course to threaten the German lines of communication by way of St. Quentin to Maubeuge and the east. It is called the Battle of Albert, and it was desperate even amongst desperate encounters. The losses were very great, but the progress recorded was but small. Once more it was seen that a frontal encounter, these days, offers small prospect of success to either side. The battle ended in stalemate and the line was built up a little higher towards the northward. The race had begun.

While the Battle of Albert was being fought other troops were hurrying northward. This point must be borne in mind. For not only had we a series of battles, we had behind the battlefields a series of races going on simultaneously with the fighting. It was seen that all the battles would be won together if only the flank of the enemy could be turned; if only one could get round behind his lines, so to speak, and attack him from behind at his vital spot—his lines of communication.

So the race went on, becoming ever more and more furious in its pace. On September 30 de Castelnau's line was extended northward by the addition to it of the 6th French Army under General Maud'huy. This new force possessed some cavalry, and this again moved northward to operate in the difficult country towards the sources of the rivers Lys and Yser.

Lille was still in the hands of the Allies. The great Manchester of France with its network of railways and canals and its forts, with its vast accumulation of wealth and of the means of producing wealth—clothing and arms and railway stock—was an asset of almost priceless value. One could travel to Lille from Boulogne in these days, or at least in the days of the Battle of the Aisne.

But the danger to Lille, now that the great rush had begun, was clearly of the most extreme character.

That danger was, indeed, apprehended; but it was not possible to guard against it effectively. It was not possible to send reinforcements to the town in time because it was not possible to withstand the on-rush of the foe and to drive him from the region of Douai and La Bassée. Lille was doomed because the battle fought by Maud'huy's Army at Arras did not result in victory.

The first runners in the race had now reached Flanders and were at grips amid the waste of the canals and flats and among the willow trees of this sorely vexed land. They were cavalry for the most part, and they fought a strange kind of guerilla warfare about which very little has been heard, because it was only the prelude to the gigantic struggle which was about to begin upon these same fields. The cavalry-men worked in small detachments according to a rough plan of campaign which was improvised largely to meet the needs of the situation, and the object of which was to hold the enemy's cavalry in check and prevent a new cloud of the dreaded "Uhlans" from sweeping down over northern France, taking possession of the undefended channel ports, and thus endangering the lines of communication.

This is a warfare, though, the usefulness of which is of the first order, the last cavalry warfare of the Western Front for long, long months and scarcely a cavalry warfare at all in the strict sense. The bands use their horses only to bring them within reach of the enemy. Then the horses are tied up beside some deserted farm-house and the soldiers creep away to shelter among the reeds and marsh of the canal banks. They lie concealed in these ungracious places during long hours, or they creep forward like hunters on the track of dangerous game. Through long days and chill nights they carry on this strange "amphibious" warfare, losing no chance of dealing a blow at the vigilant enemy, and exposing themselves to all manner of risks and dangers.

And the enemy must needs play the same game on his side, so that the early warfare in these Flanders marshes is like the old Fen warfare of our history; a bitter affair of wet and mud and cold in which men die hard in a still land that is very silent as it has not been silent these hundred years—in a land of long, long distances and great sunsets, where the heavens are spread over the earth like a cloak and the spires of a dozen village churches rise up upon every horizon, dark, among the dark willow trees.

The race is nearing its end now, and so far neither side has won it. The British Army, under General Smith-Dorrien, is at Bethune and is struggling already towards the fatal height of La Bassée soon to be writ in blood across the pages of our history. In the forest of Nippe to the north our cavalry is engaged in driving the enemy to the eastward. Antwerp has fallen, and the Belgian Army is reeling back across the good country by Bruges and Ostend towards the Yser, so that the gap between the southern armies and the sea may be closed up.

It is the hour of destiny, the moment of ruin or salvation. But the fates are still propitious, though the circumstances are well-nigh desperate. The Belgian Army, broken and battered, yet holds its courage in strong hands and casts defiance in the face of its foe. Nieuport is gained and the line of the Yser held. Red blood stains the waters of this river so soon to run with the blood and to be choked with the bodies of thousands. The line rests at last upon the sea. The race is lost and yet won, for the enemy too has lost it. Antwerp has not given him the victory which he expected of it; his hosts have not laid their greedy hands upon the coveted channel. The wall of flesh is builded about him from sea to Alps. Henceforth he must throw himself day and night against this inexorable barrier.

But the days of his strength and fury are not yet accomplished.

CHAPTER 14

The Agony of the Yser

It is October 19, 1914. Today the race for the North Sea, the race with destiny, has ended. Today the last gap in the human wall has been closed up. You may travel today from Belgium to Belfort and yet never pass from this most hideous battlefield. Like cords the lines are stretched out facing one another, and here the cords are thick where they have massed troops and there they are thin where the line is held lightly. But the battlefield stretches on from horizon to horizon, a shambles without limit or boundary, like a streak of blood across the good face of the earth.

The fall of Antwerp was the event which added the last strands of this cord and bound the forces warring among the slag heaps of La Bassée to the Yser River and the coast. The fall of Antwerp was thus perhaps not wholly for evil, though it released a large body of the enemy for service elsewhere. Thanks to their own heroism, the Belgian soldiers were able to "make good" even in that extreme hour and by their dogged courage to save the last remnant of their country from the jaws of oppression.

The position on this October day was therefore critical in the extreme. The enemy had been baulked of his immediate object, which was not so much the seizing of the Channel ports as the crumpling up of the Allied Army. He had failed to outflank the Allies. He had failed to pierce the line they built up against him. He saw before him an unbeaten foe who had indeed fought with success at Albert and Arras and was full of determination to oppose any advance even to his last man. The Germans beheld the beginning of the fortress warfare they desired so ardently to avoid. They determined, at all costs, to break down that iron wall, divide the army of their opponents, and win their way to the Channel and the capital.

And they had reason to suppose that this project was well within the bounds of possibility. Lille had already fallen and the great railway junction of the north was in their hands. The height of La Bassée—famous in the history of all wars in this region—was also theirs. Moreover, the fall of Antwerp had put new heart into their forces and had, so they thought, struck terror into the spirits of their enemies. The Belgian Army was indeed in ill plight, its commissariat disorganised, its hospital supplies scattered to the winds. The Belgian soldiers were utterly weary with long marchings and bitter strivings. They had reeled southward under the fierce blows of their pursuers, and they had come to the banks of the Yser dazed with the ordeal through which they had passed.

What a scene that was—the coming of the army of Antwerp to the frontiers of Belgium, to Furnes and Dixmude and Nieuport! A Belgian officer, who saw them, told me:

> They came like men in a dream—in a nightmare. They were smothered in mud, their faces, their eyes, their hair. Many of them were wounded, and their wounds had scarcely been dressed, so that you could see the blood dried upon them. Many of them were sick and moved with difficulty along the dreary flat roads between the willow trees. All of them held such a gaze of wonder in their eyes as made a man cold to look upon. These were the eyes of the dead, of those who have passed beyond the reach of care or pain or anxiety. These men had indeed lost touch with the world; anxiety and hardship, and strain and shock, had robbed them of their very souls.

They came to Furnes by way of Pervyse and the road which crosses the Yser near that pretty village . . . a terrible pilgrimage of sorrow, slow and without cheer. A pilgrimage moving, as it seemed, at last toward rest and safety which beckoned through the mists of a suffering scarcely to be endured.

But rest and safety were yet a long way off.

At Furnes these men learned—those of them who were able to apprehend—that urgent necessity demanded yet greater sacrifice of them—that they must turn away their eyes from the hope of rest and refreshment and must set themselves once more against the terrible enemy who was pursuing them hotfoot.

In short it was made clear to these Belgian soldiers that only their bodies stood between the German and his goal—Calais and the

Channel ports. If they failed at this supreme hour all would be lost. The enemy would pour down into northern France and attack the Allies from behind as well as from in front. The Allied Armies would be surrounded and cut in two and the doom of the Western campaign would be sealed.

The line of the Yser River is from Nieuport on the sea, inland, to Dixmude. Between Nieuport and Dixmude there are but two bridges over the waterway—one at St. Georges near Nieuport and one by Pervyse, about halfway. This latter bridge crosses just westward of the spot where the Yser River makes a bend to the northward to form a loop (*boucle*) that is like a salient thrust up to the north-east (see map).

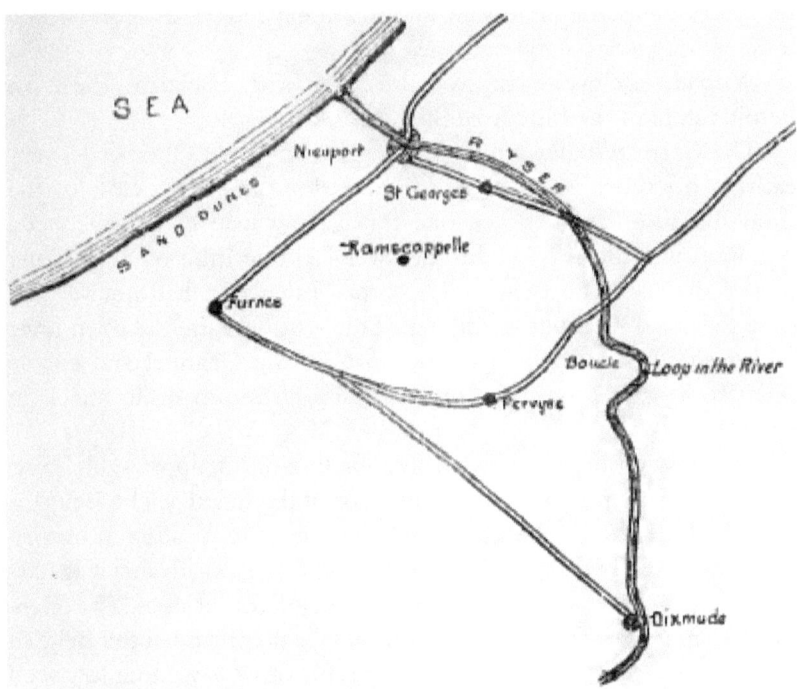

15. THE BATTLEFIELD OF THE YSER.
The Yser River was held by the Belgian troops
after their retreat from the city of Antwerp.

Of this *boucle*, or loop, history will hold long record, for it was here, as we shall see, that the fiercest hours of the battle of the Yser were passed.

It was this line of the Yser that the Belgian Army was ordered to hold at all costs in these mid-October days. The line of the Yser was the last great defensive line before Dunkirk was reached, and Dunkirk was vital to the Allied arms. The line of the Yser, too, was the last of the defensive positions in Belgium that remained to Belgians. If even a single scrap of their country was to be saved they must keep this line against the advancing and menacing cohorts of the foe.

What a gallant rally it was that they made, these weary war-worn men, amongst the willow trees and the windmills of their dear Flanders! Forty thousand men, scarce able to stand many of them from sheer fatigue—and against them 60,000 of the picked fighting men of Germany, refreshed and rested and eager. This indeed was the story of Liège over again, and with added glory—for in the forts at Liège men at least were fresh and unwearied. It was again one of the great hours of history when the impossible and the unexpected are accomplished by sheer doggedness and courage.

With the Belgian Army was the King of the Belgians, the most heroic figure in the history of this war.

The Germans delivered their first great attack on October 18 very early in the morning. They delivered it along the coast, close to the shore, because they believed that the narrow strip of sand between Nieuport and the sea was the least well-held position of all the long line of the Yser. The Belgian Army, they calculated, had not yet had time to spread itself out to this part. This was therefore the open door which should admit them to the ports of the Channel and enable them to bring discomfiture on the Allies by means of an attack in flank.

Their assault began with a heavy shelling of Nieuport, which was to be followed up by an advance in force of the infantry. The Belgians held the little town—which has been laid siege to so often in history, yet never taken by any besiegers—and the Germans advanced against it with the object of securing possession of the bridges. The Germans were under von Beseler; de Moranville commanded the Belgian troops. The Germans came to the assault furiously, expecting to sweep away very easily this feeble people and to push on without delay to the coveted land southward. A Belgian staff officer told me one night when I visited the Belgian Headquarters at ———:

> They came swarming as usual and in vastly superior force. They
> threw themselves against our people and thought to sweep us
> away by mere weight. But they had reckoned without one fac-
> tor, which was to play a great, a very great, part in the battle...
> Your warships—'monitors'—had steamed in overnight and

160

were able to open fire upon the exposed right flank of the enemy.

You can have no idea how bitter was that surprise to men who had believed themselves already conquerors. The shells from the big guns burst amongst them and devoured them. Again and again they were forced back. The little door they would have opened there, upon the dunes, had been nailed shut in their faces, and they were without the power to retaliate or to protect themselves.

(During a visit to Belgian Headquarters, I had the great advantage of a complete and detailed description of all the Yser fighting at first hand. I was able also to traverse the ground).

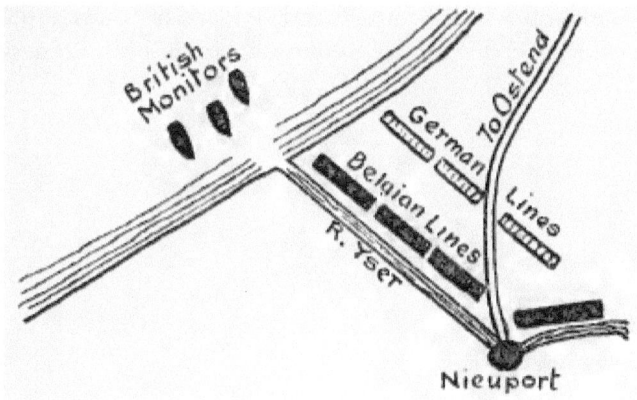

16. The narrow strip of sand between Nieuport and the sea along which the first attack was delivered. Note the British warships (monitors).

These monitors indeed, little grey ships, like "river steamers gone mad," as I heard it phrased, are saving France, and England too, under the grey skies of this October morning. They are bringing deep confusion to the enemy and deep thankfulness to the sore-tried men who stand so staunch for duty along the yellow sands while their beautiful little town is torn to pieces in their sight, and what was so lately a scene of peace and happiness is turned into a maelstrom of death and damnation.

Night falls, and now the battle is joined along all the river way by the famous *boucle* to Dixmude. Along all the river the great guns are belching their fury and steadfast men are facing them with a resolve which conquers the utter weariness of the flesh and makes men god-like in their triumph over material things. The flares leap up in the darkness, filling the long spaces of the night and lighting a thousand pools and waterways with their white flame. It is as though the world were paved with innumerable mirrors.

The battle grows sterner and more stern as day succeeds day and there is yet no decision. Will those over-weary men never yield them? Already they have accomplished, surely, the full measure of man's endurance. It is Friday, October 23, and the gate by the way of the sands remains fast closed as it was after the first attack a week ago. Today the enemy seems to despair of this passage, which has cost him already thousands of picked men, and which has cost Belgium her beautiful town of Nieuport, now a ruin terrible to look upon. He has transferred his main attack to a point further inland, beyond the reach of the terrible gunfire of the ships. It is the village of Ramscappelle that he covets now and that he will pound to ruins in his bitterness.

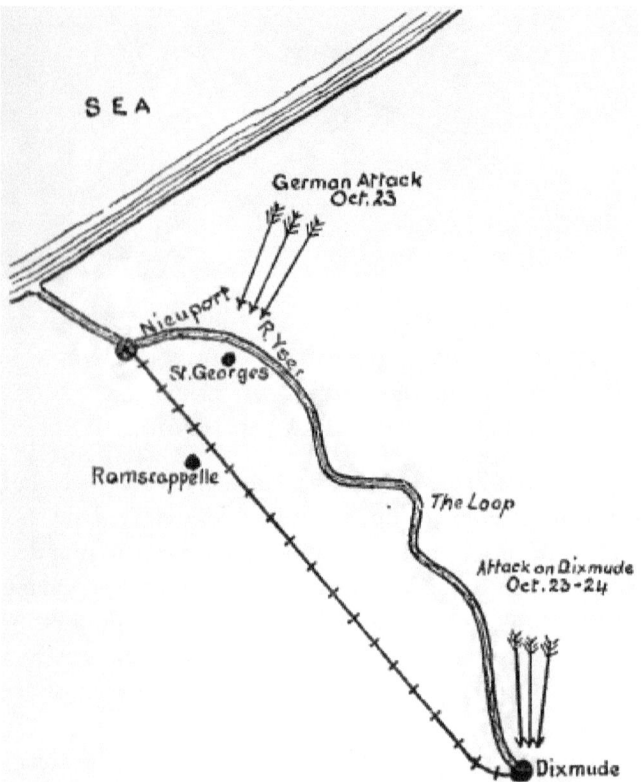

17. THE SECOND GERMAN ATTACK WAS AGAINST RAMSCAPPELLE VILLAGE ON THE RAILWAY. THE TOWN OF DIXMUDE WAS HELD BY FRENCH MARINES.

So, on this Friday, a night attack is launched across the Yser at St. Georges, and a mighty rush made along the country lane towards the Dixmude-Nieuport railway at Ramscappelle. This attack is bitter with the bitterness of anger and baulked determination. Here at any rate there are no naval guns, but only tired and beaten men to be faced. And so here they will achieve an easy victory.

The hours of that fight are written now, each one of them, upon the pages of history. The Germans crossed the river: they hurled the Belgian defenders back through St. Georges to the railway. They secured possession of the railway. And at the same time they began to launch their attacks against the town of Dixmude to the eastward. That fighting for Dixmude was amongst the most fearful of the whole war. Through all the night of this black Friday in October attack after attack was launched against the valiant Frenchmen who held the place, launched and pressed home and hurled back again. Dixmude resisted the attacks and held the foe at bay. And at Ramscappelle the men who had succeeded in reaching the railway were hurled back again across the river. My informant said:

> That effort was as dangerous as the first effort along the shore. Had they taken Dixmude then we should have been undone, because they would have burst through in all probability, and our army would have been rolled up from the flanks made by the bursting. But because the town was held their efforts were brought to nothing.

But the bitterness of death was not yet nearly passed for these gallant soldiers of Belgium. The darkest hours were to come. There remained an ordeal terrible as the ordeal of Antwerp and critical as the Battle of Ypres itself. The "men with the dead faces" had to suffer and endure through long days yet and long nights which were cold of mercy even as the days.

History will bid future generations contemplate these men, the remnants of the army of Antwerp, and hold them in everlasting honour. History will say that hope deferred—the hope of a little rest after experiences calculated to shake the morale of the finest troops—did not make their hearts sick; that their hearts were strong even when hope seemed dead beyond possibility of resurrection. History will tell how they stood in their trenches—they and their young king—shoulder to shoulder, against the terrible Würtembergers who poured against them in vastly superior numbers, and how the Emperor of

Germany himself stood far off to view that glorious stand. Men will say that if they had laid down their arms, there, in the bitter trenches beside the Yser River, it would have been only the natural failing of tortured flesh unable to endure further, and men's eyes will brighten and their hearts beat quick to know that there was no surrender, that the weakness of the flesh was less than the zeal of the spirit.

It is now Saturday, October 24—a day of rain and bitter wind. The crisis of the Battle of the Yser has come, and the fate of the battle is in the balances. Today shall see the greatest attack of all—the attack upon the two sides of the loop in the Yser River, delivered simultaneously, and delivered under the eyes of the German *Kaiser* himself.

That was our supreme moment of trial, as you will see if you regard the map.

I regarded the map—a great map unlike any other which I had ever seen. The fields were all marked upon it and the dykes and the hedges. The finger of the officer beside me pointed to the loop in the river, and then he made a half-circle with his finger and thumb, shaping them like a pair of pincers around the loop. He said,

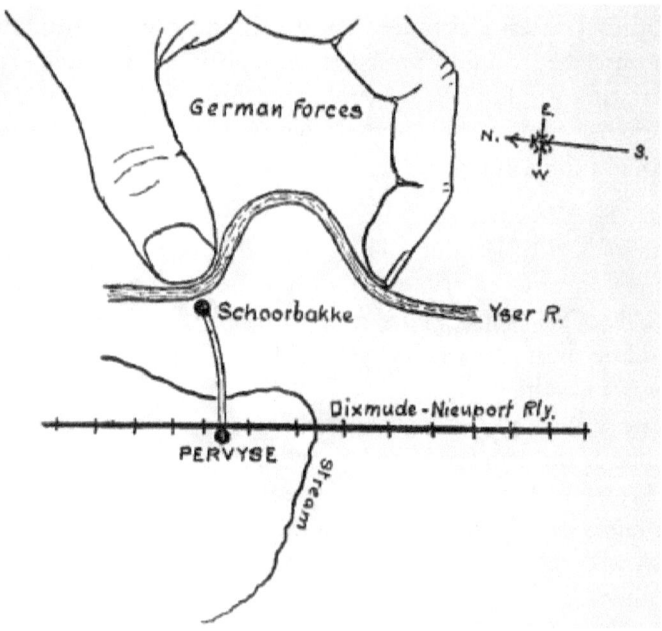

18. THE GERMAN ATTEMPT TO SURROUND AND "PINCH" THE LOOP IN THE
YSER RIVER. THE LAST GERMAN ATTACK OF THE YSER BATTLE.

They thought to pinch our force which was holding the loop and cut it off. You will judge how nearly they were successful. At Schoorbakke they made a fearful assault, drove our men back and crossed the river. The river is canalised and so the crossing was a most fearful business. But they drove our people back. They crossed also at the other side of the loop, and so our men in the loop were subjected to fire from three sides and also to the pinching process at each angle. The enemy swarmed across at Schoorbakke—eight thousand of them crossed. It was hopeless to hold the river against them and we were forced to go back. And next day, Sunday, a whole army of 18,000 men was across the Yser and was advancing through the fields towards the railway.

But our men disputed this home soil of Belgium inch by inch. They fell back because the numbers against them were overwhelming numbers, yet in the meadows they found cover to lie and shoot, and behind the dykes and among the marshes. The French had come to our help, and they fought side by side with us with most splendid heroism. We were truly an army of scarecrows, of vagabonds, but we had the good courage of our cause and of our home love. In the village of Oude-Stuyvekenskerke we made a great stand among the little gardens and the houses and behind any sheltering walls that were available, and the enemy found his advance across these sodden fields, with their bogs and ditches, no easy one. He had plucked the fruit, so to speak, but the eating of it was bitter.

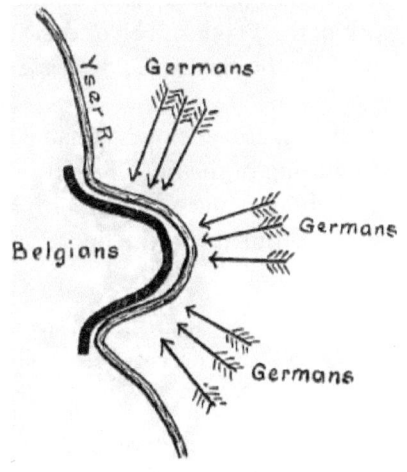

19. THE GREAT FINAL ASSAULT UPON THE LOOP IN THE YSER RIVER (OCT. 24, 1914).

Bitter indeed! For now, though the Belgians have fallen back to the Nieuport-Dixmude railway, they are fighting with a stubborn determination which seems to have undergone no abatement. The weary warriors have achieved a new strength; the strength of a new rage seems to possess them. Every inch of ground they yield is bought and paid for in German blood before it is delivered up—and only sheer weight of numbers prevails to conclude the bargain. All along the meadow lands from Ramscappelle to Pervyse the work of slaughter is continued. The bitter meadows grow rich with good blood, and the bodies of men are piled up beneath the pollarded willows.

Yet the uneven conflict cannot much longer be drawn out between these vigorous troops under their Emperor's eye and these sodden and bedraggled men who scarce know how they fight and who are "grown too tired even to run away," as they say themselves so lightly. The strained line of the Yser defence is strained now to the very breaking point. Tonight or tomorrow—at the latest tomorrow—the strained line will burst asunder and throw open the gateways of victory to the hosts of the foe.

It is the hour of destiny and upon the decisions of this hour the fate of nations is hanging. For Belgium has left to her one last resource, which in her history she has used only in the very extremities of her need. Shall she call once again upon the waters to cover her? Shall the flood gates be opened once again to lay a barrier betwixt this enemy and his goal?

It is a question very hard to ask, bitter as death to answer. For these fields are amongst the richest in a fair province, and the waters have been expelled from them only at the price of long, long endeavour and infinite patience. Shall that work of the good days be undone now in this hour and these riches gleaned by the thrifty hands of men be scattered to the floods?

But indecision is impossible, for already the enemy is at hand. Better the loss of these lands than the breaking of the line of defence and the ruin of defeat. . . . And so, with infinite reluctance, but with swift resolve, the order is given. The Yser is dammed and the floods are let loose upon the land.

Your monitors made this possible to us, because they allowed us, under cover of their guns, to close up the canalised river near its mouth.

On Wednesday, 28th October, they dammed the river and the waters rose upon the good land. The Yser was swollen with rain, soon it spread itself across the meadows, soon the hosts of the *Kaiser* were wading knee-deep in the marshes and the great guns were immovable in the lanes. The weary men breathed themselves as they watched the saving tide, and the Allied artillery swept the face of the waters, scourging them with its fury.

The battle ebbs even as the tide rises, but there are grim doings amongst the pools and swamps, these days of the flooding. Wednesday the fight goes on and Thursday and Friday. The enemy perceive now that their victory is slipping away out of their hands. . . . And so, on this Friday, across the wet fields, another last attack is launched towards the stricken villages—towards Ramscappelle and Pervyse and the railway from Nieuport to Dixmude.

One of my friends was in Pervyse during the whole period of this attack, and he has told me the story of it:

The shells were crashing into the village as thickly as hailstones. Every moment another house came crashing to the ground, blown asunder as by a fierce blast of wind. Stones and woodwork were hurled about the streets, and men rushing about their business were cut down before your eyes. The walls of the beautiful old church, which stands on an eminence between the village and the station a few hundred yards away, were thrashed down to the ground, the altar rent asunder and the furnishings torn to pieces and scattered over the tombstones in the churchyard. Even the graves themselves were desecrated and the bodies of the dead were hurled from their resting-places and profaned hideously. The village was burned up in the tornado—burned up and beaten down and razed to the ground, and the good work of patient men became a mockery even while you waited. . . . It was hell let loose upon the face of the world.
And all this within the confines of a little country village, where the milk trains used to stop of a morning to gather the produce of rich farms and smiling meadow lands. . . .

At Ramscappelle this last attack through the rising water was partially successful. The enemy seized the village on this Friday and held the railway once again. But on Saturday Belgians and French drove him out again and swept him back into the abyss of the waters.

For now the waters are coming swiftly over this land about the Yser River, since they have opened the sluices of all the rivulets and

167

of all the canals that intersect this area like a close meshwork. The waters are rising as a great tide rises, so that where the green fields were spread there is now but a field of turbid flood. And in the flood the attackers of Ramscappelle and Pervyse are struggling for life that they may win back whence they came. They are struggling horridly in the deep places among their guns and their gear, which they shall use no more upon this earth made hideous by them, and their hands are thrust up desperately out of the brown waters for salvation.

But where shall salvation be found for these men?

The big guns at Nieuport and along the railway by Ramscappelle and Pervyse are telling out the doom of this entrapped and engulfed army and speeding the labours of Death among its numbers. The big guns are shelling the broken troops as they go herding together to death among the bogs and ditches which they cannot see beneath their feet. The day is filled with the horror of their undoing, and already their ripe bodies are being carried by upon the tide. Under the pollarded willows, which rise up out of the flood, you may see their bodies clumped together grossly, like garbage—the bodies of the would-be conquerors of the world.

And under the night the waters creep up, sucking greedily amongst reeds and rushes; the waters come again to their ancient fields; they are glutted with a good feast upon their ancient fields. You can hear the lap of the waters upon the ground, and it is like the sound of an animal lapping blood. . . . But the good waters and the good guns between them have saved this day. They have barred the way to Calais and to Paris. They have frustrated once more the designs of the foe under the very eyes of their emperor.

Upon the islands which the flood has spared and which rise up out of the flood like the isles upon a great lake, the enemy has gathered—as many of him as have been able to come to these islands out of waters. Upon the islands the guns are hurling their shells now that the work of destruction and defeat be made sure. At Pervyse and at Ramscappelle they are building trenches to ensure a strong defence, and the waters have come up almost to the trenches. The danger is passed away. Dixmude, which was the key of the defence a few days ago, matters little now, for it has been held splendidly through the critical hours by the gallant Ronarc'h's marines. The enemy will take it at last (lo November), but it will be of little use to them when taken. This waste of water is indeed destined to be the boundary betwixt invaders and invaded during long, long months, in which the face of the world shall be changed and the tide of human suffering and human grief shall flow, even as the Yser tide, without limit and without restraint.

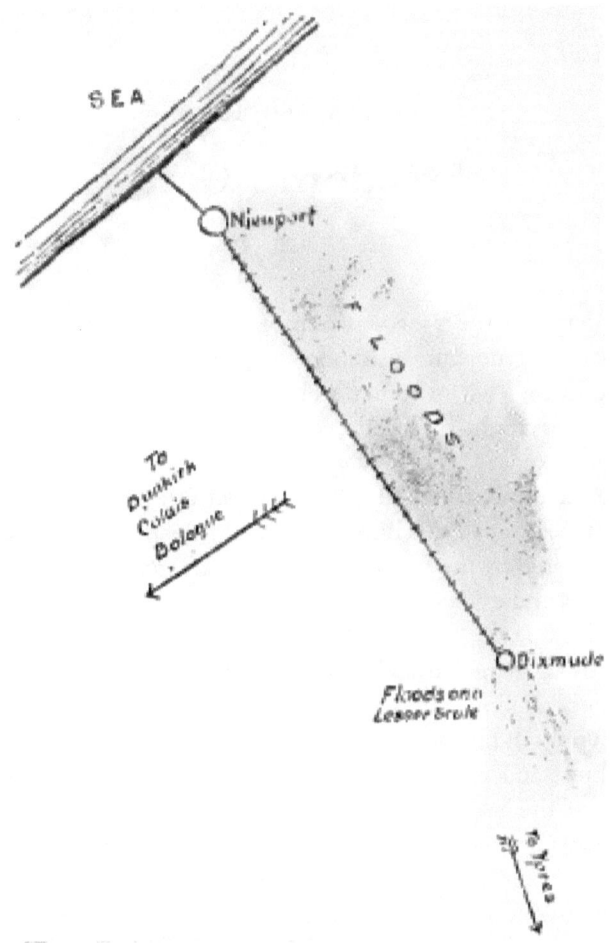

20. THE BELGIANS, AS A LAST RESORT, OPENED THE SLUICES AND FLOODED THE BATTLEFIELD OF THE YSER. THE AREA OF THE FLOOD IS SHOWN.

CHAPTER 15

Freedom's Gate

The Battle of the Yser was one of four great battles which were fought at the same time (October to November, 1914), against the same enemy and with the same object. The four battles were fought that the coast might be saved and that the Allied line might be preserved unbroken.

The Allied line stretched now (October 20) from the sea to Switzerland. But along all this line there was comparative peace, except in the area covered by the western end of it—an area measuring upwards of 100 miles and extending from the Belgian coast down to the River Aisne.

If you will glance at the diagram you will see the placing of the four battles and how the beginning of one was the ending of another—and you will be able to realise how near these battles were fought to the object and prize of victory—so near that in Calais they heard the guns of the Yser distinctly during many days and nights.—Had the Germans broken through at any of the four points the Allied line would have been rolled up and the whole history of events changed. Had they broken through at Arras the Allied Army in the north would have been cut off from the Allied Army in the south, and would have been driven in upon the Channel ports or forced to surrender. Had they broken through at La Bassée, the road to Boulogne would have been open to them. Had they won victory at Ypres, there was the road to Calais. Had they been able to seize the coast line at Nieuport, Calais would have fallen within the twenty-four hours.

So that all these battles were critical, as we have seen that the Battle of the Yser was critical, and it is almost impossible to say which was the more and which the less critical. Victory on the Yser and at Ypres would not have availed against defeat at Arras. Nor would victory at

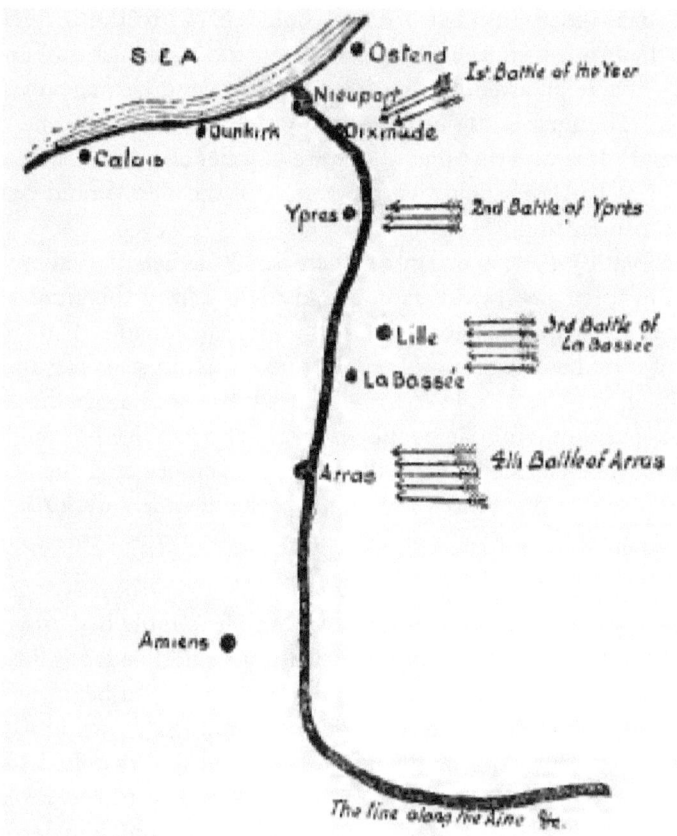

SEA   •Ostend   *1st Battle of the Yser*

Nieuport

•Dunkirk   •Dixmude

•Calais

Ypres •   *2nd Battle of Ypres*

•Lille   *3rd Battle of La Bassée*

•La Bassée

•Arras   *4th Battle of Arras*

Amiens •

The line along the Aine &c.

21. THE FOUR BATTLES FOR THE COAST (OCT. TO NOV., 1914).
NOTE HOW ONE BATTLE IS JOINED TO ANOTHER ALONG THE LINE.

Arras and La Bassée and Ypres have atoned for defeat suffered upon the yellow sands between Nieuport and the sea. It was necessary to hold all the line all the time might have been utter catastrophe.

If this knowledge is kept in mind these battles which are so difficult to understand of themselves will become quite clear. They will be seen to be, in fact, parts of the one great battle in which the three Allied Armies took equal share, and in which all the three armies won an equal glory. They may be regarded simply as a series of four doorways—the first held by the Belgians on the Yser; the second by the British under Haig at Ypres; the third by the British under Smith-Dorrien at La Bassée; and the fourth by the French under Maud'huy at Arras.

The story of the Yser has already been told, and how well the Belgians kept the faith upon that river of woe. The stories of La Bassée

171

and of Arras deserve no less careful telling. Thanks to the accident of report these great engagements have been too little heard of in this country, where all attention has been concentrated upon Ypres. Men speak of "The First Battle of Ypres" as though this alone was the critical struggle. It is well that they should remember also Arras and be not forgetful of La Bassée, and that the waters of the Yser should be ever present to their minds.

The Battle of Arras began on October 20, when the enemy advanced in force against this famous old town. Up to this time, as we have seen already, Arras had been safe against many assaults made to the north of it in the direction of Lens. But now the threat was against the town itself, and the people of Arras realised that once again the terror was come upon them. The people of Arras, who had lived through the horror of the great Retreat and the joy of deliverance after the Marne, saw before them once more only bitterness and exile and death.

One of my friends who remained throughout the battle told me shortly afterwards:

> The town was relatively quiet, however. The people had grown used to the sound of the guns by this time and heeded it little. The sound of the guns was continuous, so that you heard, as it seemed, one long-drawn roar like the ravening of a wild beast. I went out into the fields before the town and watched the battle—so much of it, that is, as a man was able to see. From the spectacular point of view it was a strange and wonderful sight. You saw first of all merely the green fields which seemed strangely empty and quite peaceful in spite of the roaring of the guns. But presently in front of you a great cloud of black smoke would rise up into the air, as though it had been loosed from the very bowels of the earth. The cloud would rise till it seemed like a pillar of smoke set upon the plain, black and solid and menacing. And then the winds seemed to come upon it and tear it asunder and it was scattered.
> 'A "Jack Johnson," sir. . . .'
> In the middle distance was a little coppice, and now over the treetops you saw a strange blue-green fire that flashed suddenly with an angry reverberation. This was shrapnel bursting and beating down upon the troops lying concealed here. As you waited you began to learn the meaning of the various sounds that came to you shrilling through the din. The long, siren-like

tone of the great shells, the shriller note of the shrapnel 've-e-e-e-e-e,' and the shrill screeching of bullets.

And then suddenly came the knowledge that these quiet fields were indeed visited of death, and that danger lurked in every footfall. It was a strange experience. I felt exactly as anybody would feel the moment after he discovered that he was in a field with an angry bull. Every instinct of mind and body prompted flight. But there came, also, with that feeling a sudden hardening of the muscles, a temper upon the edge of resolution. I looked back where the towers of the city rose up beautiful even in this hour of destruction, and I thought of the men who were selling their lives for the sake of these towers and of all they signified for France, for the world. A great happiness came to me that I was able to be joined to them here among the fields and to witness the struggle that they made so splendidly for victory.

But the fate of Arras trembles now in the balances, and the people of the city are making preparations to flee away from it. The women and the children are already passing from the doomed streets where the shells are casting down the houses and filling the roadway with debris of all sorts. The wonderful clock tower of Arras has been hit already and is being reduced to ruin, so that the memory of it shall be linked with the memory of Rheims and of the Cloth Hall at Ypres through all ages.

It is again the ancient pilgrimage of sorrow that we have seen in the streets of Brussels and in the great square before the station, that we have followed through the good lands of northern France by Amiens to the sea, that we have beheld under the moon and the stars in the Fontainebleau Forest while yet the issue of the Marne remained in doubt. The procession of the dispossessed—of the poor who have lost their all, of the women who must face a hard and changed world without protector, without even the slim protection of a home, of the children in whose eyes a great fear lingers and who ask, wistfully and without hope, why it is that all this misery and destruction is come upon them.

Who but the years shall answer the questions of these children of the stricken lands—of France and Belgium and now of Serbia? Who shall tell them all the sum of the infamy which made this thing possible in a clean world, and gave over the portion of honest men to the dogs of greed and hatred?

173

BRITISH TROOPS MAKING THEMSELVES COMFORTABLE IN A RAILWAY WAGGON IN THE NORTH OF FRANCE.

The citizens of Arras are fleeing away by the long road to St. Pol, and the walls of the Hôtel de Ville, with its clock tower, are crumbling to ruins. It is the fatal 24th of October, the Saturday of terrible memory, upon which so many mighty deeds were wrought along this far-flung line of defence. Upon this day, at this hour, the Würtembergers, under the eyes of the *Kaiser*, are preparing them for their greatest assault upon the loop in the Yser River that shall, they believe, give them all this northern France for a prize; on this day the salient at Ypres gave way under repeated blows and a British regiment was hurled back from a position defended by it with gallantry unequalled in all the history of warfare; on this day at La Bassée a furious assault threatened the whole line and drove a regiment of famous name from its trenches. It was a day of fiercest trial, of most heroic achievement, the crisis day perhaps of two out of the four battles, certainly a crisis day in the wider sense in the history of Europe and the world.

In Arras they do not know whether or not it will be possible to save the town. My friend has told me that at one time hope was well-nigh abandoned, so determined and so terrible was the onrush of the foe. But the courage of the French troops of Maud'huy never wavered. With that stoical and splendid courage which the weary soldiers of Belgium were even at this hour displaying upon the banks of the Yser they fought every inch of the ground against von Buelow and his horde of savages, and at length held him and his savages in check. Then to resistance was added attack, and the grand Frenchmen who had saved their town from the feet of the invader made it secure against his further effort. The French went forward from Arras, driving the enemy in front of them. They swept the fields clean and hurled back the huge siege guns out of range of the city.

They made the Battle of Arras a victory and a defence even as the Belgians and the French upon the Yser had made victory and defence with the flood gates of the rivers.

But at La Bassée the struggle was still raging, and British troops under Smith-Dorrien were still sore put to to hold the doorway entrusted to their keeping. La Bassée is the gateway to Boulogne on the one hand and to Lille on the other. This high ground is indeed famous in all the history of European wars, and many times have its fields been drenched with the blood of fighting men.

The high ground of La Bassée is succeeded, if one goes northward, by a valley with a road running through it and also a railway, and to the northward again of the road and railway is another high ground on

22. THE BRITISH LINE WHEN THE BATTLE OF LA BASSÉE BEGAN. AT THAT TIME WE HELD THE AUBERS RIDGE AND ALSO NEUVE CHAPELLE.

which are a string of mining villages—Lorgies and Aubers and Her-lies. They speak sometimes of this second high ground upon which are the mining villages—in reality outskirts of Lille—as the "Aubers Ridge," The "Aubers Ridge," then, looks across the valley to La Bassée (Figs. 1 and 2).

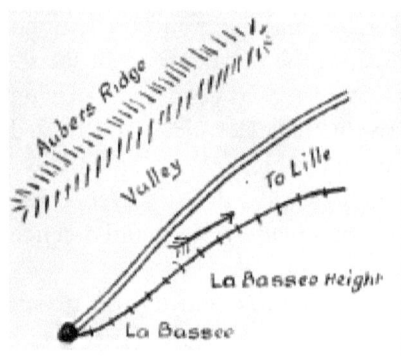

23. 1. THE LA BASSÉE HEIGHT AND THE AUBERS RIDGE.

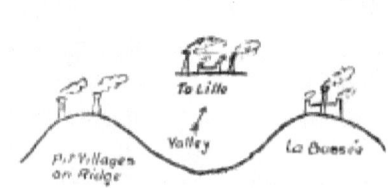

23. 2. DIAGRAM SHOWING HOW THE VALLEY LEADS TO LILLE

This height of La Bassée was indeed impossible to wrest from the enemy. Sir John French said of it that it had "defied all attempts at cap-ture either by the French or the British." So the British attack against the German positions (seeing that attack is the best method of defence) was made, as it were, along the crest of the "Aubers Ridge" by Neuve Chapelle and Aubers towards Herlies. Aubers fell on October 17 to the 9th Infantry Brigade, and under cover of night on the same day the Lincolns and the Royal Fusiliers took the village of Herlies at the point of the bayonet.

It was at this point that the counter-attacks of the enemy began along the heights and that the British force came to realise how terrible was the magnitude of the force arrayed against it. These little pit villages, dirty with the smoke of a hundred chimneys, became the scenes of bloody encounters destined to echo through the world. They became precious beyond the powers of imagination if one considers the toll of life expended in the taking and holding of them, and in the counter-attacks and defences that were made within their boundaries. Nor has the whole price exacted been paid even up till this hour. For here within a narrow radius are Neuve Chapelle and Festubert and Aubers, and, to the south, Loos. And across this grime-stained land is still stretched the long line of khaki that for upwards of a year has been seen in this terrible region. We shall yet hear these bitter but splendid names again ere the story of the great war is closed, and upon these rolling lands about La Bassée the toll of life will yet assuredly mount higher before the whole drama is played to its end.

Of that awful fighting among the brick-fields and the mean dwellings of the pit men and factory hands I have heard innumerable tales, which are too many and too like one another to set down here. Village street fighting became a commonplace, and the red hands of destruction were placed upon a thousand small homes that indeed were swept away. The line of battle oscillated for days within narrow limits, at one time being pushed eastwards by our army, and at another being thrust to the west. At the end, the salient which had been thrust forward by us as far as Herlies was driven back again and the line flattened out until the village of Neuve Chapelle was left in the hands of the Germans.

But the line held in spite of all these changes, and the door to Boulogne was not opened. In Boulogne during these October days men spoke fearfully of La Bassée and of the splendid deeds being wrought there among the slag heaps, and sometimes it seemed only too clear that the limits of resistance had been reached. But each tale of disaster was followed by another of great, of wonderful heroism. "The line holds," men said who had come down from the shambles. "Thanks to the finest soldiers who ever shouldered rifle, the line holds against most fearful odds."

But reinforcements were needed to assist these wonderful soldiers who laboured day and night among the grime and soot north of La Bassée. The fact that the enemy still held the La Bassée height made the operations tenfold more difficult and tenfold more costly. The price we paid for that unbroken line was terrible, almost beyond belief. It was essential that new strength should be added to the weary arm and new force given to the reiterated blow. New strength and new force happily were at hand. Sir John French wrote:

On the 24th October, the Lahore Division of the Indian Army Corps, under Major-General Watkis, having arrived, I sent them to the neighbourhood of Lacon to support the Second Corps.

The Indians soon showed their worth in the firing line, and great was the comfort which their coming brought to the sorely pressed British ranks. For indeed at this time the fighting had reached the very height of its desperation, and the Bavarians under their Crown Prince, were casting their all into the fiery furnace of assault. The whole of the "Aubers Ridge" was in the hands of the enemy, and from the low heights he could direct his artillery upon our positions. The foul land was strewn with dead and dying, and from behind the bodies of their dead both sides made bitter war upon one another. The "La Bassée gate" seemed to be strained to its very utmost, but it still held shut against the flowing tide of assault.

The gate of La Bassée, like the gate of the Yser and the gate of Arras, was "banged, barred, and bolted." There remained in doubt only the great gate by the city of Ypres, across the frontier of Belgium.

CHAPTER 16

The Battle of "Hanging On"

The last of the four battles for Calais and the coast was fought at Ypres, and is known now throughout the whole world as the "First Battle of Ypres," because in the spring of 1915 there was fought upon these same muddy fields another encounter of as great desperation and ferocity.

The First Battle of Ypres was "a battle of hanging on," it was a battle in which one man faced five men and was able to hold five men at bay; it was a battle of endurance rather than of wits, of dogged courage rather than strategy; it was and remains the greatest battle in the whole history of British arms.

It is not the purpose of these pages to attempt any sort of description of this battle, though the material for description was plentiful enough behind the lines at the time when the battle was in progress. The object is rather to focus attention upon the splendour of the achievement and the wonderful heroism of the common soldier, regular and territorial, to whom the victory of Ypres is wholly due.

But to understand the position it is necessary to realise the factors which led up to this terrific engagement. It is necessary to know, for example, in what manner the "Ypres salient" was formed, and how that salient became the crucial factor in the situation.

The original intention had been to push up north from Ypres towards Bruges, and so divide the German lines just as the Germans hoped to divide our lines. So a move was made to the north-east along the railways leading from Ypres to Roulers and Ypres to Bruges.

But these moves soon disclosed the fact that the enemy was here in overwhelming strength, and that defence, not attack, was certain to be the order of the day.

The Ypres salient was a bulge in the line opposite the town. If the

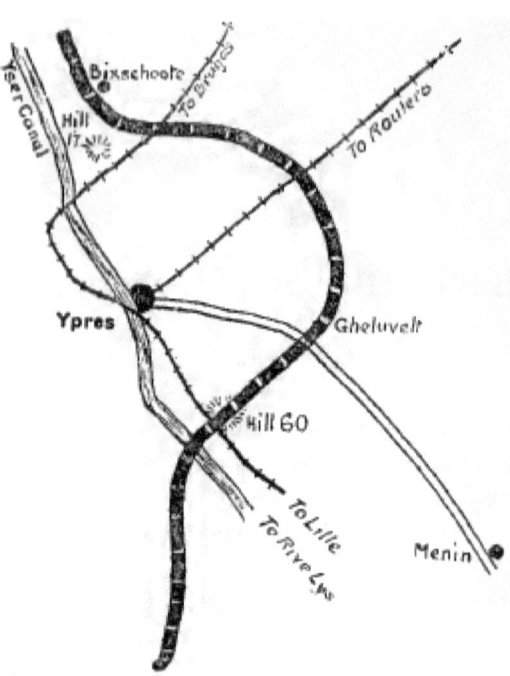

24. The famous "salient" at Ypres. The heavy line represents the
British force at the beginning of the battle.

letter D be taken and regarded as a rough-and-ready diagram, the battlefield of Ypres will be sufficiently well understood.

The danger point to the north was of course the angle between
the bulge and the straight line, and the same type of danger point
existed to the south. At the northern angle the country was flat with
the exception of one small hill near Bixschoote, which was vital to the
defence of this angle (Hill 17).

At the southern angle a substantial ridge raised itself near the villages of Hollebeke and Zillebeke—one of the mounds of which was
the famous Hill 60 of the spring campaign of 1915. (Hill 60 was not
spoken of particularly during the first Battle of Ypres, as the main
fighting was somewhat to the north of this particular eminence.) The
region of Hill 17 to the north, then, and the ridge culminating in Hill
60 to the south, were the bastions in the line of the defence of the
Ypres salient.

They enabled the country round about to be reconnoitred, they formed advantageous artillery positions, they were points of strength in a line weak beyond all the ordinary margins of safety.

The British 1st Army under Sir Douglas Haig had reached the line which was to become the Ypres salient on October 20. Next day, October 21, the battle proper opened with a fury that was surprising. Those who had come to attack found themselves forced to defend, and very soon realised that this defence was likely to become one of the most desperate and one of the most momentous in all history.

There are four distinct phases in the Battle of Ypres, the recognition of which affords an opportunity of gaining some little idea of its magnitude.

The first of these was the "phase of pure attack"; the second the phase of attacks directed chiefly at the angles of the salient and especially in the area of the lower or southern angle; the third the glorious counter-attack of the British Household Cavalry, which undoubtedly saved the southern aspect of the salient; and the fourth the supreme phase when the Prussian Guard, under the eyes of the German emperor, delivered their terrific attack along the Menin Road.

It is yet early in the battle and the first phase has but begun upon these lean fields under the towers of the Cloth Hall of Ypres. The enemy is pressing hard against the point or outmost aspect of the salient near the little hamlet of Gheluvelt, on the road between Ypres and Menin. The fighting here is bitter, without any relief such as war has been wont, of past years, to afford. War in these ditches is robbed of all her glory and rendered dull and hateful and drab.

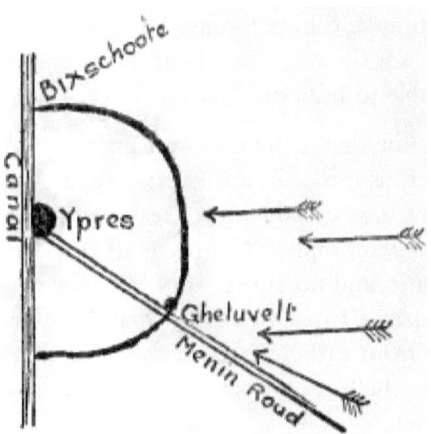

25. The D-shaped salient of Ypres. Note the Menin Road and Gheluvelt village.

181

Yet out of this drabness there is surely emerging a newer and a finer glory, while Britons are standing at bay amid the grime and mud of sodden fields, under a lashing hail of fire and with five times their own numbers advancing against them. There is surely a finer glory in the manner in which regiment after regiment is dully selling its life for the foul trenches which it will neither abandon nor yet yield.

And in the steady slaughter which goes on night and day during all this time there is at least the spectacle of utter devotion—of a devotion which has discounted life and which regards the shadow of death as a thing inevitable, near at hand, and, it may be, presaging long-awaited rest.

For the spirit of the fields of Ypres is not the spirit of these great "one-day battles" of old time. Nor is it the spirit of the Battle of the Marne, when autumn days were young and the ripe apples hung heavy in the orchards. It is a spirit in tune with the grey skies and the drab world and the driving rains and the mist—the spirit of "dull holding on"—of bitter knowledge that a man's life is completed in the sum of a man's duty.

A doctor, who fell wounded here, and whom I count among my friends, told me of this phase of the battle that it was indeed the unchaining of all the forces of death.

Men gasped with horror and surprise at first, because no man had guessed what it would be like to take part in a drama of pure slaughter carried on hour after hour and day after day upon so great a scale. But in the end men grew accustomed even to this thing and hoped only that it would be possible to hold on. That was the one thought, the one prayer, the one cry, 'Shall we be able to hold on?'

It is clear, is it not, that many times during these days holding on is becoming a ludicrous impossibility. Every day the weight of the German forces grows heavier and more heavy—the exhaustion of our British soldiers more complete. "Ypres at all costs," is the watchword of the German lines, and no effort—not even the most desperate and costly—will be spared to capture the town. The German regiments are on the move from earliest dawn to late evening. The hissing and screeching of their shells is a perpetual torment. The roar of their artillery is never hushed.

And within the gates of Ypres at the council table anxious men are discussing the chances of salvation as those discuss who know how pitiably low are the resources in their hands. They do not need to tell one another, these men in high command, that this line of the Ypres salient is unsupported and undermanned, that behind it there are no considerable bodies of troops to fill up the huge gaps made by the guns, nor that if it breaks the way to the coast will lie open and easy before the victor. These things are self-evident here, in the city of the weavers, behind the salient of death. They can ask themselves and each other only one question—for there is only one question of any import at this moment—"*How long can the British soldiers hold on, and against what odds?*"

A complete answer to that question must be awaited; but there is no need to wait for evidence bearing upon the case. Even now on this Sunday, October 25, the men in khaki are reeling under blows so terrific that it is indeed wonderful that men are found to withstand them. Along the southern aspect of the salient, as we have seen, the enemy has massed a great force, with which he is determined to seize the high ground about the canal and railway and so command the communications of the forces fighting within the salient (see Fig.). This force advances through the wooded lands about the slopes of the heights and in the area of the Menin Road. And so bitter is the fire with which it heralds its coming that for a moment the British regiments exposed to the chastisement are forced to yield ground. These weary men reel back, death and anguish upon their faces, and with shouts of triumph the German rushes forward to complete his advantage.

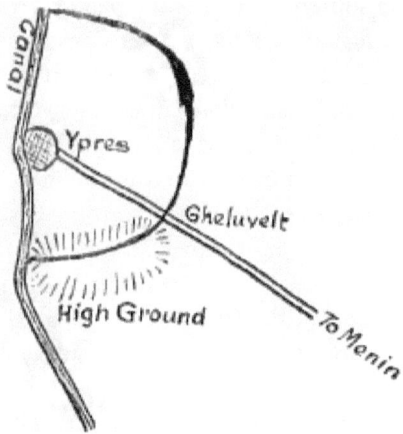

26. THE GERMANS DESIRED BITTERLY TO WIN THE HIGH GROUND TO THE
SOUTH OF YPRES AND THUS COMMAND THE LINES OF
COMMUNICATION WITHIN THE SALIENT.

But how shortlived the triumph! Reinforcements are hurried up—reinforcements literally torn from another part of the line—the Blues of splendid memory. There is a fierce encounter in the trenches, there, to the west of Zandvoorde, and the enemy are driven back once more, and once more a fleeting respite is won from the reluctant hands of fate.

A soldier told me that the impression he had of these advancing Germans was "the impression you have when you kick over an ant heap." They seemed to come out of the ground on every side just like the ants, and it was useless to kill them, because for every one that you killed there were five others ready to kill you.

So the battle rages day and night around this salient—a nightmare of attack and counter-attack, of shock and terror and alarm, of bravery shining like a light amid darkness, of wonderful tenacity that is vindicating for all time the qualities of the men of the Anglo-Saxon race, of sheer strength of will and of purpose that overrides every obstacle, defies every menace, conquers every difficulty. Who, indeed, will ever tell the whole glory of the fields of Ypres? Who will sing that saga of brave men as it should be sung—so that the strains of it echo to the very stars? Ypres is more than a place name of our history; Ypres is more than the most splendid and the most bloody of our battlefields. Ypres is the new altar of our nationhood, red with sacrifice; the covenant-shrine of a new Britain builded by the hands of those about to die, sanctified by their agony, embellished by their devotion. Ypres is holy ground, the supreme sacramental place of our nation.

The first act is played and for a brief hour there is respite across the fields of the dead. Then again they ring up the curtain of flame, and again the Angel of Death unsheathes his sword. The enemy have returned to the attack with new vigour and new spleen. They are upon every side, and upon every side the strength of the blow seems to be overwhelming. Here is the pinching movement of the loop of the Yser and the battering-ram movement of the Retreat from Mons combined. They swarm from the northward by Pilkem and Bixschoote, they swarm from the south along the fatal road that leads to Menin, they swarm from the east along the railway between Ypres and Roulers. The whole broad breast of the salient—the D that defends the city—is assailed and threatened. It is as though all the human ant heaps in the world had been emptied in the same hour.

If you will glance at the diagram you will see the nature of this mighty attack. But the ferocious character of it can be expressed in no diagram nor in any words. The cost was not counted, nor the expense in life, nor the price in human anguish. The hail of shells ceased not day or night, the shrieking of the bullets was wide-cast as the shrieking of the tempest wind. The coming of fresh *cohorts* to fill the place of the fallen was like the outpouring of an unmeasured tide. It was as though they made a bite at this salient of Ypres with poison fangs, meaning to swallow it whole in their fury; or grasped at it with iron hand to seize and crush it utterly. The stand of the 7th Division during these days belongs now to the pages of history—the story of how they held apart those terrible fingers which clutched at the very throat of our defence, at the throat of the army, at the throat of England.

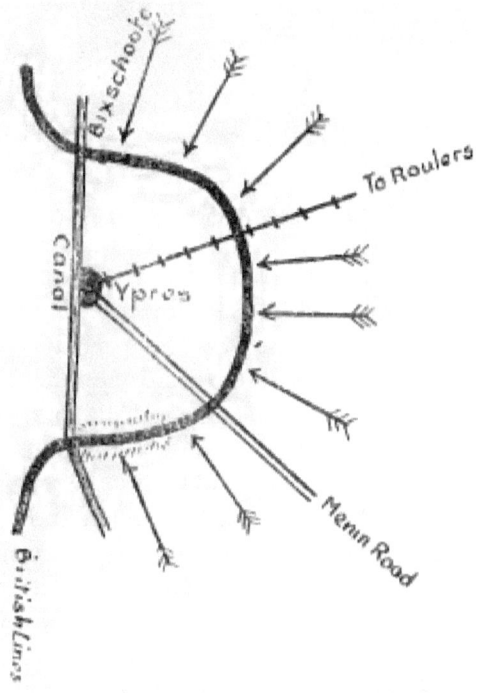

27. THE GREAT GENERAL ATTACK ON THE YPRES SALIENT.

At Gheluvelt during these days (October 29-31) trenches were lost and won again at the bayonet's point, and strong men held their breath to watch the miracle charges that stemmed the tide of assault and withered hope even in the hour of fruition. The slopes of the rising ground near the south angle where canal and railway issue from their deep cutting were stormed again and again, and once more the fate of this deadly south angle hung as by a hair. Should the enemy come to the canal and secure all these heights (we call them "heights") the days of the defence of Ypres would be ended.

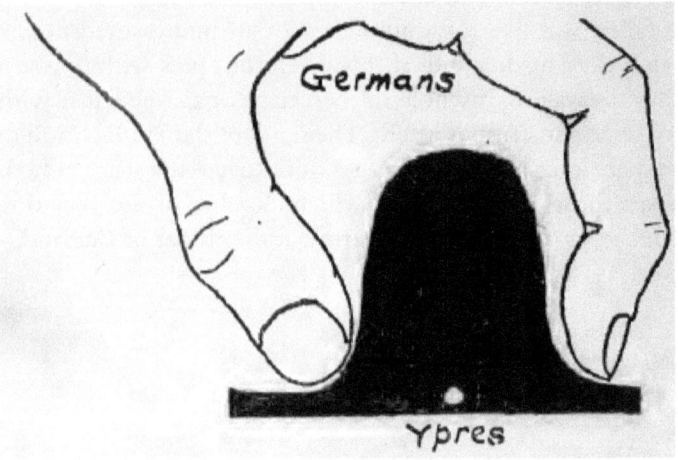

28. THE GERMAN GRASP ON THE YPRES SALIENT, OCTOBER 31.

But though the fierce artillery fire has driven our men from some of the slopes, the progress of the foe is impeded and stayed. Not even the stern encouragement of the *Kaiser's* supervision can drive these green-coats up the wooded slopes to victory on this Friday in October when "the British people is being saved amid blood and mud and horror." The night falls at last, lowering but gracious, and for an hour or two there is rest perhaps, leaning up against the soaking trench sides and with feet and legs deep immersed in the liquid ooze of the trench bottoms. But with the dawn breaks all the fury once again.

What a dawn this, of the day, Saturday, October 31, the fiercest day of all the days of the Ypres battle, and the most critical. On this morning man may well ask of man what shall be the issue and whether the hope of hanging on be vain or not. For now redoubled strength seems to have come to the foe, while the ebbing tide of our resources makes even the boldest afraid. We are bankrupt in everything except honour.

They came again, up by the road from Menin, which is, indeed, the Via Dolorosa of this pilgrimage of death. Up towards Gheluvelt they came, the village of a hundred battles. Whole regiments are cast into the fire before them, and in the fire are consumed like chaff. It seems as though there is nothing that shall stand against this onslaught.

186

BRITISH SOLDIERS ARREST A SPY IN FLANDERS.

Away to the rear the brains of this German machine are throbbing with high hope, while the nerves of those who direct the opposition to it grow tense with apprehension. . . ."How long will the British soldier be able to hang on against those fearful odds?". . .The trenches are undermanned, there is but this line, and after it nothing at all—nothing until the coast is reached and the goal of the Channel ports. And the line—how thin it is—how far outspread—how hopelessly, ludicrously insufficient! . . . Surely it is a stronger thing than flesh and blood which wrestles there among the dirt and the mire against these impossible odds! . . .The men who watch and plan and wait experience, as the hours go by, a strange exaltation of spirit like the uplifting of the morning upon dreadful night; for they know—they believe—that the supreme miracle is in process of being wrought—that the impossible is being translated into the real—that victory even now is being accomplished out of the ready materials of disaster.

There is the Menin Road to clear and the village of Gheluvelt to win again from the myriads who have swarmed into it. The bloody highway must run yet redder with good blood, the battered houses must once more be assailed and taken. . . . Eager men, who have already forgotten all their torment of weariness and anxiety, are ready to accomplish this purpose, awaiting only the order to set to work. The order is spoken. The Worcesters are up and at them like the Guardsmen of Wellington at Waterloo. The conquerors of Gheluvelt reel under the mighty blow, and the sickle of death is thrust in again deeply upon the road to Menin. Gheluvelt is won and the Menin Road lies clear.

But that is but the fringe—the bare fringe—of the mighty events which have made of this day a crisis-day in our history. On this day also General Moussy with his 9th French Corps was holding the danger area at Klein Zillebeke and reinforcing his shattered lines with cooks and scullions—with every man upon whom he could lay his hands—that salvation might be snatched from the teeth of doom.

On this day also the cavalry was fighting bitterly in the woods south of Hooge, helping to clear the enemy out of them. On this day our Indian warriors fought side by side with Allenby's Cavalry to the south by St. Eloi, and an Indian gunner—Sepoy Khudadad—won the Victoria Cross. On this day in the Headquarters at Hooge, before Ypres, and just behind the fighting line, Sir John French was with Sir Douglas Haig, through what he himself described as "the most critical moment in the whole of this great battle." He wrote, and his words are worth quoting *in extenso*:

> I was present with Sir Douglas Haig at Hooge between two and three o'clock on this day, when the 1st Division was retiring. I regard it as the most critical moment in the whole of this great battle. The rally of the 1st Division and the recapture of the village of Gheluvelt at such a time was fraught with momentous consequences. If any one unit can be singled out for especial praise it is the Worcesters.

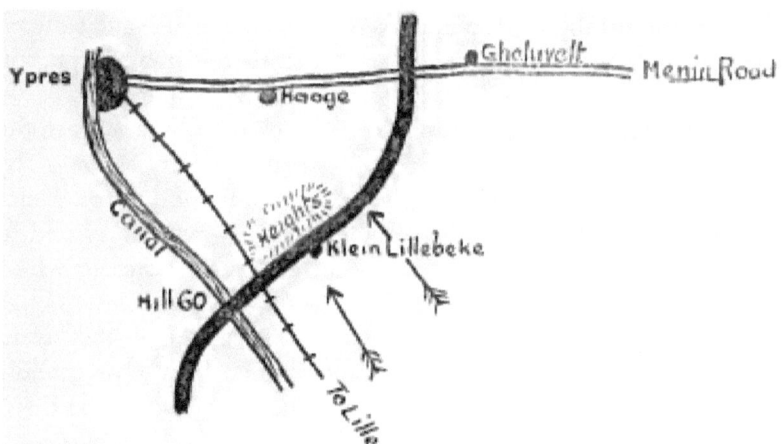

29. The danger area at Klein Zillebeke held by General Moussy with his "army of cooks," and later the scene of the charge of the Household Cavalry.

Thus closes the second phase in a flood of glory, and thus is justified the belief which every Briton cherishes concerning the armies of Britain—that they are true even to the gates of Death.

But the drama is not yet played out, the price of "hanging on "not yet fully exacted. There remain—if we pass over the intervening days with all their store of bravery and devotion—the day of the 6th of November and the day of November 11th. The day of the British Household Cavalry and the day of the Prussian Guard.

The story of the Household Cavalry at Ypres is the story of the saving of the danger angle of which so much has already been said— the angle by Klein Zillebeke, north of the canal from Ypres to Commines. Against this angle the enemy, on this Friday, launched one of those thunderbolt attacks which caused my friend, who faced so many of them, to speak of the overturning of an ant heap. The ants swarmed

189

up again towards the coveted ridge at Klein Zillebeke which commands the city of Ypres and the communications of the army within the salient.

The thunderbolt attack succeeded in a measure, and the French who held this point fell back. They sent the Household Cavalry to stiffen the French resistance—the 1st and 2nd Life Guards, with the Blues in reserve. It was like sending thunderbolt to meet thunderbolt. But then "suddenly the French returned at a run, reporting an advance of the Germans in strength. General Kavanagh doubled a couple of squadrons across the road to endeavour to stem the rush and suffered a certain number of casualties in so doing. Considerable confusion ensued, and there was a *mêlée* of English, French, and Germans."

Out of this *mêlée*, like lightning out of a cloud, was developed the charge which saved the position and perhaps the city as well. The Guards do not yield, it is their tradition to conquer or die. And so this splendid body—the very flower of England's chivalry—prepared to leap again against their foes and to avenge the transient success which had been wrested from them. It was surely a case of noblesse oblige in the finest interpretation of that idea. Wearied though they were, and mud-bespattered and sore tried, they hurled themselves grandly against the close ranks of the enemy, and the day was given to them, as it seemed, out of the very hands of God.

The battle grows old upon the plains of Ypres—the Battle of "Hanging On," which is the new wonder of the world. The flood of attack has well-nigh spent itself against this terrible barrier that is so frail yet so elastic, so thin yet so impenetrable. Wave after wave, waves of living men, has been broken asunder until hope is grown a-weary and confidence has become cold.

Yet there must be enacted a final scene, since the eyes of the War Lord are upon his soldiers. What the Guard of England has accomplished the Prussian Guard can accomplish also and in fuller measure. The day of victory, long deferred, shall yet be hasted and the fruits of victory garnered.

And so Wednesday the 11th November disclosed a strange sight about the dawning, when the light stole dimly along the bitter stretches of the road to Menin. Here surely was burlesque within the very arena of death—a spectacle of disordered minds, the apotheosis of overweening vanity. In the dim dawning of this November day the Prussian Guard upon the road from Menin are showing the goose-step to their astonished foes.

What a scene that for history to dwell upon. The long, long fields, peopled with the dead of three nations. The pollard willows weeping by a dozen misty streams.

The dank smell of the trenches, and the terrible sucking sound of the mud upon boots and legs. The voice of the wind, dismal, among the trees—far away and just visible in this pale glimmer of light the towers of the ancient city rising up like a benediction.

And along the roadway this prancing column with stiffened knees and pointed toes dancing heavily to death. Brave men indeed, and iron discipline—but can the mind of free man contemplate them without amazement that is near akin to ridicule? If a man must go to death let him go easily. Our soldiers gazed in astonishment, scarce understanding what they saw, and then on a sudden the hail of shells was unloosed upon the Prussian Guard, and the work of butchery was begun.

They came by the road from Menin—the road that is paved with the bodies of the brave and cemented together by their blood, and though their sublime courage carried them through the lines of our army in some places it was upon the road from Menin that they perished. The guns pounded them, the bullets mowed them down, the bayonets drank of their blood. Broken and withered they were cast back again—the remnant that remained—to the feet of their Imperial Master, whose behest they had so signally, yet so nobly, failed to accomplish. . . .

The Battle of "Hanging On" is ended, and the long winter comes bitterly to the plain before Ypres city, where in other days good husbandmen prepared the soil over against the coming of spring. Another husbandman has these fields now in his keeping, and his harvest is rich under the weeping skies.

CHAPTER 17

"Tommy"

The four battles for the sea are ended, and the wall is builded against the coming of the terror. Of the young bodies of men they have built this wall and the stones of it are bound, stone unto stone, by the noblest blood in all England. Behind the wall the affrighted cities rest in safety; behind the wall the husbandman returns to his task and the peasant to his cot; behind the wall the world is rebuilt and men breathe themselves and look again toward the future, and are joined again to the number of those who possess the world.

We sit in a little hall, under an arc lamp which bears upon its white shade the name of the German maker; in front of us is a fish pond wherein three goldfish move perpetually through a labyrinth made of concrete and sea shells, and adorned with fern plants of sickly growth. Upon the walls are the calendars of shipping companies, showing great steamships riding upon impossible waves, and the advertisement of a brand of cigarettes which takes the form of a picture of a French *marquise* of the great days strolling amid flower gardens.

In the hall there are a few British officers, a few Belgians, some war correspondents, and some French doctors attached to the health department of the town. We are sitting at a little table after dinner and there are coffee-cups on the table and a box of chessmen. But the chessmen have not been in use these many days, and who knows why they are always placed in readiness for the game which does not come?

We are a mixed company—men of many types and professions, but there is with us a man who has come down from the Ypres battle this very day, and it is to him that we are listening as perhaps we have never listened before in our lives—for this is the first of the news of Ypres which has come to us from the very trenches of Ypres themselves.

Our informant is a soldier whose name is very well known. But he speaks tonight not of the great men of this battle; he speaks to us of one man only, who is the one great man of the battle, though he is known under many distinguishing marks. He speaks to us of "Tommy," and he lingers upon that name fondly, as though it holds for him a world of gracious and sacred memories. He repeats it very often, and often when he repeats it he smiles. Sometimes—if such a thing were possible—you imagine that his voice is a little shaky when he speaks this mundane British name that is half a jest in itself. His eyes are bright anyhow, and his face is keen with the keenness of a father who regards a gallant son, he is saying:

Tommy is wonderful beyond all the wonders. He is the miracle that has happened; the impossible thing that has come to pass. He is alone in his greatness and there is nothing like him upon the face of the world.

Who won the Battle of Ypres?—Tommy! Who confounded the plans of the enemy?—Tommy! Who brought confusion to all the wise men who knew—because it was a case of knowing in all seriousness—that the defence of the city had become a wild impossibility?—Again Tommy! It was Tommy's own battle this and it belongs to him only. There are good generals and great leaders and heroic officers—we have all of these—but without Tommy what are they? When the hour of hours seemed to have struck, when even the most sanguine were giving orders which should safeguard the retreat of the guns, what was Tommy doing? Tommy was driving the enemy from the captured village of Gheluvelt and hurling him back down the road to Menin! And so the orders that were to safeguard the retreat must be countermanded, because forsooth Tommy had been first with his own orders—the orders that a man dies at his post but does not surrender it.

Do you realise what this battle has been? It has been pure murder prolonged over days. It has been the holding by one man of five men, and the five men have had a gun power behind them better in every respect than that behind the one man. You talk of a line . . . but what you mean is a series of single men with a gap of twenty yards each side of them, with no supports behind them, and with all the ingenuity and all the ferocity of the greatest army in the world before them.

When the enemy came against Tommy he came in droves, in solid masses, and attended by all the keenest and newest weapons of war. He came against lads who knew little of warfaring after this pattern, the lads standing twenty feet apart, tired to death, unsupported, unrelieved. It was like a hurricane sweeping down upon a castle of cards.

Until it had happened. . . .

They tried the goose-step and they tried their singing, and they tried a hell of fire that seemed to devour the very earth and threaten to 'crack the floor of heaven'—as Tommy said—but they did not impress Tommy in the very least. Tommy stood in the trenches and ridiculed them even in their most solemn moments. He called the Prussian Guard a 'bunch of waiters' to their faces, and he begged them to bring him a 'Scotch and soda, waiter, please!' even while he mowed them down or was mown down by them. To have seen Tommy in these hours is to have no fear for the future. A race which can breed Tommy can rule the world—must rule the world. At the very height of the battle, when things looked blackest. Tommy's cheerfulness overflowed and his heart sang. He invented a limerick which ran along the trenches like the news of a great victory, (This limerick has been printed in some newspapers. I can vouch for its origin as stated):

There was once a young fella' of Wypers
Who was hit in the neck by the snipers;
He made such a noise
That the Allemand boys
Thought they were in for a charge from the pipers.

In the most desperate moments Tommy's good nature and his joy did not desert him. In one trench where fourteen men had fought their last fight the fifteenth stood, bleeding, among the bodies of his comrades to light a cigarette. The relief party coming to his help saw him hold the French sulphur match with an expression of great disgust and heard him say in tones of reproach, 'These matches will be the death of me yet.'

The plain of Ypres has been mapped afresh by Tommy with his inexhaustible store of nicknames. He nicknames everything and everybody, and most of all the men he trusts and loves. When the sun shines he is a terror—full of grumble and complaint, and the men he loves have the worst of his temper and suffer bitterly. But let the rain pour and the floods come and Tommy's humour grows mellow as good wine. He is easy to handle then and splendid to control—he is the truest, the bravest and the most devoted of friends.

Can you doubt the truth of this eulogy in face of the stories of the Marne, of the Aisne, of the fields of Ypres? If still you doubt its truth, see again that scene by the château of Hooge, when Sir John French and Sir Douglas Haig walked together upon the Flanders road on Saturday, the 31st October, about two o'clock of the afternoon, waiting for news of the battle. See the horseman who dashed up to them at full gallop with report that the battle line was broken and the enemy about to advance upon the town. See the preparations that were made to save the guns, and see the populace of Ypres streaming out by the western gates of the city in full flight. . . . And then cast your eyes where the Worcester Regiment is throwing itself into the death struggle to save the day and selling life thriftily that the line may be held intact. This is Tommy at his very grandest, when he rises above the mere stature of a man and is joined to the heroes who go easily in the high places of the battle.

And come now to the hospital wards of the Hospital City and see how Tommy bears the pains that are come to him because of his devotion. The Hospital City is busy these days as never before it has been busy in all its history. Feverish activity prevails upon every hand. All day and all night the long trains are coming to it from the battle-field, not the trains of cattle trucks which came to Amiens from the plains of Mons, but luxurious hospitals rolling easily upon their springs. The trains are crowded to overflowing, so that doctors and nurses know not where to begin in the mighty task that has been so suddenly forced upon them. All manner of men are here, and all manner and degree of injuries. There are the dying and the sorely wounded whose last fight is fought, and the less severely wounded who hold their courage in both hands that they may bring cheer to those more severely afflicted than themselves. And those who die, die splendidly in the bare stations or in the hospitals that are only just opened and have not yet been furnished—die indeed as "Tommy" has taught the world how to die; "with a stiff lip, unless indeed the lip be bended in a smile."

What a scene of activity the old town of Boulogne presents, and what changes are in process. Here they are converting the gay Casino into a vast hospital, and already the floors of the great *salons* are thronged with stretchers; there a huge hotel is being rebuilt inside so that wounded officers may be housed comfortably in it. The streets are full of ambulance men with their red-cross brassards, and a long line of motor-ambulances moves perpetually between the station and the hotels.

This is not the Boulogne of the Mons days, when all was gaiety and hope and good courage; nor is it the Boulogne of the bitter days and nights of the Retreat, when fear of the impending doom gripped every heart as in a vice. It is not the city that lay naked to its enemies so that the streets stood empty and all the hotels were wide and silent. It is a new city, engendered, it would seem, of a new purpose.

That was splendid—the devotion of the battlefield. But this devotion, though unarrayed in grandeur of effect, is not less splendid. These terrible wards with their never-ending spectacle of woe, are indeed the battlefields of a more holy warfare. They too demand all that a man has to give of love and patience and resolution, and all that it is within the power of men and of women to give is being lavished here with prodigal hand. The very speed with which they equipped the place for work is a testimonial to their devotion. . . . For the Hospital City was born in a single night.

Through the long nights of pain gentle hands are ready to administer comfort and tender hearts are open to smooth the poor lads' way to the Darkness. Men bless their comforters here with their dying lips, in great, crowded wards that lie like a field of slaughter under dim lamps. . . . Here, where once on a time men and women laughed through the soft hours. In these wards heroic bravery is a mere commonplace of everyday life. You may see the most wonderful courage here almost at any hour—the courage of pain borne without excitement to dull the edge of pain—borne with a jest that rings grandly from white lips.

In the harbour the hospital ships are waiting that shall carry these broken men back again to England. What a contrast is the sailing of these ships from the coming of the great troopships only a few months ago while yet the scythe of death was idle over these good lands. About this sailing is no glamour of romance, no mystery of expectation. These ships go silently upon the flood bearing their precious freight tenderly. The men are gathered about the decks in little groups, scarcely speaking while the vessel moves so slowly away from the quays. Their eyes are turned towards home, towards England, the

196

goal of all their aspirations. There is a strange light in their eyes and a strange eagerness upon their faces as they pass away to the open sea from this land of France, and their thoughts are of the gallant comrades who fought side by side with them through the long days amid the grime and the reek of blood and who never again will sail the seas to England.

The night falls as you wend your way back through the narrow streets. But the procession of woe is not ended. It seems indeed to be a procession that has no end. In front of you and beside you and following you are the motor ambulances bearing each its living freight of devoted warriors. The cars creep so slowly over the rough paving-stones that are a perpetual trial to wounded men; as they go their tyres make a curious ripping sound that will haunt you, you think, during all the days of your life. And again there are other cars passing swiftly back from the hospitals to the station.

And if you would know all that this war means you must go and sit by the bedsides of these heroes and listen for a little while to their talk. You must be prepared to listen to stories that have little relation to war and to the affairs of war—most soldiers I find are reluctant to speak of the things which they have seen—to stories that concern home ties and the doings, real and conjectured, of children—queer sentimental stories woven around old ideas, like the Christmas idea and the idea of home.

They will fill you with wonder at first, these unwarlike tales, because they belong to the truly unexpected. War against this background of human feeling becomes grotesque and unreal. It seems to recede into the distance so that the sun may be set free upon the green fields and a man may speak wholesomely of the good things which God has given to men to speak of and think about and rejoice in.

This poor fellow who is so clearly wounded to death will tell you of his home away in an English village where the doings of the vicar and the squire are the big events of every day. Upon that subject he is ready to pour out his very soul. He will tell you of his wife and his children—and with oh, what wistfulness of his children—and he will even continue to make merry as his strength will let him over the little troubles of his home life that still bulk large and important in his eyes. He will tell you how his children play and how they work and how, of an evening, it is his joy to play with them, the merriest of the group, so that his wife reproaches him with being more of a child than any of them.

BRITISH SNIPERS SNIPING FROM A WELL IN FLANDERS.

And this man has come down from the salient of Ypres, where that salient is cut by the bloody road to Menin. This man has stood day after day in the bitter trenches and faced all the hell of modern artillery and massed infantry. He has played his glorious part in the greatest battle of British history!

It is incredible almost—one of those truths that rise up and smite a man between the eyes because of his unbelief in the essential goodness of human nature....

He has no hard thoughts for the enemy, either, this wounded man. "They fought well," he will tell you readily—"they are brave men" —and sometimes he may add in those weary tones which doctors and nurses know so well yet never quite become accustomed to, "they have their children too, away at home, poor devils."

★★★★★★

The hospital ships come and go across the Channel, the ambulance cars move in perpetual procession along the narrow streets. Week follows week and yet the whole sum of this human agony is not reckoned, its measure is not accounted. The Angel of Death still broods over the fields of the dead.

And upon this far-flung scene of hate and fierce anger dawns once more as of old time the Christmas morn. ... In England, where Christmas has meant and means so many different things, the ancient sweetness of the season may well appear to have turned to bitterness at a moment when the world is fuller of wounded and broken men than ever it has been before in its history. But out here where the war is a commonplace of life, things are different. The personal value of the great feast still holds as it held of old time. That cannot indeed be debased so long as courage and good humour remain to mankind. The Christmas spirit is greater than a thousand sorrows....

In the trenches they knew the truth of this and called to one another and made merry together, Briton and German, in spite of all the indignation of those set in authority over them. They knew that it is not well, nor meet, to raise the hand against one's fellows upon this holy day. For an hour or two the bonds of nation and of blood were merged in the common bond of humanity, and brave men accepted one another as the children of the same Spirit....

They are keeping Christmas in the hospitals and there is much joy there over the simple festivities. And there is joy along all the lines where the breath of the good Spirit has been breathed. For the com-

199

mon soldier has the heart of a little child and he is merry, in season, as children are. His good mirth is like a cleansing of a world befouled.

But to some the day breaks heavily enough and without light; as you may see if you will linger in the long narrow street of the town that leads to the hill where are the graves of the fallen. It is the hill of fate by which they went away in the autumn days to the dreadful ordeal of battle. Now it is strangely quiet and lonely and deserted—for the camps that were so joyous are forsaken.

Under the flag of England they are bringing the dead to their rest upon the hill over against the sea.

The procession passes, going heavily upon the *pavé*. Behind each of the rude hearses there are a few men with weary faces, and perhaps a woman whose grief is written upon her face so that all may see it. . . . The townspeople cross themselves and turn their eyes away. "Will the good God have mercy upon a brave man."

But you do not turn your eyes away. Because there is something in this spectacle which thrills you to the very marrow, and fills all your heart with awe and wonder. That Union Jack bound upon the body of the young dead who have died for England, is it not a symbol at once strange and moving and terrible?

CHAPTER 18

The Way to Calais

In one of his bitterest and most terrible war-cartoons Raemaekers, the Dutch artist, has depicted a weary flood filled with the bodies of dead men which float easily under some stunted pollard-willows. The cartoon is entitled "We are on the way to Calais."

It is of this way to Calais, as I was privileged to see it, that I wish to write in this chapter, because though the face of the war may change out of all recognition, yet the great fact of the way to Calais will never change . . . and, so long as men live upon the world, the memory of it will never be suffered to grow cold.

It is a moonlight night in February, 1915, and the land of north France lies chill and silent in its long flat expanses. You come out of Calais by the north gate and take the road between the poplar trees toward Dunkirk. The road is crowded tonight with all manner of vehicles that pass in great processions, some going northward and others returning towards the town. The night is full of the grinding of heavy wheels and the throbbing of motor engines. Suddenly far off, down the straight road that lies white under the moon, you see the flicker of a lanthorn which swings slowly from left to right.

It is the lanthorn of one of the sentries who guard the way to Calais. He comes to you slowly along the highway, carrying his rifle with bayonet fixed. You note that he is of the French territorial army, a tall fellow with a drooping moustache and dressed in the long blue overcoat with the turned-up flaps with which the whole world is now so familiar. He takes your papers and scrutinises them closely by the light of his lantern, examining all the stamps and signatures. At last he is satisfied. He stands back and salutes. You go on again into the night.

And so by Gravelines, where King Louis thought to put a curb on the vaulting ambition of England in the brave old days, to Dunkirk, silent within her great grey walls that have withstood the storms and stresses of so many hundreds of years of this same bitter warfaring in the low countries. They are very busy in Dunkirk these days and a little excited too, for a couple of nights ago a Zeppelin came to the old town and dropped bombs, and many times the enemy's aeroplanes have buzzed over the central square like wasps, while they rang the tocsin that warned the good citizens of their danger and sent them to seek shelter in cellars and basements. The Hôtel des Arcades in the central square, over which Jean Bart, of adventurous memory, presides upon his pedestal, is full tonight of English and French and Belgian officers. They sit together over their coffee after dinner discussing the latest news from the front and the prospects during the coming summer toward which all hopes are beginning to turn, one says:

We have held them now for more than six months. Their great offensive is spent, their numbers are depleted. Soon it will be our turn. We shall break that line, believe me, and roll the two ends of it backward so that Belgium will be uncovered and France cleansed. And after that the Rhine.

Brave words—and words that in these days find many an echo. France and England and Belgium too have the same hope, the same expectation. At this moment men have not envisaged the fearful hours of Neuve Chapelle and the bloody trenches of Festubert, they have not guessed at the second Battle of Ypres, with its hideous accompaniments of gas and suffocation and slaughter. The terrors of Gallipoli and Serbia are far indeed from their thoughts, and the dream of the Russian "Road Roller" is still present to every mind.

So they are merry in the Hôtel des Arcades at Dunkirk, these officers and airmen, who meet of a night within its hospitable walls after the day's adventures, or who return here from the bitter trenches along the Yser, that are so near yet seem, under the painted ceilings and the electric lights, to be so very far away. You may hear in these rooms strange tales of flights across the Belgian frontier by Nieuport towards Ostend, of how they dropped bombs on the "Archibalds" concealed along the coast, and on the military works of the enemy at Zeebrugge, of how, one day, a German submarine was hit at the latter place, in her dry dock, of how a minelayer perished suddenly just as she left the shelter of the harbour from a bomb that struck her fairly amidships, of how the famous "mole" at Zeebrugge was broken so that the storms might complete the good work of destruction.

And you may hear also of thrilling escapes, up there among the clouds, with the enemy's shrapnel bursting like balls of gossamer all round about. There is a tale of a machine that flew very low over Zeebrugge so that the work it was engaged upon might be the better carried out. They shot very near to that machine, for they cut the controlling wires that hold the steering gear. . . . But the wires were duplicated. . . . There is another tale of a boy in his machine hurling down bombs upon a great arsenal, and when his bombs were exhausted, for sheer joy of his emprise, emptying his pockets of small coins and odds and ends.

These cavalry-men of the air are cheerful company, because they seem to have no care and no apprehension. They are good fellows in the true sense, brave and modest. The little stories they recount are never of themselves, but of mysterious "friends" who remain nameless and whose accomplishments are spoken of offhandishly, as though they were the most commonplace events in the whole world.

But you will not tarry long in this good circle, because a chance has been given you of seeing the whole of the way to Calais right up to the banks of the bloody Yser itself. So you return to the car that awaits you in the square and are soon creeping out again through the iron gates of the city on the long white road that runs by the canal to the northward.

'Tis the very blood-channel of the army, this road, and it is thronged, day and night, with vehicles of every description. There are the huge forage cars bearing food to the army of the Yser, to the men in the long trenches beside the floods, and there are the hospital cars moving delicately on the rough surface, fearful of causing their freight undue pain. There are, moreover, the staff cars, in which officers pass swiftly backwards and forwards upon what business no one is permitted to know.

The convoys are very long, so that you must wait patiently while they creep past you, great waggon after great waggon grinding heavily through the mud. Sometimes it seems as though there was indeed no end to them at all, and the whole visible stretch of the road is full of them. Then they look like a huge black snake winding slowly across the white fields under the moon.

By the side of this way too are derelicts, the wreckage of this high channel of supply. These wrecks are strange and even moving sights as they stand, leaning giddily towards the ditches, where days, or it may be months, ago they were abandoned. A broken wheel, a "seized" engine, a hundred and one forms of breakdown have determined the end of the car's "life "in this land where the fittest only survive and where for the weak and incapable there is little room or consideration. If the car will not go it is left and another car is secured. Time is too precious to waste it upon a faulty engine. . . . So the derelicts lie under the moon, strange objects of desolation, their members falling asunder, their structure the prey to wind and rain and storm.

You come thus to a little village which a hundred years ago was witness of as strange scenes as those presently being enacted. These drab houses and this beautiful old church looked down once upon a time on the black travelling carriage with its four swift horses which carried Napoleon from battlefield to battlefield. In this same muddy street the marshals of the First Empire rode together while yet that Empire was stretched across the face of Europe. Today a king has come to it whose stainless honour has made of him the type and symbol of the perfect knight in the eyes of all men—a king by the side of whom the most ambitious and powerful of the emperors is mean and trivial.

There is an ancient moated house near the village, and here you will have a chance of seeing something of the way in which a great army is controlled. You will see business-like men, dressed as for work, sitting at little tables engrossed in the task each has to accomplish. There are many telephones in the room and many papers—but otherwise it is like a thousand rooms, plain, and humble, and busy.

Yet these telephones make it possible to communicate with the remote outposts away upon the islands in the flooded Yser district, and with the brave men who are the eyes and ears of the army and whose duty it is to keep vigil day and night lest the enemy succeed in springing a surprise. By these telephones have come, in the days that are passed, strange messages of life and death. "The enemy are advancing in force. We can hold him but a moment or two. . . . Our resistance is at an end. . . . " . . . The far-away voice will be heard no more on this earth. . . .

There are other cars waiting in the roadway to continue the strange journey. These carry no lights, for you are now entering the fire zone and must move with extreme caution. Along the miry by-roads, that were but farm tracks before the war made them important, the heavy car swings at a slow pace, seeming to feel its way. A single false move and the car will leave the centre of the road and slip into the terrible quagmire which threatens upon either side—and from that quagmire it may be utterly impossible to extricate it. Happily the moon, tonight, has largely solved the problem, and so progress is relatively very good except during the showers.

You pass by numerous hamlets, some of which seem to be still awake, for there are men to be seen near the cottage doors—men who stand together darkly in groups, seeming to talk, yet, so far as can be heard, uttering no sound. . . . At length the car stops. This is a village as big as the village where were the telephones and the busy officers.

You alight and are conducted to a schoolhouse near at hand. The building looks deserted, but there is a sentry with a fixed bayonet at the door, a big bearded Flanders man with the kind eyes and warm smile of this hospitable country. He opens the door, and suddenly you are confronted by a scene so strange that you scarcely know how to interpret it.

The hall is dimly lighted by a lamp which burns smokily from an iron hook in the roof. At one end a great fire burns, throwing a glow across the darkness and casting long shadows. Eddies of smoke curl and twist across the firelight and, rising to the roof, seem to darken the ceiling like a heavy fog.

On the floor, lying side by side, are a great number of soldiers in the blue uniform of Belgium. And between the rows of the soldiers are their rifles, stacked together in groups of three, with the keen bayonets thrusting up to catch the flicker of the lamp and the glow of the fire.

The soldiers are not all asleep, for some of them are gathered into little groups. If you approach these groups you will discover that they are playing cards. Here and there, too, you will see a man reading, and the smoke is curling up from a very great number of cigarettes and pipes.

These men came down from the trenches today. They will rest here a day or two before returning. Some of these men fought upon the terrible loop of the Yser River, and all of them have stood guard over the chill waters that set the limits upon the advance of the foe. . . . You note, yet, how cheerful they are and how little their cruel ordeal seems to have affected them. Many of them are fair-haired youths with pink and white faces like English lads, and these are the merriest, for the most part, and give an Englishman the most cordial welcome. You realise now—if you have not already realised it—how fine and honest are these Belgian soldier men, and how simple of heart. They are always good-natured, even in the most trying circumstances. They lie here on their beds of straw amid the gloom and the smoke as though they lay upon rich couches. Their jests are as merry as of old, their smiles as genial, their words as full of welcome.

From the little village it is but a stone's throw to the fire zone, where the great shells have been doing their work these many, many months. You come to the fire zone quite suddenly, scarcely realising the transition. Perhaps a farm-house which had seemed so tranquil under the moon is revealed to you as a mere shell, already torn to pieces and gutted. Or you see with a thrill of dismay that walls which seemed solid support no roof, that they are torn in many places by great holes that gape out towards the night, that here and there they have fallen in upon the interior, bringing down floors and ceilings in the general wreckage. You see the abomination of desolation revealed suddenly in all its most poignant manifestations; life has been extinguished in this land, and death has come to rule in her habitations. The face of death grins at you from empty windows and shattered doorways, as though peering out to see who is bold enough to intrude upon his chosen place.

This is the village of ———, and that building which looks so graceful with the moonbeams slanting upon its turrets is the remains of the church. Go a little nearer and you will see that the church is sharer in the universal desolation, that it too has been smitten and shattered and destroyed. The car has been stopped and drawn to the side of the road—it is in order that a body of men coming from the trenches may be free to pass without danger of slipping into the terrible gutter which awaits the unwary by the side of every road in this land. The soldiers march stolidly, looking neither to right nor left. They are very tired after their long stand in the front line, face to face with the enemy. It is a good thing to be going back again to a little rest and a little comfort.

Now you are come to another of the white farmhouses. This one, it seems, has been spared so far by the enemy shells, why it is impossible to discover. At any rate the roof of the building is still intact and the walls are unbroken. A door is opened very gingerly, so that no gleam of light may be shed abroad, and suddenly you find yourself within the narrow entrance-way, where in happy years the farmer's wife did the family washing at a great tub set for the purpose upon iron trestles. The door is shut quietly behind you, and you are invited to pass on to the living chamber at the back. Another door opens. Suddenly you are in the presence of the colonel of artillery, who makes his headquarters in this little farm.

Colonel —— is a soldier with a great reputation in the army of Belgium, and you know that this is an honour which has been accorded to you. He rises to greet you with outstretched hand. "*M'sieur* is welcome." He bids you be seated among the officers of his staff gathered around the table. He places before you the simple fare of soldiers—the bully beef, the bread, the biscuits of the trenches. "It is all that we have, *M'sieur*, but we eat with a good appetite and a good conscience."

You may be excused if your appetite is not less good after the long drive through the keen night. You glance around the table at the faces of the men who are holding this northern door of the world against the world's enemy through the long winter days and nights. Kindly faces, quiet faces, strong faces . . . the faces of men who have held life at a cheap price but honour at a high. And you think that such men are strangely alike all the world over, whether they wear the dark blue of Belgium, or the *culottes rouges* of France, or the khaki of the king.

This is the artillery headquarters of the ——. Out there are the trenches—*M'sieur* will see. Ah—that was a gun, of course. . . . No, the enemy are not active tonight; had *M'sieur* come two nights ago, for example. But one never knows, of course. This place has a charmed life perhaps—but how long? Still, '*à la guerre comme la guerre.*'

The simple meal which it was an honour to share is ended. You go out again into the night, this time on foot. The night is full of the moon now, and the level stretches of the country lie before you sweetened under the mysterious light. Far off to the northward you can see lights winking along the horizon—where the enemy has his lines across the flood on the other bank of the Yser. . . . For yonder flows the Yser River, and there is the loop, the *boucle*, of terrible memory.

It is the very field of war, this strange, quiet land under the white moon. This land of ruined houses and shattered hopes, this weeping land over which have come again the ancient floods so long held at bay by patient and tireless effort of human hands—this land of the dyke and the pollard-willow—this land of death and of great glory.

You must go now very warily, neither speaking nor venturing to light a cigarette, for you are coming within range of the deadly sniper, and the moon is bright. So you follow in silence the going of your guide across the flat meadow land, by the narrow path that leads directly to the trenches. He has warned you already that should a "flare" go up you must throw yourself down upon the ground, or at least bend very low. But though far away the guns are booming fitfully, and though in the distance night is pierced by the fierce light, the need for this added caution does not arise. You come to the railway—the famous railway betwixt Dixmude and Nieuport—in great safety.

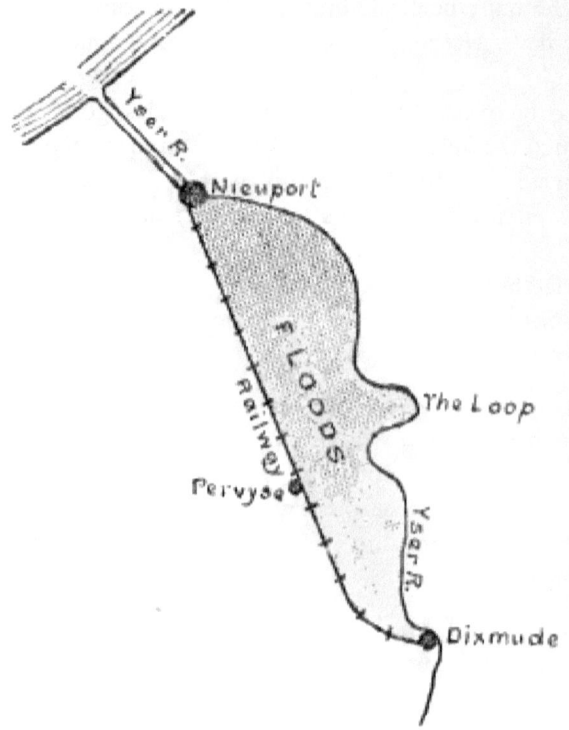

30. THE FLOODED AREA OF THE YSER AS SEEN IN
FEBRUARY, 1915.

This line of the railway marks, as we have already seen, the high-water line of the German advance during the period of the Battle of the Yser. The enemy came to this railway and even crossed it in places (Ramscappelle), but he made no real progress beyond it. The Belgians held the railway at first with their bodies and later with the waters which in their extremity they were forced to call to their help.

The railway at this place runs upon an embankment, and in the railway embankment they have built their third line of trenches. You go down into the cavern, the roof of which is made of the sleepers and the iron rails, and you creep along until suddenly you are in a long

208

narrow chamber, very low and very small, in which vigilant men are keeping guard day and night. There is some straw on the floor, and the place is much dryer than you had expected. They will show you things here of which even yet it is impossible to write, and you will find here the same spirit of cheerfulness which you met in the schoolroom and the farmhouse away to the rear. Nor rain nor storm nor cold has damped the enthusiasm of those gallant men who hold now the last acres of their beloved Belgium against the despoiler.

Across the railway is the house of the points-man—now turned to other uses, and beyond that the road leads to another line of trenches, and yet a little farther, to the front line of all. The moon is very bright now and it is a fairy-land spectacle that discloses itself.

You are standing by the edge of what appears to be a mighty lake, the silver waters of which stretch far away into the distance. A light breeze plays upon the surface, darkening it here and there and causing little waves to rise like sword gleams under the moonlight. A little way out from the shore there is an island which seems of comparatively large size, and you can see that upon the island there are a few houses, and that amongst the houses a church tower rises up, very white and graceful, as it appears, amidst surrounding trees. But you can see also even at this distance that the church tower is shattered and broken and that only a small fragment of it remains. The island is like a blot of ink upon the fair silver of the flood.

But as you stand entranced by this vision there comes to your nostrils a terrible taint of death that robs the scene of all its illusion of peace and beauty. It is the smell of corruption distilled horribly from these greedy waters; the dread memorial of the struggle in the Oc-tober days, when 18,000 men went down to death just here, even as Raemaekers the cartoonist has told so bitterly—"We are on the way to Calais" —you grow faint almost as the truth comes to you, and you touch your guide upon the arm to know if he too has become aware of it. He smiles a little and shakes his head. . . . And then you see him shrug his shoulders. . . . They were Germans who perished in these waters upon the way to Calais.

Behind the front-line trenches they have kindled fires in huge iron braziers, and these fires glow strangely now against the white world around them. There is a farmhouse to the left with open doors and empty windows. The walls are broken down and the roof has vast rents in it. A door still left upon its hinges swings with a creaking noise that is altogether desolate. You approach the trenches, which are not trenches at all, but merely ramparts built up of sandbags and rendered waterproof by a rough roofing. You lift the flap that covers in this strange tent, and behold men are sleeping peacefully here, as though danger were far away from them. The barrels of many machine-guns gleam darkly along the "trench way," and you can see the strap with the ready bullets hanging idly from each of the breeches. You gaze for a moment in silent wonder.

This is the front line of the defence, is it? And this line is stretched in almost unbroken continuity from the North Sea to the Alps! These tall sentries who march to and fro in front of the rampart of sandbags with their fixed bayonets are the guardians in fact of our whole civilisation. And then, as you are about to turn away with this great thought in your mind, your eye detects a cat lying curled up beside one of the machine-guns upon the straw of the trench bottom ... the cat, perhaps, which in better days lived in the ruined farmhouse close at hand. And the incongruity of it all tempts you suddenly to mirth, which it is hard to hold in restraint.

But the journey is not finished, for you have permission to go beyond the front-line trenches to the *avant poste* on the island in the Yser. There is much barbed wire in front of the trench and you must thread your way carefully amongst its web-like meshes. Then you will win free to a narrow cobbled roadway, which runs by the side of the water along a promontory of land which juts out at this place into the flood. If only there was not this terrible stench it would be a scene of utter loveliness, but you cannot escape the stench, and you cannot forget the meaning of it—and even if you would forget there are dark objects apparently floating in the water which serve to keep memory active!

From the end of the promontory a dark line stretches across to the island. This line is made up of bundles of small twigs bound firmly together and laid side by side in the shallow water—for the water is shallow at this place where the road used to run towards the village of ——.

Caution must be redoubled in crossing this causeway, for now the sniper has you within his range and his eye is quick and his aim certain. So you go warily and alone, picking your way. And at last the quarter-mile across the flood is accomplished and you stand under the church tower amongst the brave men who are keeping this far outpost, which is not more than fifty yards from the outposts of the enemy. You walk with them through the little village—a hamlet, no more, and they show you the narrow belt of water on the far side of the island which separates it from the next island, whereon is the enemy lying in wait. Only a week ago the enemy held this island also, but he was driven out of it at the point of the bayonet. Perhaps the attack will be pressed still farther at some future time. Meanwhile daring men are mapping out the floods—finding, that is, the safe and the unsafe places—the places where the water is deep and the places where it is shallow. Over there, by that tree, they have their snipers usually, so it is well to have a care.

The church is utterly destroyed, so that you can scarcely find even the foundations of it. Only a little part of the chancel remains, and a little part of the tower, that is sharp like a needle because of the manner in which it has been broken. By the side of the church is the grave of a soldier who fell here and was buried where he fell. But the cross they have placed over him has been smitten too and is broken in one of its arms.

And so back across the causeway to the trenches, and from the trenches to the road. It has been a wonderful experience and Fortune has been kind indeed. Your guide is frankly astonished. "I do not understand it," he tells you. "They are too quiet tonight. I do not altogether like it. . . ." The car is waiting, and once more begins the journey along the narrow road that will bring you within a few minutes to the village of Pervyse, the very storm-centre of the Yser battle.

It is well to alight at Pervyse, even though the chances of being shelled are considerable—since the enemy shells this area with a regularity that is monotonous. Pervyse is the symbol and sign of Belgium at this hour; its battered streets and broken-down buildings, its gutted houses, its terrible staring windows, its empty rooms, its ruined church, its opened graves are all of a piece with the desolation which has come to the heroic land. Pervyse the stricken is a microcosm of Belgium—and the horror of Pervyse will stand as a judgment of this enemy inscribed in stone for all the world to see.

You will walk through the village street and mark the effect of the shells. That house there belonged to the doctor and his brass plate is still upon the door. Note how a shell has opened the front of his drawing-room and set this sofa bulging out towards the roadway. This house was a private residence. All the floors have been battered down. The church there is utterly destroyed, and some of the coffins have been dug up out of the graves by this never-ending bombardment.

The railway station is just beyond the church, and beyond the station again are the trenches. It was here in these fields before the station that some of the fiercest fighting of all the battle took place. Here it was that the floods caught the triumphant host which had won its way across the loop in the Yser River and had come to the railway. Men died here as flies die in a frost, men were drowned here as rats are drowned.

You tarry in the trenches, spellbound by the strangeness of it all, and while you tarry another shell goes hurling into the village: the shell fails to burst, but you hear the crash of falling masonry. The booming of the guns comes fitfully along the vale. ... A chill wind carries the sighing of departed spirits. . . .

CHAPTER 19

Devil's Warfare

To understand the series of battles which have marked the course of the campaign of 1915 it is necessary to bear in mind the configuration of the country around the principal storm centre, La Bassée. In a previous chapter I have shown that La Bassée may be regarded as the southern boundary of a valley of which the northern boundary is formed by a string of dirty little villages leading towards Lille. The valley carries a canal and the railway, but the way of the valley is barred, on the one side by La Bassée and on the other by the villages along the ridge which is usually spoken of as the ridge of Aubers—from the name of one of the villages. To the west of the Aubers Ridge stands the village of Neuve Chapelle, wrested from our men towards the close of the great battle of La Bassée, when the Germans were striving to break through here to the coast in the October days of 1914. Neuve Chapelle therefore formed an obvious target for a first shot at Lille.

All the world knows the story of that shot, the splendour of it, the grim courage, the success and the failure. Neuve Chapelle was taken—and that was all. Lille, the object of this attack and of all those which succeeded it, remains still in the hands of the enemy.

It is no part of my purpose to offer criticism concerning the strategy of this battle—supposing that I were in a position to do so. But it is not possible to pass it by without pausing for a moment to contemplate the sheer heroism of it.

Never perhaps have British soldiers so distinguished themselves, never has the "red badge of courage" been worn with such indisputable right. On this cruel field men acted as men have prayed God in every age and under every sort of condition that they might act—without fear and without reproach.

213

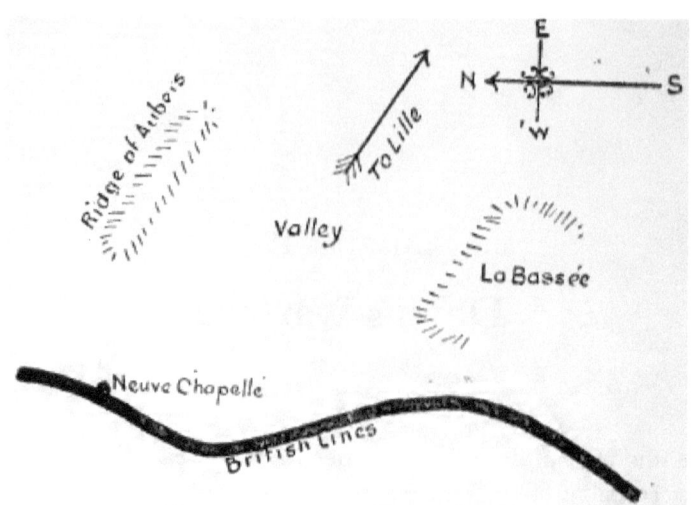

31. THE WAY TO LILLE. NEUVE CHAPELLE WAS THE FIRST STEP.
FOLLOWING UPON IT CAME THE BATTLE OF THE AUBERS RIDGE.

Alas! those boys who charged over the fields towards the little village and who will charge across the fields of France no more, those boys who gave all without a whimper, without a backward glance—though life was a rare vintage only just tasted by eager lips. We shall not look upon their like again. And those of them who returned across the ranks of the dead under a hot fire,—they came slowly, almost carelessly, so that the enemy might see how a Briton takes care of his life. Some of them stopped to light cigarettes before they strolled back across the ranks of the dead—as a German who saw them has testified.

But heroism does not of itself win battles, and so the great hopes which were aroused by Neuve Chapelle were doomed to disappointment. The stubborn height of La Bassée remained to the foe, and so also did the dreary ridge of Aubers and the little villages and the brickfields, and the great city of Lille beyond them all.

The battle here has no end indeed, though you may pick out special hours of intense fighting and call them battles. The fighting at Festubert in May was of a piece with this same advance upon Lille, and so was the fighting at Loos in the autumn days of last September. Also the great effort of the French at Arras, by Carency and Souchez, which had as its object the taking of Lens, was really but another phase of the struggle for the "Manchester of France" with all its wealth of material and industrial resource.

Yet let it not be supposed that these terrific conflicts, the history of which is as yet almost unwritten—at least as regards details—were without value because they have not yet been crowned with success. This battle is not of a day, nor yet of a week. It is a battle of years. The Battle of the Aisne, we say, ended in three weeks. But the truth is that the Battle of the Aisne is not yet ended. So the Battle of La Bassée is not yet ended, and the Battle of Loos, and the Battle of Souchez, and the Battle of Arras—all of which are in reality the "Battling for Lille." Years hence men will see this work whole who have not been forced to wait through weary months for some completion, and then they will know how much or how little value each of these separate phases of the struggle really possessed, and be able to see in what way this perpetual warfare contributed to the great final result.

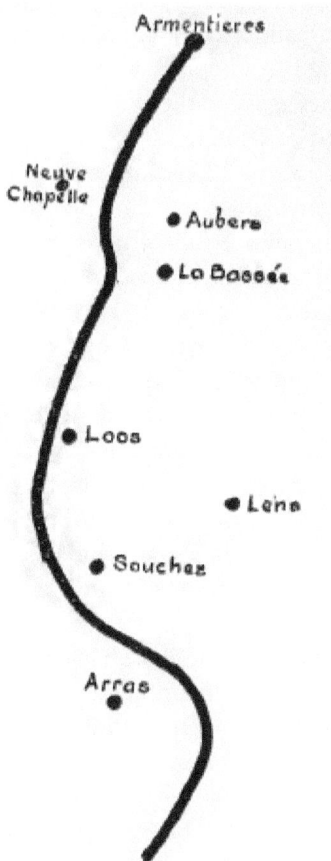

32. THE LINE FROM ARMENTIÈRES TO ARRAS DURING THE SPRING OF 1915. LOOS HAS SINCE BEEN TAKEN, AS ALSO HAS SOUCHEZ.

They will study this line from Armentières to Arras with new vision, and the conclusions which they will draw will assuredly be different from those which today are apt to compel our attention.

But if I may not dwell upon this heroic struggling for Lille, I must indeed invite my reader to return to the terrible salient before Ypres, that we may follow, however imperfectly, the second assault made by the enemy against this hapless city. For the second Battle of Ypres is like the first battle in one respect only—the fact that it was fought over the same ground. In all other respects it is a battle by itself—standing alone in the history of our warfare alike by reason of its devilish ferocity and by reason of the fact that in this encounter Britain's great colony was the direct means of her salvation.

It is the month of April, and as the days lengthen out a great peace comes to this land of Flanders. It is the peace of spring, full of the new gladness of awakening life. The days are sunny and the skies clear, and a genial warmth comes again to the trenches where men have suffered all the chills and pains of winter.

This day, Thursday, April 22, is almost perfect in its serenity. Not a cloud is in the sky. Scarcely a breath of wind disturbs the wide silence. The men in the trenches are full of good spirits; and you may hear them singing as they go about their work in the rest-stations behind the lines and in the great depots at the bases. The afternoon grows old under a rich sky that, as it darkens, is filled with gorgeous colourings, crimson and saffron and gold, spread like a banner to the western horizon. . . . With the sunsetting comes a light breeze, blowing softly from the north-east over the rolling lands by Roulers towards Ypres.

The salient about the city of Ypres is held on this night by troops drawn from the very ends of the earth. The north of the salient is guarded by the French Colonials, and linked up with them are the Canadians, who again join hands with the British farther south. The Canadians are holding 500 yards of trenches from the Ypres-Roulers railway to the Ypres-Poelscapelle road. The Third Infantry Brigade of the Canadian Division joins hands with the French Colonials, the second with the British, while the third is in reserve.

The Canadian soldiers are new as yet to this game of war, and are therefore glad that the enemy seem to be resting in their trenches and that the ordeal of battle has been delayed. On this exquisite April evening they have little thought of any danger—for the very beauty of the sky, which all these men remember so well, seems to be a guarantee that no ill shall befall.

But suddenly an uneasy thrill runs along the crowded trench. "What was that? Did you hear it?" Men look at one another anxiously, every man aware that something has happened, no man understanding exactly the nature of the misfortune. Away to the left there is sound of heavy firing—though that in itself is commonplace enough—and suddenly the "buzzer" in the trench is sounded vigorously. In a few moments these Canadian lads know that this telephone message is of most serious import. The order is passed, "You are to hold the trench at all costs." A boy who passed through those terrible hours told me a few days later:

We stood there, and our hearts thumped against our ribs. So at last we were in for it. We didn't know even yet what had happened, because we were not near enough to the end of the line to see the retirement of the French Colonials, and the reason of their retirement. Each man had his kit strapped to his shoulders and his rifle loaded.

You cannot realise what those moments of acute tension are like unless you have lived through them. Then a man feels a coward in the most abject sense, and he wants to run away more than anything else in the world. All sorts of queer notions come thumping into his mind—thoughts of home and happy thoughts of happy days—and then wonder that he should be here in this dreadful position, and anger—great anger that it should be so. I have seen men almost go mad just with this anger. . . .

You want to run away . . . but somehow you don't do it. Somehow you manage to laugh and talk nonsense to the man next you, and pretend it doesn't matter a little bit, and that you like it and have hoped it would happen—if only you could keep your knees from trembling so and your heart from shaking you as a dog shakes a rat.

And then all of a sudden the ground in front of us seemed to open, and up sprang the enemy, of whom we had seen so little, and began to run straight at us with fixed bayonets. It was a most strange and horrible sight. The Germans were shouting, and they seemed mad in the short moment that you could see them. For a moment our curiosity nearly got the better of our discretion. Then we settled down to give them a real Canadian welcome. We shot and shot till our gun barrels were almost red-hot—but the more we killed the more of them there seemed to

217

be. And meanwhile, of course, shells were bursting all about us. I don't remember much more. I know there was an awful gassy smell that seemed to draw all his breath out of a man's body, and then I remember a loud order to retire to the trench behind by way of the communication trench. The new trench had water in it, but we got back all right, and we took our wounded with us. After that I don't remember much. We fought and fought. Some of the gas got to us, and some of our men went down with it. Our eyes were red and inflamed and our brains were on fire. We were covered with mud from head to foot, and our faces were flaming red with hate and rage, and the awful fumes made us double up with coughing.

But we fought on. We fought and fought as we went back, so that our rifles jammed and were useless, and we threw them away and took others from the bodies of the dead. I saw one great fellow stand up above the trench and kick the bolt of his rifle home, and he didn't get a scratch. We hung together till the night came down, and then we lost ourselves till we came to the road which, I think, was the road to St. Julien.

This boy had been spared the worst torment: it is not so to the left, near the place where the French Colonials have been driven from their trenches. For here the poison cloud of the enemy has come in all its terrible strength—the deadly chlorine gas which devilish minds have conceived in calm hours and have launched, as the result of deliberate calculation, against foes who stood all unprepared against it.

If you have doubt of it look at the men as they lie huddled in the trenches tearing at their throats for breath the while their eyes bulge fearfully from the sockets and their faces grow grey and then black under the torment. See the blood foam on their lips and behold how with dying hands they tear at the sides of the trenches, breaking their nails upon the wooden boards. And then see the German "conquerors" rush upon them, when the cloud has gone by, and bayonet them swiftly while yet they writhe in this agony. Is it not a sight for eternal remembrance? And see at another part of the line upon what hell's work are they engaged!

This man whom they have taken is a Canadian sergeant, and because he has fought bitterly against them and because they dream that at last, by means of their gas, Ypres will fall, they are having their vengeance upon him yonder by the door of this ruined homestead. See them force him against the wooden door and hold him outstretched in front of it. See them drive their bayonets through his outstretched palms and through his feet as the accursed of old times drove the iron nails upon the hill at Calvary. And hear the mockery with which they greet his dying sorrow. . . . It is enough, is it not, to wring tears from the very stones that are the silent witnesses of it? And in what days will the men and women of our race forget the things which are afoot under the still sky before the towers of the old town in Flanders?

The French Colonials are driven back, since no man may live in this inferno. The salient of Ypres, so long intact, is broken. The line, which in the October days was cemented with blood, is a line no longer. In its course, now, there is a huge rent. The line is smitten asunder. The Canadian left hangs at this hour unsupported, "in mid air."

The position indeed as the night falls is desperate. Great masses of the enemy are advancing against the line determined to push on to the possessing of the coveted city. An inferno of shells embroils the retreating troops. "Gassed" men crawl like spent animals along the fields and byways, dying miserably in their tracks as poisoned vermin die. As the night falls there is wild confusion upon all the roads leading to the town. The St. Julien road presents such a scene as the eyes of men have rarely witnessed. It is strewn with dead and dying men, with dead and dying horses. The Canadians are retreating along this road and they are fighting bitterly as they go. At one point the advancing Germans come almost to the muzzles of a detachment of artillery, and the appalling sight is witnessed of the big guns firing at point-blank range into this mass of reeling and screeching human beings. The Germans are mown down like corn and fall in a heap that lies writhing under the pale sky. The crying of the sorely wounded and the groans of the dying are mingled with the roar of the battle.

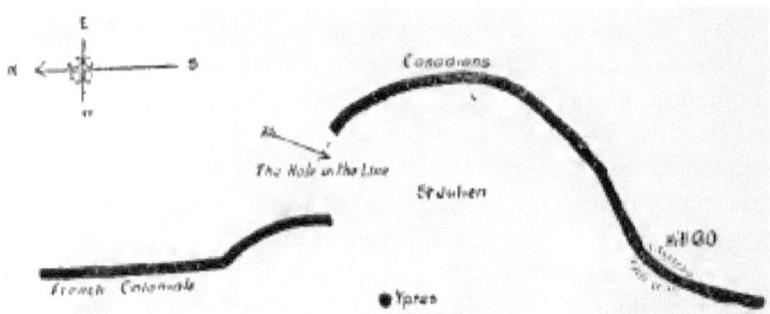

33. THE HOLE IN THE LINE AT YPRES MADE BY THE POISON GAS.

Meanwhile, to the west of St. Julien, the Canadian Scottish are at work recovering the four British guns which were lost earlier in the evening. What a feat this is for the world to wonder at! There is a moon, and the men can see the dark wood quite clearly in front of them.

Their officers form them quickly into four lines. The first line rushes forward with fixed bayonets and regardless of the bitter fire which is poured into them. Then the second line follows, passing on through the first line and carrying well past it. And then the third line after the fashion of the second; and then the fourth.

The bugle sounds: and then all four lines rush again to the charge together. The Germans fight fiercely enough, but they are unable to stand this final blow. They dwindle away. . . .

And so on until the guns are taken. . . .

And all this Thursday night, unbeknown to the fighting men, a great movement is being carried out which tomorrow will resound through all the continents of the world. This is nothing less than the shutting of the open door in the face of the enemy and the plucking away from him of the advantage given by his cloud of poison.

The Canadians are being brought back with a swiftness which is almost miraculous—they are defeating, with every step they take to the rear, the purpose of the enemy. Villages must be abandoned in this retreat, and points of vantage given up. But what of it? The salient shall be saved; Ypres shall be saved; the Allied line from the sea to the Alps shall be saved.

This closing of the door is, indeed, a great achievement, the importance of which it is impossible to overestimate. It is so swift, so sudden, so thorough that a man can only regard it with amazement. There is no praise too high for it and no thankfulness too profound. . . . Yet what sacrifices are being made that it may be carried out!

They fall back to the village of St. Julien, a devoted band who will sell their lives, here in the muddy street, but will not yield them. Gas is poured upon them by the advancing enemy on these days, Friday, 23rd, Saturday, 24th—and again the fearful scenes of Thursday are witnessed, only it would seem in greater profusion. But the men do not break; they do not yield. Never have such stubborn fighters stood in the way of the *Kaiser's* ambition as upon these days.

The situation becomes more and yet more critical, and it is seen that if the closed door is to be held a further retirement must be carried out. St. Julien must be evacuated. *And a rearguard must be furnished.*

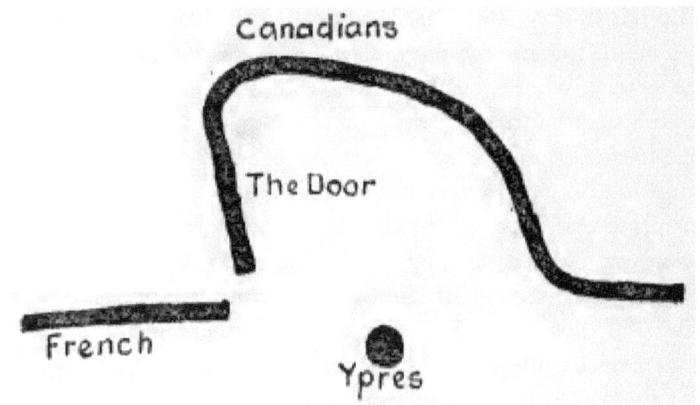

Canadians

The Door

French

Ypres

34. How they shut the door at Ypres and saved the line.

Who will stay to guard the rear, in this village of death, and with no hope of salvation?

The official record is cold and formal, as are all official records, but perhaps, in these circumstances, it is enough: "a gallant handful" was left in the village for this purpose. They are left to die, and every man of them knows it ... to die hard and bitterly, and as slowly as may be possible ... to die fighting, with their backs to the wall and their faces towards the enemy.

It is reported that they have indeed fulfilled their contract.

And so this Saturday night is witness of one of the most shining examples of heroism in the whole campaign, a heroism like that of Horatius at the Bridge, like that of the Gracchi.

The line is closed at last and the acute danger is ended, though there are terrible days to be encountered yet before this second Battle of Ypres shall be ended and the last assaults upon the town repelled. Ypres itself is like a shambles. The townspeople have fled away from it and the splendid town-hall is reduced to a battered ruin. The glorious towers are riddled and torn by innumerable shells, the houses surrounding are thrashed to pieces by the iron hail, all the roadways leading into the town are under a perpetual bombardment. And in the streets dead men and dead horses lie piled together in confusion. As an artilleryman wrote in his diary:

Valley of the shadow of death. You must gallop with all your might through the town, as the enemy have guns laid on all the cross roads and bridges. Takes a cool head to go through.

The battle ends and a new battle begins. Having failed to burst in the salient the enemy attempt to retake Hill 60 at the south angle of the salient, where the Ypres to Commines canal goes southward through a deep cutting. To the north of Ypres they have already succeeded in crossing the canal at Het Sas—the so-called "Yperlee" Canal, running between Ypres and Dixmude—and if they can but cross in this place also they will be able to isolate the town.

So a bitter warfaring is begun for the hill, and also for the salient, the attacks alternating with almost monotonous regularity, yet without any real success. . . . For success is no longer possible. The gas attack has failed, and now measures are being taken to provide the men against the gas danger, while away to the southward at Festubert and Arras our troops and the French are bringing heavy pressure to bear against the German lines and so rendering it necessary to draw away troops from the area of the bloody salient.

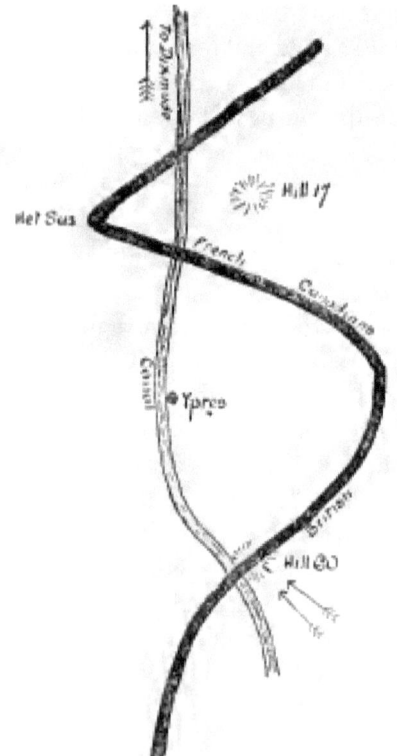

35. The re-formed Allied line, showing the crossing of the canal effected against the French by means of the first gas attack and the later attacks on Hill 60.

Ypres is spared once again. But once again her fields are drenched with rich blood, and once again, between the trenches, the unburied dead look up to the fair sky. Yet they died not in vain. For here on the fields of Ypres the world has been reborn of their blood and the serpent of tyranny and oppression has been scotched. In the days to come the losses of these fearful days and nights will be made good— the French have already cleared the western bank of the canal to the northward of the town, and once more Hill 17, near Pilkem, is in our hands. In the days to come others will reap where these sowed, and reap too a great and glorious harvest. Their blood will indeed prove itself the seed of a new, a better world, as the curse of their undoing will be laid for ever at the door of their murderers.

CHAPTER 20

Ring in the New

It is once again the old town, with the hill rising up behind it, and the road leading away over the hill across the mystery land of France. And once again the old town is awaiting the coming of men from over the sea who shall join in the good combat against darkness for the light. And once again there are little knots of spectators in the dark streets, under the moon, talking together anxiously of the great doings beyond the hill.

But on this night you may mark many features which were not a part of that other coming long months ago, as it seems, in the green youth of the world, before they wrought the horror that has changed all things. On this night you may see, for example, the slow ambulances coming forth from the railway station, each with its little flickering light, and moving at snail's pace over the cobbles to the wooden swing bridge, and so along the harbour wall to the hospitals. And you may see the long ambulance trains with their red crosses drawn up outside of the station to await fresh orders, and you may see the tall masts of the hospital ships lying in the harbour.

But you are accustomed to it all—to the ambulances and the trains and the ships, and also to the perpetual stream of doctors and ambulance men that flows across the wooden bridge, surging from the hospitals to the hotels and the stations. And so you scarcely notice these things. Your eyes are fixed rather upon the great flares that they are lighting now upon the quay-head to be a guide to the brave feet that will so soon be set ashore upon this land of France.

And as you wait there comes a sound of marching that is like the sound of waves beating pleasantly upon the shore. And then into the ring of the dancing light, like dream figures, they emerge, rank upon rank, regiment upon regiment, the young men of the New Britain that is awaking overseas and stirring itself towards mighty endeavour. The light gathers them, as it were, within a golden circle, picking out their faces beneath their caps and their knees where they shine white below swinging kilts.

A thrill goes through you for very joy of this great spectacle.

What men these who have given themselves freely to the service of their country, not as conscripts, but as saviours! The very faces of them are a triumph and an inspiration, lean hard faces that glow in the red light with the beauty of strength and health. The faces of such a breed of men as this world has but seldom known in all its ages.

They are forming up quickly into two long lines that stretch away to the utmost limits of the circle of the light. They stand stiffly at attention, heads raised, bodies erect; they have all the pride of a great people in their eyes; and all the modesty of boys who are but just come to manhood. Their officers move about amongst them, arranging and inspecting.

Suddenly a sharp word of command rings out in the stillness of the night. The ranks begin to march towards the old wooden bridge. You hear the heavy boots resounding upon the timbers. A voice from the crowd cries "*Vive l'Angleterre*," and from the ranks a voice answers "*Vive la France*." A woman sings the chorus of the forgotten *Tipperary*, and the lilt of it comes strangely, reviving old memories.

And then suddenly there breaks out, like a great cry upon this night silence, the wailing of the pipes of Lochiel that the Cameron men may march worthily to their ordeal. ... It is such an hour as men dream of but are seldom privileged to live in; an hour when a man's heart is called forth in full flood and his spirit is glorified within him.

Oh, do you hear the pipes wailing and storming their way through the grey streets and by the dark, bastioned walls? Do you hear them take the road that is the road of glory and of death? Do you hear the calling of them from the heights that lie over against the battle?

They are telling of a new world, these pipes of the men of the new Army. They are telling of a world of stirring faith and high endeavour, of great adventure and of fair chivalry. The young men have indeed seen visions who follow the pipes through the streets of the French town, and who will follow them to the bitter trenches and the stricken field. The old order is already changed, the old values already discredited. All things are become new. It is the dawn. . . .

www.ingramcontent.com/pod-product-compliance
Lightning Source LLC
Chambersburg PA
CBHW032143020726
47496CB00003B/692